THE FIRST WORLD WAR

Twentieth-Century Wars
Series Standing Order ISBN 0–333–77101–X

You can receive future titles in this series as they are published. To place a standing order please contact your bookseller or, in the case of difficulty, write to us at the address below with your name and address, the title of the series and the ISBN quoted above.

Customer Services Department, Macmillan Distribution Ltd
Houndmills, Basingstoke, Hampshire RG21 6XS, England

THE FIRST WORLD WAR

Gerard J. De Groot

palgrave

First published in 2001 by
PALGRAVE
Houndmills, Basingstoke, Hampshire RG21 6XS and
175 Fifth Avenue, New York, N.Y. 10010
Companies and representatives throughout the world

PALGRAVE is the new global academic imprint of St. Martin's Press LLC
Scholarly and Reference Division and Palgrave Publishers Ltd (formerly
Macmillan Press Ltd).

ISBN 0–333–74534–5 hardback
ISBN 0–333–74535–3 paperback

This book is printed on paper suitable for recycling and
made from fully managed and sustained forest sources.

A catalogue record for this book is available
from the British Library.

Library of Congress Cataloging-in-Publication Data

De Groot, Gerard J., 1955-
    The First World War / Gerard De Groot
        p.   cm. -- (Twentieth-century wars)
    Includes bibliographical references and index.
    ISBN 0-333-74534-5 (cloth) -- ISBN 0-333-74535-3 (pbk.)
        1. World War, 1914-1918. 2. World War, 1914-1918--Campaigns--
Western Front. 3. World War, 1914-1918--Campaigns--Eastern Front.
I. Title. II. Series.

D521 .D35 2000
940.3–dc21
                                                                00-030891

10 9   8   7   6   5   4   3   2   1
10 09 08 07 06 05 04 03 02 01

Typeset by Aarontype Limited, Easton, Bristol
Printed in China

To my mother
who has reason to hate war

Contents

List of Maps

Preface

War is a difficult subject to write about briefly. In outline, it is dull: units attack or retreat like the arrows and boxes on a strategist's map. The detail of war is where its fascination lies. What did the individual British soldier feel at the moment, on 1 July, when he left his trench to attack well-entrenched German defences on the Somme? What did the German machine gunner feel when the orderly lines of British infantrymen came within his range? How were millions of soldiers on the Eastern Front kept supplied with munitions and food, despite the obstacles of poor transport and atrocious weather? How did they react when supplies ran thin?

The hardest part of writing a short book about the First World War is resisting the temptation to make it twice as long as the publisher wants. It is terribly frustrating to leave out material which would undoubtedly add to the book's interest. A book is like a body; it needs a skeleton to keep it upright. But dry bones provide little interest. In writing this book, I have tried to give the bones just enough flesh to give the subject some life and vitality. There is, of course, an enormous amount missing, but that is in the nature of a short book. I hope that this book provides sufficient stimulus to inspire the reader to investigate more deeply.

I would like to thank Professor Jeremy Black for asking me to write this book and for providing guidance along the way. Dr Corinna Peniston-Bird helped with a great deal of the research, often without realizing she was doing so. Dr Elspeth O'Riordan provided valuable guidance on the Versailles Peace. But I would especially like to thank the students who have taken my classes on the Great War at the University of St Andrews over the last fifteen years. I feel privileged to have been blessed with such bright and energetic students. In teaching them, I learned a great deal about the war and what it means to generations born after it.

GERARD J DE GROOT
St Andrews
December 1999

Acknowledgements

All maps drawn by Donald S. Frazier, are taken from *The Great War* by Spencer Tucker (UCL Press, London, 1998).

We have been unable to trace the copyright holder of these maps and would appreciate any information that would enable us to do so. We would be happy to include any further acknowledgement in future reprints.

1
Origins

Approximately nine million combatants and twelve million civilians died during the Great War. The damage to property totalled perhaps $36 billion. All this death and destruction began with an assassination carried out by a hapless adolescent on the streets of Sarajevo on 28 June 1914.

The period from the assassination of the Archduke Franz Ferdinand of Austria to the outbreak of war on 28 July is one of the most contentious months in history. Thousands of historians have studied it, graduate schools and professional journals have been formed with it as their sole focus, and millions of pages have been written. The argument over the origins of the Great War contributed to the outbreak of the Second World War. The war-guilt clause forced upon Germany in the peace settlement of 1919 was later used by Adolf Hitler as a focus for German resentment. The 'appeasement' of the 1920s and 1930s was inspired in part by a widespread feeling that Germany had been unfairly required to shoulder the burden of blame for the Great War. Since the Second World War, the pendulum has swung the other way, with prominent historians arguing the case for German guilt. The argument, though lacking the vitriol which once characterized it, continues to attract obsessive interest.

In the study of history, inquests are more appropriate than prosecutions. In the case of the Great War, the attempt to prove guilt encourages a blinkered view. Simple explanations are sought, usually where they are woefully inappropriate. Subjectivity becomes obstructive. By focusing on a single culprit, one loses sight of co-incidental forces and accessories to the crime. Only through an inquest into the state of European politics, economics, culture and society can one begin to understand why most of Europe (and much of the rest of the world) went madly off to war in 1914.

A popular myth relating to the origins of this war must first be discussed. It is commonly held that the war was caused by secret treaties and an alliance system that placed European diplomats, at the moment of crisis, in a strait jacket. As with most myths, this one has an element of truth. A small (though important) argument in the Balkans did start a chain reaction of nations honouring solemn commitments to defend other nations, with a pan-European war eventually resulting. But treaties and alliances do not by themselves cause wars. History provides many examples of countries breaking agreements when war does not seem a sensible option. In 1914, for instance, Italy blatantly ignored its solemn commitment to Germany. Self-interest is the most important factor influencing any decision to declare war. Thus, the countries of Europe plunged headlong into the conflagration, not out of any commitment to an ally, but because, at the point of crisis, entering the war seemed to offer greater promise than staying out. No country went unwillingly to war, cursing an ally for tying its hands.

In 1914 the international system broke down. A century of peace ended in disastrous war. The failure of the system seems massive because the war it produced was so huge. But at the time war seemed no catastrophe and peace was not an obsession. If the actions of European leaders seem, in retrospect, terribly reckless, we must bear in mind that few of them expected such a terrible war. As the great military thinker, Karl von Clausewitz, argued in 1833, war was 'a mere continuation of policy by other means'. After the war, Osbert Sitwell reflected:

> We were still in the trough of peace that had lasted a hundred years between two great conflicts. In it, such wars as arose were not general, but only a brief armed version of the Olympic Games. You won a round; the enemy won the next. There was no more talk of extermination, or of Fights to a Finish, than would occur in a boxing match. [33, p. 25]

Europe after the Franco-Prussian war

Victory in 1871 left Germany triumphant and France humiliated. All of Alsace and half of Lorraine were taken by the Germans as the spoils of war. Both regions became symbols of French humiliation and, later, of their desire for revenge. It is important to note that the population of Alsace was almost wholly German, while that of Lorraine was virtually entirely French.

The war was followed by a period of unusual peace in Europe, engineered by German Chancellor Otto von Bismarck. Harmony resulted not from a 'balance of power', but an imbalance. Germany was the strongest country in Europe. As long as she was able to keep her rivals apart, her domination would continue, and so would the peaceful state of European politics. Treaties with Austria-Hungary, Italy and Russia kept France isolated. With Germany's two great rivals – Russia and France – safely separated, Germany could feel secure. The rest of Europe felt safe because Germany felt safe. The treaties were complicated and sometimes contradictory, but that did not matter as long as peace was maintained.

The other great European power, the United Kingdom, was content to remain aloof from European politics. Within Europe she was a bit player, but in the rest of the world she was a superpower. Britain did not wish to threaten German continental hegemony, and so did not feel the need of an army for that purpose. Germany might have wanted to threaten British imperial hegemony, but did not yet possess the navy to do so. Rivalries certainly developed, but the issues involved were never so important to justify a war.

Peace brought prosperity. Though the depression of the 1890s caused genuine suffering among the working classes and those who had invested unwisely, these were on the whole boom years. Despite deep suspicion, the countries of Europe got on rather well with each other. Borders could easily be crossed without passports; and an English traveller could write a cheque in Berlin, Paris or Rome. The interconnectedness of the European economy caused some economists to speculate that war on the continent had become obsolete. The pacifist Norman Angell attracted a huge following (and a small fortune) when his book *The Great Illusion* presented just such an argument. In a speech to the Institute of Bankers in London on 17 January 1912, he argued that

> morality after all is not founded upon self-sacrifice, but upon enlightened self-interest, a clearer and more complete understanding of all the ties that bind us the one to the other. And such clearer understanding is bound to improve, not merely the relationship of one group to another, but the relationship of all men to all other men, to create a consciousness which must make for more efficient human cooperation, a better human society. [56, p. 12]

In other words, henceforth, the bankers would restrain the war-mongers.

To many Europeans it seemed a golden age. Crime was under control, and decency governed the affairs of civilized folk. Medical advances and a general rise in the standard of living improved life expectancy and reduced child mortality. Across Europe, real wages rose by 50 per cent between 1890 and 1913. Progressivism, in varying degrees and forms, characterized European domestic policy. Germany was a leader in social reform, demonstrating that Liberals did not have a monopoly on welfare provision. The reforms were in part an attempt to keep up with the demands of an increasingly educated, cohesive and assertive working class. Improvements in health care, education and housing mollified the workers but also proved an effective way to prepare for war, producing a population more able and motivated to serve.

But beneath the surface calm tensions existed. Militant feminism, syndicalism, radical socialism, religious sectarianism and antagonism between social classes disturbed the social harmony in all the countries of Europe. There was, at one and the same time, a sense of exhilaration and of *malaise*. The exhilaration arose from the excitement of these times: the relaxing of social mores, the sense of fluidity and the apparently irresistible force of progress and technology. The *malaise* arose from an understandable uncertainty as to where all the change would lead and what form the modern industrial nation would take. 'Modernism', a much-debated notion, provoked both excitement and fear. This cacophony of emotions was reflected in more expressionistic modes of artistic expression. Musicians and artists were on the one hand more assertive in the works they produced, but those works often evoked bewilderment and paranoia. Within some groups there arose a belief, which stemmed from the ideas of the German philosopher Friederich Nietzsche (1844–1900), that only through a profound shock (like war) could the sterile complacency of capitalist life be transcended and a more sublime spiritual state be realized.

Social change contributed to, and was fuelled by, advances in literacy and communication. The press flourished, which meant a more aware public, but also one more easily manipulated. Greater political awareness inspired a consciousness of oppression among certain groups. This consciousness was not merely a phenomenon of the class system, though that is where it seemed most threatening to the established order. Oppression could be personal or political – the oppressor could be a violent husband or a domineering nation. Within a country, consciousness might be expressed in class or gender terms, while within Europe as a whole, ethnic groups became more aware of their common heritage and more inclined to assert nationalist sympathies.

Nationalism is profoundly important to an understanding of the origins of the First World War and of the character the war eventually assumed. It redefined the relationship between the individual and the state, thus superseding the more parochial identities that might have existed within that polity. Individuals began increasingly to identify themselves as French, German or Italian, whereas they might once have thought of themselves as Burgundians, Hanoverians or Tuscans, and had little concern for affairs outside their limited locale. Heightened nationalism meant that citizens shared in the success or predicament of their countries to an unprecedented degree. Thus, the German people felt proud and assertive after their victory in 1871, and the French in turn felt the humiliation of defeat. In a situation akin to a sporting contest, Britons and Germans cheered from the sidelines as their respective countries raced to outdo each other in warship construction.

This evolution of national identity transformed the nature of citizenship. The citizen was increasingly assumed to have a responsibility to the state, and the state, in turn, to the individual. If the state found itself in danger, the citizen had a duty to come to its aid. The state, likewise, assumed greater responsibility for the welfare of the individual. As has been discussed, this was not simply altruism on the part of governments. Rather, it was widely understood that a healthy, educated population was essential to national survival.

Nationalism helped bring into being the concept of the citizen army and, in some countries, the introduction of compulsory military service. Stated very simply, heightened nationalism ensured that any future European war would be big, costly and long. It would also involve the homefront population in a way heretofore unimagined. The people would feed, clothe and arm the soldiers, and would pay for the war through higher taxes. Their support for the war would have to be manipulated through the control of information – censorship and propaganda. In future, war would no longer be a contest between armies, but between peoples.

Nationalism was strongest where the nation was least well-established. Thus, it was most keenly felt in those regions where groups of people found themselves within a state that did not reflect their ethnic identities. They did not have the benefit of a bona fide nation to express their nationalism. Ireland is a useful example: because an Irish state did not exist, Irish nationalism was strong. East of the Rhine and south of the Alps, where the rise of nationalism came after the formation of supranational states, ethnic identity was a particularly volatile force. In the Austro-Hungarian and Ottoman Empires, it posed a serious threat to internal stability and thus to European peace.

In ethnic terms, the Austro-Hungarian Empire was neither Austrian nor Hungarian. It consisted of Germans, Magyars, Ruthenes, Poles, Romanians, Serbs, Croats, Czechs, Italians, Slovaks, Slovenes, Armenians, Bulgars, Greeks, Albanians, and an assortment of Gypsies and Jews. (When war broke out in 1914, mobilization orders had to be printed in 11 different languages.) The government was composed of two kingdoms united by a common emperor. Each kingdom had its own prime minister. There was a ten-year renewable treaty which covered mutual concerns like commerce, finance, foreign affairs and defence, but otherwise the two entities handled their own internal affairs. There was no Austro-Hungarian nation and thus no Austro-Hungarian nationalism. In such a supranational state, foreign and domestic policy could not easily be separated, since the definition of what was foreign and what domestic differed according to the perceptions of the various ethnic groups. For instance, a hostile policy towards Italy annoyed Italians within the Empire. The Italians, Greeks, Serbians and Romanians who lived under Hapsburg rule posed especially serious problems because each group had a nation with which to identify outside the Empire.

The Empire's weak structure and unstable politics encouraged paranoia among her rulers. The fear of spies, secret societies and subversion was endemic. Suspicion was focused on independent Slav states like Serbia which, it was feared, were a focus for Slav nationalism within the Empire. But, despite its difficulties, the Empire was reasonably prosperous and quite progressive. Most ethnic groups enjoyed a better standard of living than their compatriots outside. It was probably the best system of government that could have been devised in a turbulent, ethnically diverse region, but that was little consolation to those who despised its power and craved their independence. In an age of nationalism, the Empire was an anomaly. In addressing threats to its stability, the Hapsburg government had to toe a line between aggression, which might bring disaster from outside, or passivity, which might encourage disintegration from within.

Austria-Hungary was nevertheless a model of stable government compared to the Ottoman Empire. Here there were at least twelve ethnic groups with the same strange dynamic between foreign and domestic policy. Again, the central authority was extremely fearful of those who threatened internal stability. But the main difference between the Austro-Hungarian and the Ottoman empires was that the former was prosperous and progressive, while the latter was authoritarian and impoverished. A weak economy sapped the strength of the government and widespread poverty fuelled ethnic passions. Repressive policies exacerbated internal tensions.

The Ottoman Empire, in contrast to Austria-Hungary, had no firm allies. This meant that she was at the mercy of small aggressive states like Serbia that had designs upon her people and territory. Since no European power was actually dependent upon the survival of the Ottoman Empire, none felt overly motivated to save her from disintegration, as they had in the mid-nineteenth century. But that disintegration, especially after 1910, let loose forces which imperilled stability on the continent. Jackals like Serbia and Bulgaria grew strong from feeding on the Ottoman carcass. This had important implications for Austria-Hungary, since an assertive Serbia or Bulgaria spelled trouble for her internal politics. In addition, the Ottoman Empire's geographical position was immensely important. Russia, for instance, coveted control of the region in order to ensure access to a permanently ice-free port and to influence politics in the Mediterranean.

Aspirations of the Great Powers

The underlying instability of European politics, especially after the collapse of the Bismarckian system toward the end of the nineteenth century, caused all of the European powers to look for ways to harness the forces of change. In order to do so, the Great Powers had to contemplate proactive policies, perhaps to the point of war. Competing aspirations inevitably led to animosity and distrust.

France was motivated by a fear of Germany and a desire for revenge. As the years passed, the humiliation of 1871 gave way to a militant desire to recover Alsace and Lorraine. In order to accommodate this aspiration, the French military was expanded and modernized. France, with a population of just 40 million people, decided that she would have an army the equal of Germany, a nation of 60 million. French plans for war assumed a more aggressive character. If attacked by Germany, France intended not just to defend herself but rather to use the opportunity to launch an offensive to recover the lost provinces. As in all European countries, external threats proved a convenient distraction from internal problems. The discontented, chief among them the workers, were diverted from their political goals by the aim of national resurgence. Militant patriotism was an effective way to neutralize working-class discontent.

Russia tried a similar ploy, with less success. She had been severely humiliated in the 1905 war with Japan. That defeat, when combined with the revolution of the same year, had seriously weakened Russia and in the process destabilized the European balance of power, since a strong Russia was essential as a check upon German ambitions. Since that time, the Russian military had improved significantly, but progress seemed remarkable only because the starting point was so low.

Russia was concerned by what the tide of pan-Slavism sweeping the Balkans might mean for the aspirations of ethnic groups within her own Empire. She could not allow Serbia to provide an inspiration for internal discontent. But she could not simply crush Serbia, since aggression toward any of the small Balkan nations would only spread alienation at home. Russia instead hoped to contain pan-Slavism by proving herself a friend of the Slavs. But internal instability after the 1905 revolution made it difficult for Russia to assert herself internationally.

Germany was the most prosperous and industrialized country on the continent, but she also had severe internal problems which were increasingly difficult to camouflage. Her governmental system was both weak and top heavy, capable of being manipulated by a genius like Bismarck or a buffoon like Wilhelm II. German unification had come about because her phenomenal industrial growth had allowed her to win wars and dominate continental markets. Bismarck's policy of 'blood and iron' strengthened the nation but also rendered it more indebted to the workers, who began to flex their muscles by meddling in radical politics. Jews, Catholics and Liberals also felt dispossessed.

Wealthy industrialists, on the other hand, were ecstatic at Germany's phenomenal rise and keen to see it continue. War (or even the preparation for war) made some men very rich. They pushed for continued expansion of the Empire, either within Europe or in Africa and Asia. Imperial expansion naturally implied a burgeoning military, an idea which delighted the big arms manufacturers. There were many Germans who felt that a contest between the Teutonic and Slavic races was inevitable. It seemed in the nation's best interest that the 'final reckoning' should come sooner rather than later. Time did not seem an ally, since, with each passing month, Germany's enemies would grow stronger and more friendly toward each other.

Britain had little desire to become involved in European politics. Her small army of just over 100 000 men was minuscule in comparison to the massive continental conscript forces. But her navy and empire provided a sense of security and splendid isolation. Most Britons thought that they could safely ignore events on the continent. This idea of a *Pax Britannica* was, however, a dangerous delusion. Rather than being a source of unmitigated strength, the colonies were becoming an increasing burden with each passing year. It was difficult to balance imperial commitments with the need to maintain Britain's security within Europe. The colonies also aroused jealousy among the great powers, producing points of conflict around the globe, all of which had to be monitored assiduously. And Britain was a great deal more dependent on continental markets than she ever accepted. The proportion of trade with Europe was steadily increasing in relation to trade with the colonies.

Entangling alliances

The brilliance of Bismarck's diplomacy lay in the way he was able to keep France isolated from Russia. But after Bismarck's departure in 1890, the new Chancellor, Count Caprivi, complained that Bismarck's system was like 'keeping five balls in the air at once'. He and others close to Kaiser Wilhelm II (1859–1941) sought a 'simpler' foreign policy. [15, p. 164] The carefully constructed network of agreements began to unravel. In 1890, Germany refused to renew the Reinsurance Treaty with Russia, causing France and Russia to drift together like two lonely hearts. They forged an alliance in 1894. Thus, just four years after Bismarck's departure, Germany found herself in the position that the former Chancellor had devoted his career to avoiding. She was surrounded by two hostile powers and faced with the prospect of a two-front war.

The erratic Kaiser also managed to alienate Great Britain. Bismarck, by leaving the British virtually alone, had kept relations peaceful and usually friendly. As long as Germany's empire was continental and Britain's colonial, the two could peacefully coexist. With Bismarck gone, and Germany increasingly interested in affairs outside Europe, points of friction began to develop. These were handled with considerably less dexterity than had characterized the Iron Chancellor. In particular, Germany's desire for a large navy annoyed the British, who did not appreciate foreign boats on their lake. A new generation of advisers at the Foreign Office, prominent among them Eyre Crowe, repeatedly warned of the danger which Germany posed. The British press chipped in with frequent references to 'Britain's secret and deadliest foe'. 'There is an inevitable conflict of ideals between Germany and Great Britain', the *Spectator* argued in 1911, 'between the satisfied nation and the unsatisfied nation, between the nation which desires to maintain the *status quo* and the nation which desires to alter it'. [59, pp. 119, 129]

By the turn of the century, 87 years had passed since Britain had fought a war on the continent. She was the world's leading industrial power and had amassed the largest empire in history. At least as far as European affairs were concerned, Britain was a peaceable kingdom. True, she was an aggressive imperial power, but her aggression was carefully directed. Two points deserve emphasis: first, it was not the natural British reaction to intervene in a continental quarrel and, second, because Britain was inclined to be peaceful, she was militarily weak.

The War Office official Sir Henry Brackenbury warned in 1899: 'We are attempting to maintain the largest Empire the world has ever seen with armaments and reserves that would be insufficient for a third-class power'. The only conceivable response to this predicament was diplomatic. Britain took the crucial step of entering into entangling agreements, the avoidance of which had been central to *Pax Britannica*. The first significant departure from diplomatic custom came with the Anglo-Japanese agreement of 1902. Under its terms, Britain agreed to remain neutral in a war between Russia and Japan alone, but promised to provide support to Japan if Russia were joined by another European power. Japan's ambitions were thus safely contained, as were, more importantly, those of Russia.

Next came France. After two world wars, the Entente Cordiale of 1904 seems a natural expression of Anglo-French accord. At the time, however, it constituted an abrupt change of heart. Less than a decade earlier (in 1898) the British and French had nearly come to blows during the Fashoda crisis. The Entente was again a pragmatic attempt by Britain to protect her imperial interests through compromise with a rival. Warm feelings were absent; there was little that was *cordiale* about the Entente. It dealt with specific areas of competition, in particular Morocco and Egypt, and was not, as far as Britain was concerned, supposed to affect European relations. In other words, it was not directed against Germany. Nevertheless, within Parliament, there was a growing feeling that Britain could not afford a second defeat of France by Germany. The government feared that this 'would end in the aggrandisement of Germany to an extent which would be prejudicial to the whole of Europe, and it might therefore be necessary for Great Britain in her own interests to lend France her active support should war of this nature break out.' [59, p. 125]

France saw the Entente as a way to isolate Germany and was therefore keen to cement ties with Great Britain. Military commanders from both sides met in secret talks designed to find ways to facilitate cooperation in the event of war. In other words, what began as a convenient arrangement designed to solve difficulties in the Empire was evolving into a full-blown military alliance centred on Europe. This reveals both the *naïveté* of British diplomacy and also the dangers of agreements borne of desperation. At the price of peace in North Africa, Britain was drawn into the European vortex.

By 1898, the biggest threat to the British Empire was not France, nor Germany, but Russia – or so it was thought. Russian interests in Persia threatened the imperial jewel, India. The Committee of Imperial Defence warned that the Army would not be able to defend India in the event of a determined Russian invasion. The massive size of Russia's army was a problem, but even more daunting was the fact that she was the one power in Europe virtually invulnerable to Britain's naval might. The Anglo-Russian convention of 1907 resolved this predicament satisfactorily for the British, but, again, at the cost of pulling Britain deeper into European affairs.

The safety of the Empire was ensured, but with the result that Britain herself was more at risk of entanglement in a European war.

These agreements are far more important to Britain's decision to intervene in August 1914 than are any of the manifold instances of Anglo-German antagonism that occurred after 1890. One should not discount entirely the significance of the naval rivalry, the bumbling intervention of the Kaiser in the politics of Southern Africa, the Agadir Crisis, or the building of the Berlin–Baghdad railway. But those problems pale in comparison to the much more pressing dilemma of protecting an Empire that, it seemed, could no longer be protected by the usual means, namely military power.

The formation of the Triple Entente of Russia, France and Britain sowed distrust within Germany, where a feeling of isolation and persecution grew. Attempts were made to revive the treaty with Russia and to divide Britain from France, but all to no avail. Europe had been peaceful while Germany felt confident. Suddenly that confidence had evaporated.

Germany was still allied with Austria-Hungary, but the new European alignment meant that she was now dangerously dependent upon an unstable partner, leaving her little room for manoeuvre in international affairs. She could not let the Dual Monarchy crumble. As a result, the Hapsburg tail wagged the German dog. Austria-Hungary's interests, particularly in the Balkans, were not enthusiastically shared by Germany. Bismarck, it should be noted, once remarked that the area was not worth the 'bones of a single Pomeranian [German] grenadier'. But because Germany needed an ally, she had to tolerate her ally's whims.

For Germany, the future looked bleak. With time, her allies were bound to grow weaker, while her enemies grew stronger and more united. Faced with the prospect of a two-front war, the Chief of the Imperial General Staff, Count Graf von Schlieffen, decided that Germany would have to defeat France quickly (within six weeks or so) and then move her forces east in time to meet the advancing Russian hordes, before they could seriously threaten Eastern Prussia. Schlieffen decided that a lightning-quick invasion through Belgium (where a flat landscape aided advance) would permit a quick defeat of France. The invasion would approach Paris from the west, thus attacking the capital from the rear, bypassing the static defences which were designed to meet an attack from the east. The plan was technically brilliant but politically foolhardy, in that it committed Germany to a two-front war and did not contemplate the implications of violating Belgian neutrality. It was also a

strategy of abstraction which did not take into account the fact that
Germany did not possess the men or munitions to achieve the aims
Schlieffen proposed.

Austria-Hungary and the Slav problem

Austria-Hungary was worried about what the spread of nationalism
in the Balkans would do to the internal stability of the Empire. Her
concern focused primarily on Serbia, the most assertive and
powerful of the Balkan states. She at first tried to control Serbia
economically by imposing crushing tariffs on her main export, pork.
But the plan backfired: the main effect of the 'Pig War' of 1892–95
was to enhance the appeal of Serbian nationalism, both in Serbia
and throughout the region. This failure increased the determination of the Dual Monarchy. Though it is easy to criticize the
foolishness of its foreign policy, it is difficult to see an alternative.
A stable Austria-Hungary could not coexist with a strong Serbia.

In 1908 came the first serious threat to stability in the Balkans, the
Bosnian Crisis. At this stage, though Germany considered Russia an
enemy, Austria-Hungary was not quite so antagonistic toward her.
The Hapsburg Empire wanted to annex Bosnia and Herzogovina,
two provinces over which she had exercised a protectorate since
1878. Vienna gained Russian acquiescence to the annexation by
agreeing that the latter might place warships in the Dardanelles.
But the deal was formed in a vacuum; it did not take into account
the objections of Britain, France and Serbia. Britain and France
abhorred the idea of Russian warships in the area and vetoed that
part of the deal. Serbia disapproved of the Bosnian annexation,
because Bosnia was heavily populated by Serbs, and because the
area figured prominently in her plans for an enlarged Slav state.

Austria-Hungary nevertheless went ahead with the annexation.
Russia felt duped, since she was unable to secure her part of the
deal over British and French objections. But she was too weak at
this stage to act upon her annoyance. As a result, Russia and Serbia
were drawn closer together in their mutual distrust of Austria-
Hungary. The latter, in turn, grew more hostile toward Russia. Fear
of Russia caused Austria-Hungary and Germany to begin active
military cooperation. Within the Hapsburg Empire, a feeling grew
that survival depended upon the destruction of Serbia. War seemed

the only solution to the erosion of Hapsburg unity. The Chief of the General Staff, Conrad von Hotzendorf, repeatedly reminded his Emperor that 'only an aggressive policy with positive goals can save this state from destruction'. [45, p. 10] The entire affair also cooled relations between Vienna and London. Until that time, Britain had been interested in maintaining a stable Austria-Hungary as a check on Russian ambitions in central Europe.

South-eastern Europe remained relatively quiet for the next few years, but tensions nevertheless bubbled. The revolt of the Young Turks in 1908 seriously destabilized politics in the Ottoman Empire, much to the delight of those who coveted Turkish territory. In 1912, the Balkan League, consisting of Montenegro, Bulgaria, Serbia and Greece, attacked Turkey like a pack of wolves devouring an injured deer. The result was the almost complete disappearance of the Ottoman Empire in Europe and the consequent growth of Slav confidence. In the subsequent peace negotiations, Serbia demanded a port on the Adriatic, but was blocked by Italy and Austria-Hungary. The difference between this incident and the Bosnian Crisis lay in the actions of France and Germany. Both were now willing to contemplate a wider European war and both urged their respective allies to assume a tough line. Europe was slipping toward war when, at the last moment, Austria-Hungary backed away from active opposition to the Balkan League and Russia failed to support the Serbian demand. Feeling herself out on a limb, Serbia wisely decided not to pursue her claim to an Adriatic port. The crisis ended with no one happy.

Dissatisfaction over the settlement of the First Balkan War led to the second, in 1913. Bulgaria, now brimming with confidence, attacked Serbia, on the pretext that she had received a better division of the spoils. Bulgaria was nominally supported by Austria-Hungary, who was keen to see the Serbs taught a lesson. Serbia was joined by Greece, Romania, Montenegro and Turkey, the latter interested in recovering its lost territory. The Bulgarians were taken down a peg, much to the annoyance of Austria-Hungary. Maps were redrawn and, again, no one was really happy. Serbia, again frustrated in her desire for a port on the Adriatic, then turned on Albania in October 1913. Austria-Hungary stepped in, Russia stood aside and Serbia backed down. Russia, humiliated, realized that at some point she would need to demonstrate that she was indeed a friend of the Slavs.

The Balkan Wars resolved nothing. They grew out of a cauldron of ethnic antagonism which still boils to this day. The wars are important not for what was decided, but for their effect upon opinion across Europe. A number of important conclusions could be drawn. First, the wars led to the creation of truly independent Balkan states, that could not be controlled by the great powers. Serbia had doubled in size, and the trouble it could cause Austria-Hungary increased exponentially. Pride and anger ran deep among these new states and territorial aspirations were pursued with reckless intensity. Second, while Slav confidence had risen, the Dual Monarchy had reacted in a manner best described as faint-hearted. Serbia, not Austria-Hungary, seemed to control affairs in the region. Third, Russia also appeared pusillanimous, having failed on two occasions to come to Serbia's aid. Russia had trumpeted the idea of a Slavic brotherhood in order to gain a foothold in the region and to quiet ethnic tensions at home. Yet the Serbs had reason to question Russian sincerity. Fourth, Germany and France were both alarmed by the vacillation of their respective allies. Neither could afford an ally who failed to deliver. Both desperately wanted a rapid resolution of the Balkan crisis. As a result, after the wars, both urged their allies to take a tough stand in any future disagreement and promised that support would be forthcoming.

Finally, the military character of the Balkan Wars is immensely important. Both involved lightning quick campaigns with a great deal of mobility. (The exceptions to this model, like the entrenchments which protected Istanbul, were conveniently ignored.) In other words, the wars seemed 'normal', a fact immensely reassuring to military planners. Schlieffen, for instance, had assumed that France could be defeated quickly. The Balkan Wars seemed to demonstrate that his assumptions were well-founded.

The July crisis

On 28 June 1914 the Archduke Franz Ferdinand of Austria, visited Sarajevo, capital of Bosnia. Though this was billed as a mission of goodwill, it was more likely a deliberate act of provocation on the part of Austria-Hungary, since it happened to be Serbia's national day. The Serbs were understandably annoyed at the idea of the Archduke effectively gate-crashing their party. While the Archduke's motorcade passed through the city, a group of conspirators stood in wait. In fact, the term 'conspirators' assigns them a legitimacy they hardly deserve. They were little more than a motley collection of post-pubescent hooligans whose penchant for mayhem was legitimized because of the nationalist atmosphere in which it was expressed. They were sympathetic to, but probably not members of, the secret society known as the Black Hand, which continues to foment tensions in the area to this day. In another era, they might have thrown eggs or paint bombs at a football match. But in their society, at that violent time in history, the availability of bombs and guns gave deadly expression to xenophobic hatreds.

There followed a sequence of events which might have been funny had its consequences not been so tragic. As the Archduke passed by in his car, the first young assassin failed to get his revolver out of his pocket in time to get a clear shot. The second was spooked by the close proximity of a policeman, who would obviously have disapproved. The third lost his nerve when he saw the Duchess Sophie, sitting next to the Archduke. The fourth decided he was not cut out for the life of a terrorist and went home. The fifth threw his bomb, but missed. The sixth conspirator, Gavrilo Princip, heard the bomb, decided that the plot had succeeded and sat down feeling smugly satisfied. He then saw the Archduke's car speed by and rued the passing of his heroic moment.

The Archduke went on to the town hall loudly complaining about the rude welcome he had been given. For reasons which remain unclear, his chauffeur shortly afterwards retraced his route back through the old town, directly into the path of the disgruntled Princip who, needless to say, could not believe his luck. He walked out of a café, pulled out his pistol, jumped on the running board of the car and shot the Archduke. He then aimed at the Governor of Bosnia sitting in the front seat, but missed, hitting instead poor Sophie.

It was hardly the shot heard round the world. Most people had never heard of the Archduke and could not place Sarajevo on a map. But the blast was sufficient to stir Austria-Hungary from her timidity. The assassination seemed to present an ideal opportunity to teach Serbia a lesson and to reassert Hapsburg dominance within the Balkans. But disagreements quickly surfaced within the ruling hierarchy as to how far to go in punishing Serbia. The Austrian Foreign Minister, Berchtold, and Conrad wanted to use the assassination to punish Serbia for its very existence, and spoke of wiping her off the map. The Emperor was largely in agreement, so much so that he decided not to invite the crowned heads of Russia and Britain to the Archduke's funeral, in case they might use the opportunity to seek a compromise solution to the crisis. But the Hungarian Prime Minister, István Tisza, was considerably less eager. His reservations arose primarily because he did not want any further annexation of Slav territory, which would only exacerbate ethnic tensions within Hungary. The Austrian inability to act quickly and the unwillingness to act unilaterally transformed a relatively small local crisis into a huge continental war.

Advice was sought from Germany, and, as in the past, the Germans urged their ally to be tough. Germany was concerned about its own interests, not Hapsburg ones, nor indeed of the need for harmony in the Balkans. Wilhelm promised full support in any action taken against Serbia, even if 'serious European complications' should result. The Chancellor, Bethmann-Hollweg, made it clear that he thought war 'the best and most radical solution' to the Balkan problem. He also stated quite openly to his advisers that if 'war [is] unavoidable, the present moment would be more advantageous than a later one'. [45, pp. 15, 21]

Germany definitely prodded Austria-Hungary, but the latter was quite keen to be pushed. When the Common Council of Ministers met in Vienna on 7 July, the mood was decidedly in favour of war. Politicians approached war with their eyes fully open to its possible consequences. Though they hoped for a quick strike against Serbia, they expected a wider war. Count Alexander Hoyos, Berchtold's personal emissary during the crisis, confessed that 'it is immaterial to us whether a world war comes out of this'. [45, p. 16] The Chief of the German General Staff, Helmuth von Moltke, spoke of a war which would 'annihilate the culture of almost all of Europe for decades to come'. Equally apocalyptic, General Falkenhayn reassured Bethmann-Hollweg that 'Even if we go under as a result of this, it still [will be] beautiful'. [45, pp. 36–7]

At that moment the French President, Raymond Poincaré, and Prime Minister, René Viviani, were in Russia. The Germans did not particularly want French and Russian leaders to be together when the crisis broke, since German plans depended upon a slow reaction by their enemies. In any case, a large proportion of the Austro-Hungarian armed forces were on 'harvest leave' and would not return to barracks until the 15th. Nothing was therefore done until 23 July when a timed note was sent to Serbia with demands, which, if accepted, would have virtually meant the end of Serbian independence. The British Foreign Minister, Sir Edward Grey, called it the 'most formidable document that I have ever seen addressed by one State to another that was independent'. [45, p. 25] But the note was not an ultimatum, since it did not make clear what consequences would transpire in the event of a Serbian rejection. Nor did the Germans or the Austro-Hungarians begin mobilizing.

The Serbian reply was a diplomatic masterpiece. By accepting most of the demands, they made their adversaries seem unreasonable, particularly if Austria-Hungary then decided to secure the remaining points militarily. But the response may have been too brilliant in that it left politicians in Vienna feeling they had been painted into a corner. They now felt that they had no real option but war. Serbia, keen to get a head start in the coming conflict, began to mobilize.

The Russians decided that they could not let the Serbs down again. They saw the Austro-Hungarian action as masking a German desire to control the Balkans and squeeze out Russian influence. Moscow therefore decided to call a 'preparatory to general mobilisation'. It was not an actual movement of troops but was instead designed to show Austria-Hungary that Russia would not stand aside. It was, in truth, the last act of diplomacy and the first act of war. Since neither Germany nor Austria-Hungary could afford to allow the Russians to get a jump on them, the Russian declaration, in their opinion, deserved a warlike response.

After the Serbian reply, the German Chancellor Bethmann-Hollweg urged his ally to take decisive action. Germany, it seems, hoped that Serbia might be crushed quickly, before Russia could intervene. Austria-Hungary complied, declaring war on 28 July and shelling Belgrade later that day. This put Russia in a difficult position, since her mobilization plans called for a war against Austria-Hungary *and* Germany. The Russian Foreign Minister, Sergei Sazonov, warned the Tsar that a partial mobilization against Austria-Hungary alone was out of the question since it might endanger the agreement with France. The French could not be given an excuse to remain neutral. Alarmed at this prospect, the Tsar reluctantly approved full mobilization on 30 July.

The Russian mobilization allowed the Germans to pretend they were the victims of naked aggression, a propaganda point of some value in establishing unity at home. Germany could not, however, allow a day to be wasted, since she had to defeat France before the

Russians arrived at her back door. The Kaiser, fearful that Britain might side with France, asked Moltke if it might be possible to mobilize against Russia only, but the latter replied that such a last minute change of heart would inevitably spell chaos. Germany therefore responded to Russia's declaration of war by demanding French neutrality. When the French refused, Germany declared war on both her enemies and put the Schlieffen plan into operation. The Kaiser told his people that 'the sword is being forced into our hands', a lie, but a stirring one nonetheless. [56, p. 81] The Italians, it should be noted, decided for the moment to remain neutral, hoping that they might eventually sell their services to the highest bidder. Moltke, angered at this betrayal, promised that Germany would, in time, 'settle accounts with these scoundrels'. [45, p. 32]

The French can hardly be blamed for acting hastily; they were fully aware of the dangers of delay. Joseph Joffre, Chief of the French General Staff, warned his government that every day's hesitation in announcing a general mobilization would result in the enemy penetrating an additional 25 kilometres into French territory. A similar haste was apparent in all the European capitals. No one wanted to miss the train. Once war became inevitable, the European nations obeyed the dictates of the stationmaster's whistle.

Up to this point, the British had had little influence upon events. But, as Crowe pointed out, Britain could not realistically stay out of the war:

> Should this war come and England stand aside, one of two things must happen: (a) Either Germany and Austria win, crush France and humiliate Russia ... What will be the position of friendless England? (b) Or France and Russia win. What would then be their attitude towards England? What about India and the Mediterranean? [20, p. 7]

Neutrality would jeopardise the carefully constructed web of agreements designed to protect the Empire; neither Russia nor France would see any reason to behave themselves in India or Africa if Britain let them down in Europe. But, at least as important, Britain could not stand aside while the war produced a dominant European power – such as Germany – determined to exploit British vulnerability. In addition, free British access to the Belgian ports of Ostend and Zeebrugge were essential to British trade. *The Times* recognized that intervention was 'not merely a duty of friendship.

It is ... an elementary duty of self-preservation ... We cannot stand alone in a Europe dominated by any single power'. [59, p. 139] But the German invasion of Belgium was a godsend to the British government. Selling the war to the British people became infinitely easier. A war of hegemony was transformed overnight into a war of morality.

By the end of the first week of August, some 44 declarations of war and mobilization orders had been sent by the various belligerents. The paperwork was complete, and the business of killing could begin.

Militarism and the mood for war

On hearing of the declaration of war, Sigmund Freud commented 'all my libido goes to Austria-Hungary'. The novelist Thomas Mann wrote that he was 'tired, sick and tired' of peace. War, he was certain, would provide 'purification'. [45, pp. 34–5] In 1928, the British social scientist Caroline Playne reflected on the way a war fever had gripped Europe:

> the thoughtful, no less than the others, were under the spell of an immense crowd infection even before it finally took hold of them in the hot dog-days of 1914. The desire went out from the more primitive-minded, those to whom force made a supreme appeal – militarists, chauvinists, imperialists. The mental contagion – it was a contagion, something more immediate than a suggestion – swept down the mindless, expectant, half-frightened, wondering crowds, and ... swept down progressives, earnest people, intelligent people as well. [88, pp. 329–30]

Kurt Riezler, Bethmann-Hollweg's secretary, recorded how 'The incomparable storm unleashed in the people has swept before it all doubting, half-hearted and fearful minds'. [25, p. 63] Maurice de Bunsen, British envoy to Vienna, witnessed the city in 'a frenzy of delight, vast crowds parading the streets and singing patriotic songs till the small hours of the morning'. Perhaps 1.5 million patriotic war poems were penned in Germany in 1914 alone. [45, pp. 17, 33] What is striking is the way people of all classes embraced the war not just out of a sense of duty, but with positive alacrity.

It is easy from this evidence to conclude that the war arose from a herd emotion, that Europeans plunged to their deaths like millions of lemmings. A short leap of reason leads one to the realm of inevitability. But since we know that war did break out, the factors and emotions that contributed to it seem obvious and important and those that worked against it seem insignificant. We ignore, for instance, the tremendous impact and popularity of Angell's pacifistic book *The Great Illusion*; the enormous progress made in international cooperation, especially in banking, transportation and communication; the worldwide interest in the Olympic movement; the civility which the Hague Conferences of 1901 and 1907 brought to international relations; the popularity of pacifist groups, especially those socialist-inspired; and the fact that the Anglo-German naval rivalry had eased significantly by 1912. Had war not occurred, historians would today point to these phenomena as clear harbingers of a dawning era of peace.

Furthermore, there is a fundamental misconception in the arguments of Playne and those of her ilk, namely that the popular will can carry a nation into war. In any country, foreign policy is formulated by a very small group of individuals who contemptuously ignore popular opinion. Governments go to war not because of mysterious forces swirling in the air but for purely pragmatic reasons. The people's will is important; politicians will usually hesitate before committing a nation to a war which is decidedly unpopular. But no amount of 'war fever' will drive a government to wage a war not in the national interest.

But popular emotion was important to the way the war was fought. For many the conflict provided a release and a spiritual cleansing. Herman Hesse welcomed war as an escape from a 'dull capitalistic peace'. Even after a few hard months in the trenches, Franz Marc was still able to proclaim: 'Let us remain soldiers even after the war ... for this is not a war against an eternal enemy, as the newspapers and our honourable politicians say, nor of one race against another; it is a European civil war, a war against the inner invisible enemy of the European spirit.' [25, p. 94] These were times when manliness was elevated to a Christian virtue and war seemed the ultimate test of masculinity. For many Germans, the uniform provided potent sexual stimulus. French boys dreamt of a martyr's death in Alsace or Lorraine, and British schoolboys absorbed H. A. Vachell's vision of noble death in *The Hill*:

To die young, clean, ardent; to die swiftly, in perfect health; to die saving others from death, or worse – disgrace – to die scaling heights; to die and to carry with you into the fuller ampler life beyond, untainted hopes and aspirations, unembittered memories, all the freshness and gladness of May – is not that cause for joy rather than sorrow? [118, p. 236]

Hill's and Hesse's fantasies did not cause the war. But the war fever, such as it was, did ensure that when war broke out there were millions of men across Europe ready to die a glorious death in the pursuit of national honour.

2
The Western Front, 1914–17

For most people the Great War brings to mind muddy trenches, demoralizing stalemate and the 'strategy of attrition'. The advance of the dead was more successful than that of the living; cemeteries occupy more ground than was won in battle. The foetid swamps of the Western Front swallowed the myths of glorious war which had so inspired the young soldiers of 1914. Because the war seems incomprehensible, acceptance of the losses has been difficult. This lack of understanding has encouraged the easy judgement that the commanders must have been stubborn incompetents.

The war on the Western Front is unique but not very interesting. It is no wonder that there are so few good films or war novels about it. Quite simply, it is difficult to construct a plot around 44 months of stalemate. But there is a story to be told. Little happened, but millions died. Too often, amateur analysts have tried to cast the war in a different scenario based upon an imagined solution to the trench deadlock. The responsible student of the war should avoid such fantasies. Instead of imagining what might have happened, it is better to explain what did.

One should start from the premise that the war's progress was determined not by men but by machines. Technology put men into trenches and kept them there for three years. It narrowed the scope for imagination and good command. Both sides developed a remarkable proficiency for going nowhere. There is little point, therefore, to spend time describing in detail the various battles that occurred on the Western Front up to the end of 1917. They differ in scale, but hardly in achievement. A more illuminating approach is to explain why the war took on the static character that it did and why that character proved so immutable despite determined efforts by all combatants to achieve a breakthrough.

The State of the armies

In the second half of the nineteenth century, the German (or, rather, Prussian) Army had imposed its dominance upon continental Europe. This dominance was founded upon a highly organized professional system with a well-trained General Staff that acted as the 'brain of the army', formulating new strategies and exploiting new weapons technologies. The deep patriotism of a proud, newly emergent, nation meant that Germany could rely upon a ready supply of men in whom the idea of service and sacrifice ran deep. In 1914, Germany had a standing army of around 800 000 men, and perhaps another four million in the reserves, drawn from a population of around 65 million. These men were trained to a remarkably high standard and supplied with the finest weaponry, including a more formidable force of artillery than existed in any other army. The Germans were also the first to grasp the enormous potential of the machine gun and to develop tactics suited to it.

The German military maintained its hold on the individual for a very long time, which in part explains its strength and cohesiveness. After two or three years of full-time service, the soldier moved to the regular reserves for another four or five years and then served in the Landwehr for 12 years and finally the Landsturm until the age of forty-five. In contrast to the other belligerent armies, German regular reserves were first-class troops. They were used in combat from the opening days of the war, much to the chagrin of the British and French, who expected a smaller German army. The technical knowledge and leadership skills of long-service officers and non-commissioned officers (NCOs) rendered them far superior to their rivals in any other continental army. Thus, the German army possessed both the command structure and raw material necessary for rapid expansion in wartime. A rigid system of discipline ensured that the force remained cohesive and morale high even during periods of great adversity.

The Germany army was big because it had to be. German leaders knew they would have to fight a war on two fronts, and planned accordingly. Thus, the army was not only prepared for the challenges which might face it on the battlefield, it was also capable of quick mobilization and efficient transport. The railway system had been built with the specific need for transferring large numbers of troops from East to West in mind. But there were limits to German preparation. In 1912, the army rejected proposals to expand its standard peacetime contingent of 800 000 men because it was feared that this would disturb the social cohesion of the officer corps. And, on the eve of war, ammunition reserves were between 20 and 50 per cent below required levels.

The French army was also massive, but not quite as formidable as the German. In 1913, in anticipation of war, the French government had passed (over the bitter opposition of the Socialists) a bill extending the period of conscription from two years to three, effectively expanding the standing army by 50 per cent. Despite the fact that France's population, at around 40 million, was much smaller than Germany's, her regular army was roughly similar in size, at 813 000 men. France conscripted 86 per cent of men of military age, Germany just 50 per cent. This meant that the French were effectively over-mobilized, a fact of little importance in a short war, but crucial in a long one. French industry was not well equipped to support a huge army in a protracted war.

France could call upon 2 887 000 reservists. Though quite a few of the reserve divisions were of suspect quality, the regular troops were first class. They were blessed with modern artillery, and the best gun in the war, the French 75 mm. It possessed the highest rate of fire of any gun in the war. But the very existence of this gun exacerbated an already unhealthy emphasis upon the offensive, to the detriment of defensive training and preparation. Generally speaking, the obsession with moral factors, or *élan,* encouraged blindness to the physical factors which were of such significance in this war. It is unwise to go into a technological war believing that the human spirit will always prevail.

The British army was both modern and antique. It was a professional army, not unlike that of today: small, highly disciplined and very well trained. The logistical apparatus was first rate, allowing quick mobilization. Soldiers could trust that they would be well supplied and that they would be provided with fast and effective medical care if wounded. The main purpose of this army had been to act as an imperial police force, a function it had performed well in the countless small wars of Victoria's reign. But officers reflected the class divisions of wider British society. The educated middle-class officer usually ended up in the artillery or engineers, the two arms that required a high level of technical expertise. The elite classes went into the infantry or more prestigious cavalry and enjoyed the lion's share of prestigious commands. For this group, authority was a birthright and good breeding was thought to be more important than good education.

While the British were busy fighting Dervish, Zulus and Maoris, the nature of European war changed radically. Highly accurate, long-range weaponry allowed anonymous soldiers to fight each other at great distance. The British thumbed their noses at this depersonalization of war by continuing to rely on leaders who were instinctively suspicious of technology. The dominance of cavalry officers meant that strategists planned battles conducive to cavalry operations. Success in colonial wars encouraged a false sense of security – war still seemed small, noble and heroic. The Boer War disturbed this cosy confidence, but only briefly. Setbacks in South Africa caused considerable worry, and some reform. But by 1907 cavalry traditionalists reasserted themselves, as evidenced by the re-introduction of the lance, which had been abolished immediately after the war.

Victory, it was presumed, was mainly a test of character, which explains why new weapons were not fully exploited. The mantra of the cavalry officer was that 'the moral is to the physical as three is to one'. In truth, the 'moral' only wins battles if the physical will allow. The British seemed loath to accept that their superb morale resulted not from superior character, but from greater wealth and development in comparison to their colonial adversaries. This advantage would not be replicated on the Western Front.

On paper, the Entente Powers were numerically superior and could rely upon greater industrial capacity. They had a combined population of 279 million; the Central Powers just 120 million. In 1914, they could field 199 infantry and 50 cavalry divisions, compared to 137 and 22, respectively, for Germany and Austria-Hungary. On the Western Front, the French fielded 46 infantry divisions and 10 cavalry divisions in August, with another 25 divisions in reserve. The Belgians and British contributed another six and five divisions, respectively. Germany put the bulk of her forces in the West, fielding 78 divisions.

Despite their numerical inferiority, the Central Powers did enjoy interior lines of communication, which eased the transport of troops and supplies. In contrast, British troops had to be moved by ship to the battlefront, which implied a huge effort in keeping sea lanes open. On the other side, Russia was cut off from her allies – getting supplies to her was extremely difficult. It was impossible to transport large numbers of troops from the East to the West, or vice versa. No system of unified command had been established on either side. But, in contrast to Germany, no one power within the Entente was sufficiently dominant to impose its will upon its allies.

Battle plans

Strategic plans are formed by military staffs who apply past experience to present political aspirations. Unfortunately, past experience is often irrelevant and political aspirations often unrealizable. Wars seldom follow blueprints because blueprints are seldom appropriate. In this conflict, no country planned upon a defensive war. Staff colleges across Europe had produced identikit commanders all wedded to a cult of the offensive. In Germany, Schlieffen preached that 'attack is the best defence'. British officers, taught that defence was unmanly, devoted little attention to its study. Even the French, who did not seek a war, were determined to attack if one came. Joffre claimed that his army 'knows [no] other law than the offensive'. [45, p. 36] 'For the attack only two things are necessary: to know where the enemy is and to decide what to do', preached the influential Colonel de Grandmaison. 'What the enemy intends to do is of no consequence'. [28, p. 35]

   Long before war broke out, the French had decided that the most important goal was to recover Alsace and Lorraine. Even though they had long known of the Schlieffen Plan, they had no intention of waiting in northern France for the German blow to fall. Instead, they put the bulk of their troops in the South, in preparation for a campaign of conquest. Their confidence was sufficiently robust to assume that a relatively small force, allied with the British, could stop the German steamroller. This strategy was called Plan XVII.

   Germany, as was discussed in the last chapter, had long planned upon a two-front war which would be won by quickly defeating France, whereupon troops would be transferred eastward to meet the advancing Russian horde. There were a number of somewhat shaky assumptions behind this strategy, including the obvious one that a quick campaign could be won in an era of huge armies and massively powerful weaponry. It was also presumed that the capture of an enemy's capital would automatically result in outright victory. While such a scenario was certainly characteristic of classical war, whether it still held true in the modern age was uncertain.

The British had a strategy called 'Business as Usual'. Often seen as merely an attempt to reassure industrialists and financiers that war would not disrupt commerce, it was in fact a cohesive and purposeful plan for military and economic victory. The British started from the assumption that they could not avoid involvement in the war but must not suffer too extensively. The small army was to be deployed on the left flank of the French, where it would maintain a token presence, thus demonstrating that the British were 'doing their bit'. Meanwhile the Royal Navy would impose a blockade on Germany, designed not only to stop goods from getting in, but also to hinder trade from getting out. Britain would, in other words, be the arsenal, larder and banker of the Entente, but the French and Russians would do the dying. While the Germans were preoccupied with the fighting, the British would take over German markets in the rest of the world. The war would end with Britain victorious and rich. But in order to pursue this strategy, Britain had to avoid 'tremendous drains on our labour supply in war' – in other words, she could not afford to have industrial workers dying on the battlefield. [20, p. 55] Unfortunately, no one bothered to inform the generals. They had in mind a very different war, which involved an immediate expansion of the army. When Field Marshal Herbert Kitchener took over as Secretary of State for War just days after hostilities began, he quickly called for 500 000 volunteers, a demand he quickly doubled and then doubled again. Overnight, workers became soldiers. 'Business as Usual' was dead on arrival.

Across Europe, plans were formed in a vacuum, and took little account of enemy (or even Allied) intentions. Strategists did not properly consider the state of military technology, the size of the various armies, the difficulty of terrain, and the popular commitment to war which nationalism implied. They stuck instead to classical concepts of war, in which the aim of any army was to out-manoeuvre the enemy force, envelop and defeat it. But this type of war was not entirely relevant to the age of nationalism and huge citizen armies. Though there would continue to be manoeuvre warfare (particularly in Eastern Europe), the war would not be confined to the battlefield alone. The contest was no longer between armies but between nations. Success would go to the side which imposed its will upon the other and destroyed the enemy's will to fight. This goal involved military action, but was not exclusively military. Equally important was the ability of a nation to supply its army, pay for its weapons, feed its people and keep them believing in victory.

The shape of war

A short war was always unlikely. The longer the war lasted, the more important industrialization, organization, social stability and political leadership became. Likewise, as the war dragged on, technology would impose its autocratic will on the character of the fighting. This meant not only that modern weapons would dominate the battlefield, but also that victory would go to the nation or nations able to produce those weapons in vast quantities and transport them to the battlefield.

Industrialization had affected war in ways that military leaders did not fully understand. Long-range rifles, machine guns, barbed wire, gas, powerful explosives, smokeless powder, accurate artillery, and a host of other lethal developments had changed the character of warfare. It was technology, not idiotic commanders, which put the armies on the Western Front into trenches and kept them there for three years. Soldiers have always dug trenches to protect themselves from enemy fire. They wait in their holes until an opportunity for advance presents itself, usually achieved when one side establishes superiority in a given locale. That opportunity did not arise on the Western Front until 1918, despite repeated efforts by both sides to create the conditions for it. The men stayed in the trenches for three years because it was the only safe place for them.

Warfare is shaped by the interplay of firepower and mobility. When firepower is in the ascendancy, the war is static. When methods of movement allow the battlefield to be crossed with sufficient speed and protection, the war is mobile. In this war, mobility came in the form of primitive motor transport, the horse, or – the most common form – men simply walking. Movement was impeded by the boggy, shell-churned ground which made the battlefield inaccessible to trucks and motorcycles, and slowed the pace at which a fully equipped soldier could walk. The Western Front was also very crowded with soldiers. Crowds move slowly.

The combatants, on the other hand, had access to a wide variety and virtually limitless supply of lethal firepower: artillery, rifles, mortars, machine guns, bombs and mines. In other words, firepower was dominant. The advent of slow-moving and unreliable tanks in 1916 did not markedly alter the firepower/mobility dynamic. There was little a soldier could do to advance against this firepower, therefore the natural response was to dig a hole. When millions of men dug holes the result was a trench system stretching from

Switzerland to the English Channel. Because technology forced men into the trenches, but did not provide a way to get them out, the soldiers instead directed their energies to improving their trench systems by making them more impregnable. Thus, mobility became even less likely as the war progressed.

Opening battles

The war was not, however, immediately characterized by trench stalemate. During the first three months, the combatants fought a classic war of movement. The Germans, as Schlieffen had planned, attacked through Belgium and northern France. [Map 1] In their path stood a stubborn Belgian force, some French divisions and the tiny British army, which managed to mobilize with impressive speed. Meanwhile, a huge concentration of French troops attacked eastwards, into Alsace and Lorraine. The effect was not unlike a revolving door. French troops left France just as German troops entered. Because both sides attacked relatively weak sectors, initial results in both cases were encouraging.

But the real danger occurred in the North. The Germans encountered stiff resistance in Belgium, to which they responded with consummate cruelty. The atrocities committed during the first week of war would provide Entente propagandists with good copy for the rest of the war. But little Belgium could not sufficiently throw the German juggernaut off course. It seemed that Schlieffen would indeed be pronounced a genius. But Moltke altered the original plan by approaching Paris from the north rather than from the west. He also weakened his right wing, when two army corps and a cavalry division were dispatched to East Prussia to meet a Russian threat which had arrived much more quickly than had been anticipated. Was Moltke's diversion from Schlieffen's precepts a demonstration of courage or wisdom? The original plan was sufficiently risky to strain the nerves of any mere mortal. Moltke perhaps could not stomach the idea of his massive force, so deep within enemy territory, relying upon a long and vulnerable line of communication. If the plan had worked, Germany might have won the war. But, if it had failed, a huge German army would have found itself deep in a hole from which there was no ready escape.

The Germans and British collided at Mons on 23 August rather like a truck hitting a porcupine. The British were severely shaken

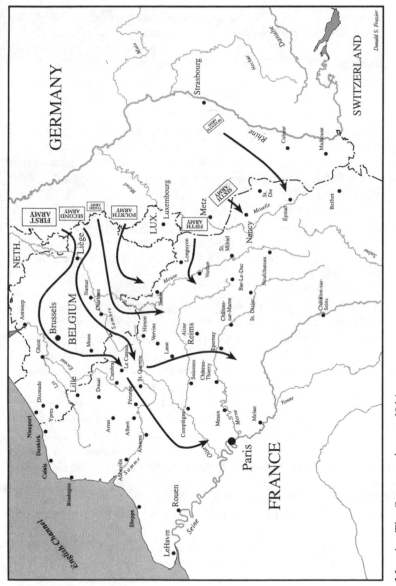

Map 1 *The German advance, 1914*

but still managed to throw the Germans off course. A German soldier later recorded his impressions of coming under British fire:

> No sooner had we left the edge of the wood than a volley of bullets whistled past our noses and cracked into the trees behind. Five or six cries near me, five or six of my grey lads collapsed in the grass ... Here we were as if advancing on a parade ground ... away in front a sharp hammering sound, then a pause, then a more rapid hammering – machine guns! [56, p. 109]

The fire, in fact, came not from machine guns but from British infantrymen, trained to fire at speed. But it was not enough. In the centre and on the left, the British and French were forced into full retreat. Joffre cabled his War Minister:

> We are ... compelled to resort to the defensive, using our fortresses and great topographical obstacles to enable us to yield as little ground as possible. Our object must be to last out, trying to wear the enemy down, and to resume the offensive when the time comes. [56, p. 110]

Joffre managed to hold Entente forces together as they moved back to the Marne, by no means an easy task. As the Germans drew to within artillery range of Paris, plans for defending the city were put into effect. Though it had been agreed that Paris would be defended to the last man, the French government thought it prudent to make for Bordeaux. Some 500 000 Parisians followed their leaders. Meanwhile, Anglo-French forces hung on by their fingernails. Soldiers were ferried in taxis across the city in order to plug gaps in the line. By 1 September the German momentum had dissipated. Meanwhile, the French offensive in Alsace and Lorraine also ground to a halt.

Moltke had diverged too often from Schlieffen's plan. When decisive victory did not come, he found himself in a highly vulnerable position. Recognizing his opportunity, Joffre ordered a counter-attack upon the German right flank:

> Now, as the battle is joined on which the safety of the country depends, everyone must be reminded that that this is no longer the time for looking back. Every effort must be made to attack and throw back the enemy. A unit which finds it impossible to advance must, regardless of cost, hold its ground and be killed

on the spot rather than fall back. In the present circumstances, no failure will be tolerated. [115, p. 483]

The resulting Battle of the Marne was a stunning victory, with the French and British eventually pushing the Germans back to the River Aisne. The lacklustre Moltke was replaced by Erich von Falkenhayn.

What followed has been wrongly called a race to the sea. It was actually a series of attempts by both sides to outflank each other. They eventually ran out of room and reached the Channel. By November, the combatants found themselves on a line that would remain largely unaltered until March 1918. [Map 2] The losses on all sides were staggering. By the end of the year, the French had suffered 995 000 casualties, the Germans 667 000, the British 96 000 and the Belgians perhaps 50 000. Soldiers and politicians began to consider what to do about this incomprehensible war. 'I don't know what is to be done', Kitchener confessed, 'this isn't war'. [99, p. 70]

Fighting a static war: the battles of 1915

The Germans, the most modern and least hidebound army before 1914, adapted best to this new type of war. They organized defences that relied, as far as possible, on materials rather than men. Huge concrete fortifications were built, and firepower was intelligently applied to the best advantage. Unlike the British and French, they were also willing to surrender territory in order to retreat to more secure defensive positions. But both the fortifications and the ability to retreat arose from the position in which the Germans found themselves once the war became static. To advance was not of great importance, since they occupied enemy soil and it was up to their enemies to evict them. Physical possession of French and Belgian land would be an enormous advantage if the war were to end by diplomatic rather than military means. For the Allies, retreating meant surrendering more land to the Germans, which was politically dangerous and bad for morale. Likewise, building solid fortifications made little sense, since trenches were supposed to be launching pads for attacks, not defensive positions to be held permanently. Since the Allies had no intention of remaining in one place, they were not overly concerned to build fortress-like emplacements.

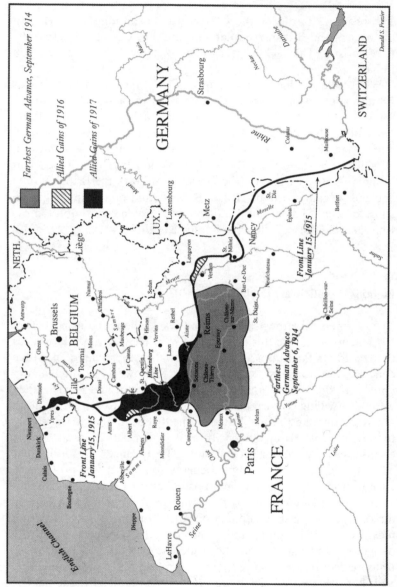

Map 2   *The Western Front, 1914–17*

The British and French responded to the stalemate by applying old principles of warfare. Battles in the past assumed a standard pattern: the artillery would 'soften' a section of the enemy line, whereupon the infantry would attack. The cavalry would then charge into the breach and turn the flank. Allied commanders assumed that this was still possible, despite the formidable strength of the German defence and the difficulty of movement on the Western Front. When they failed to achieve a breakthrough, they did not change their strategies, but instead merely intensified their attack. As the war progressed, offensives grew larger, bombardments longer and casualties greater, but the depth of advance remained depressingly small.

It is now fashionable to criticize the Entente commanders, and Douglas Haig in particular, for fighting an unimaginative, costly strategy of attrition. In fact, most of them assumed that, given sufficient men and munitions, they could restore mobility to this war. They should, therefore, more appropriately be criticized for trying to fight a war of movement when movement was impossible. In wars of attrition, the body count is all that matters. Capturing ground is immaterial, and can be counter-productive if the advance leaves the attacking force in a position that subsequently proves costly to hold. The aim in attritional warfare is to kill as many of the enemy as possible, thus weakening him physically and destroying his morale. The British and French never quite grasped this very basic fact. Though they fought a war of attrition by default, they would have fought a more efficient (and perhaps less costly) one had they accepted the immutability of stalemate.

During 1915 both sides attacked with considerable ferocity, but were not able to sustain their efforts for very long. Offensive action was limited by the fact that demand for artillery ammunition outstripped supply. The combatants had expected a war of movement and an army on the move uses far fewer shells (of smaller calibre) than static operations demand. Furthermore, a static war required massive amounts of high-explosive shells for blowing apart enemy entrenchments. These were in short supply, since shrapnel shells seemed more appropriate to the anticipated war of movement in which artillery would be used to cut down advancing soldiers in the open. It would be some time before the factories at home could begin to satisfy the demands of their rapacious armies, especially since the manufacture of high-explosive shells was more difficult and dangerous than shrapnel. Thus, early in 1915 the progress of the war was determined not by the ability of the belligerents to put men in the field, but by the capacity of the factories to supply them.

On 20 December 1914, the French began an offensive in the Champagne region. Forward thrusts were launched sporadically until mid-March, but no significant gains were made. French losses doubled those of the Germans. Then, in March, the British struck toward Neuve Chapelle in the first set-piece attack of the war. Haig, the First Army commander, carefully studied German positions and meticulously planned his attack, including the placement of 342 guns. As would become typical of battles on the Western Front, a preliminary bombardment sought to soften the defences and destroy the German wire. But shortages of ammunition limited the bombardment to 35 minutes. The British nevertheless managed a momentary breakthrough on a narrow frontage. But they lacked the reserves to exploit this modest success, while the Germans quickly brought troops forward to plug the gap. The battle was nevertheless profoundly important because it convinced Haig that breakthroughs were possible. 'I think that the main lesson of Neuve Chapelle is that given sufficient ammunition and suitable guns we can break through the enemy's line whenever we like', he told a friend. [21, p. 183] Henceforth, the battle provided a model for future British operations. But Haig failed to realize that success had been achieved because of, not in spite of, the short bombardment. The brief barrage allowed the element of surprise to be maintained. A longer bombardment would destroy that advantage.

The Germans then attacked near Ypres, primarily to give the impression that they were still strong in the West and to camouflage the steady movement of troops eastward. Their assault in April 1915 was notable for the first systematic use of poison gas. Because the new weapon came as a complete surprise, its effects were impressive. The German penetration was significant, at least by the standards of this war. They also won the body count, suffering just half the casualties of the British and French combined. The attack further narrowed the salient formed during the previous year when the Allies had stubbornly refused to surrender Ypres. That salient was now extremely dangerous. A more sober analysis might have dictated abandonment of the town. But the Allies hung on, eventually consolidating a useful piece of real estate on which to die in large numbers.

Joffre now turned his attention to the area around Artois. Progress in the war can be measured by the steadily increasing size of battles; on this occasion the French collected 1200 guns and fired 700 000 rounds. On 9 May 1915 the French infantry attacked Vimy Ridge with considerable ferocity but limited results. A British thrust upon the Aubers Ridge, timed to coincide with the French action, did little to disrupt the stalemate. Attacks continued until mid-June when exhaustion and ammunition shortages finally dictated a halt. The Germans emerged from the fray convinced that they had mastered the art of defence. The French and British, on the other hand, were certain that, given a steady supply of men and munitions, a breakthrough could be achieved.

The stalemate caused considerable unease among those who would decide the fate of the Entente armies. Opposing schools of thought bickered over whether the Western Front held any promise at all of significant movement. 'Westerners' like Haig and Joffre decided that the answer lay in concentrating all effort in France and Belgium in the hope that more of everything would eventually cause the Germans to crack. 'Easterners', in contrast, argued that it was better to attack Germany by way of the Mediterranean theatres. Self-proclaimed strategists spoke of 'knocking out the props' on which the German war effort rested. They looked longingly at the 'back door', 'soft underbelly' and other imagined weak points in the enemy fortress, the exact location of which was never firmly established. The two sides would argue for the rest of the war, a stalemate not unlike the issue over which they argued.

Over the summer the British Expeditionary Force expanded steadily. Territorial and New Army (the new units raised by Lord Kitchener) reinforcements arrived, and a Canadian Corps was added, allowing the British to take over 32 kilometres of French line. In September, the Westerners got another chance to buttress their case. A simultaneous offensive was launched by the British and French in Artois and by the French alone in Champagne. Joffre wanted the Artois attack to concentrate upon Loos, but Haig and Sir John French, the British commander-in-chief, thought the area ill-suited. They were overruled by Kitchener, who argued that 'We must act with all energy and do our utmost to help France in this offensive, even though by so doing we may suffer heavy losses'. [67, p. 196] The French attack in Champagne was at first quite successful, penetrating to a depth of over two kilometres. It then went the way of earlier attacks, with further movement stifled by German reinforcements. An immutable law of static war had once again been demonstrated. Any advance merely pushed enemy troops closer to their reinforcements, while lengthening the distance that the second wave of attackers had to travel in order to consolidate or extend the advance. The problems of capitalizing upon an initial success would plague armies for the entire war.

Further north, Entente forces achieved some local successes, but mainly encountered the battlefield equivalent of a brick wall. At Loos the British deployed gas for the first time, but, so rigid were their plans, it was used despite the absence of a favourable wind to carry it toward German lines. Some British attackers were incapacitated by their own gas. German soldiers were astonished at the way British infantry walked forward in perfect order to their death: 'Never had [our] machine guns had such straightforward work to do'. [56, p. 218] The initial thrust on 25 September penetrated to a depth of four kilometres on a frontage twice that length, but then quickly stalled. Two New Army divisions were then thrown into the battle on the following day. In their first experience of combat they were slaughtered by crack German troops. When the battle sputtered to a close, German casualties totalled just over 50 000, while French and British were over twice that many.

An argument subsequently raged between French and Haig. The latter thought that he had achieved a breakthrough only to see it squandered by French's failure to release the reserves in time. 'We *were* in a position to make this the turning point of the war', Haig later claimed, with no hyperbole intended. [21, p. 208] Haig's argument was overstated, but French made an ass of himself by vehemently refusing to accept blame for a minor misjudgement. The commander-in-chief had proven himself unsuited to this type of war and, since a ready replacement existed in the altogether more impressive Haig, a change was made. French was a good man and a competent commander, but too sensitive to direct affairs in a war of such appalling tragedy. Haig, in contrast, had what the war demanded, namely an iron nerve. His irrepressible optimism encouraged a sense of invincibility which was further reinforced by a sycophantic staff who worshipped him. Haig's confidence was further bolstered by his sincere belief that he had been chosen by God to lead the British army to victory.

By December the front had altered little. Nothing had changed, but thousands had died. The year 1915 is often neglected in annals of the war since the offensives seem minuscule in comparison to those that would follow. But one easily forgets just how much the French in particular had to endure. On the Western Front, they suffered 1.3 million casualties, twice as many as the Germans and nearly five times as many as the British. Attrition was taking its toll upon the French in a way not appreciated by the new British commander, whose prejudice often made him confuse French exhaustion with cowardice.

Big battles

The weakened state of the French army did not escape the notice of the Germans. Early in 1916 they attempted to force attrition to its logical conclusion. They had decided that the way to win the war was to bleed the French white so that they would surrender, whereupon the British would quickly lose their will to fight alone on French soil. The Germans sought to do this by attacking the rail junction of Verdun which it was presumed the French could not bear to lose. The city was protected by a series of strong fortresses but these were not as well-manned or heavily armed as had been the case earlier in the war. The narrowness of the salient around Verdun meant that the Germans could train artillery fire upon it from three sides.

'The object', Falkenhayn stressed, 'is not to defeat but to annihilate France'. [45, p. 184] With a troop superiority better than two to one and an artillery advantage of three to one, the Germans attacked on 21 February. French lines quickly collapsed and by the end of the month Fort Douaumont, the cornerstone of the city's defence, was captured. The Germans anticipated that the French would go to supreme lengths to defend Verdun, and would launch repeated counter-attacks to recover lost ground. The French played their assigned role to perfection. The Second Army under General Henri Pétain was moved into the area for the purpose of holding Verdun. The city became a symbol of national survival.

Pétain did not hesitate to sacrifice troops to hold Verdun. But his defence was not the blind rage of a cat cornered. He understood the importance of morale and the inherent strength of fresh troops. Units were, therefore, moved efficiently in and out of the battle, their condition carefully monitored. He relied heavily on superior French counter-battery fire. French gunners acquired a lifetime of skill and technique in a few short months. But the battle itself was bigger than any commander; it consumed men like an insatiably hungry beast. German attacks and French counter-attacks continued throughout the spring, summer and autumn. The French gradually imposed their patriotic will upon their enemy, finally recovering all of the fortresses by December.

In eleven months of battle, the two sides hurled 10 million shells at each other. The annals of war provide few battles to equal Verdun's savage destruction. As a meatgrinder, Falkenhayn's operation was very nearly a success. The incessant German attacks did come close to breaking French will. But attrition went both ways. In the original plan, the German artillery was to provide the main offensive thrust. But Falkenhayn got carried away with the prospect of actually capturing Verdun and poured in unit after unit of German blood. Under his original plan, three Frenchmen were supposed to be killed for every German. He did not come close to achieving that proportion. The French suffered perhaps 400 000 casualties, the Germans slightly fewer. The French army was never the same again, but did survive. The same could not be said for Falkenhayn, who had exhausted the patience of his government. In came Hindenburg and his sidekick, Ludendorff, whose exploits in the East seemed to suggest that they might be able to work miracles in the West.

Verdun is synonymous with French martyrdom, the Somme with British. Haig had long hoped to engineer a massive offensive in Flanders, an area he was convinced was uniquely suited to a breakthrough. But he had to bow to Joffre's preference for the Somme, and had to launch his attack six weeks earlier than he wanted. The proposed offensive was supposed to be a joint Anglo-French effort. But, as Verdun took its toll on the French, the Somme offensive became more distinctly British. Unfortunately, the battlefield, originally chosen because it was the point at which French and British forces joined, was ill-suited to the aims of the battle. Movement was difficult and the defenders had the high ground. Nor did it help that Haig made little effort to conceal his intentions from the Germans.

Haig thought that German strategy, specifically the emphasis upon attrition, lacked imagination and ambition. He instructed his subordinates to 'prepare for a rapid advance' and specifically directed that mounted troops should be ready for a breakthrough. [21, p. 248] This annoyed General Sir Henry Rawlinson, the Fourth Army commander, who preferred the 'bite and hold' strategy employed by the Germans at Verdun. One of his staff described Haig's scheme as 'an academic plan that would have been given good marks at the Staff College'. [114, p. 171]

Eighteen divisions were committed to the attack, 11 of them raised from Kitchener's New Army volunteers, who had little or no experience of battle. The bombardment began in the last week of June, with 1.6 million shells, a good many of them duds, dumped on German lines. 'The men are in splendid spirits', Haig wrote on the eve of the battle. 'Several have said that they have never been so instructed and informed of the nature of the operation before them. The wire has never been so well cut, nor the Artillery preparation so thorough'. [21, p. 251] It is not clear how he came upon this information, since he had little direct contact with the men in the trenches. Subsequent events suggest that his optimism was based more on blind faith than actual evidence.

Around 750 000 men were assembled along the attack frontage when the 'Big Push' went forward on 1 July. Over 57 000 casualties were suffered on the first day, with over 19 000 killed. The Germans, many of whom were safely ensconced in bunkers over nine metres deep, mowed down British soldiers with depressing efficiency. After two weeks of fighting, British losses were prodigious, and gains minuscule. Yet Haig remained confident:

> I think we have a good chance of success. If we don't succeed this time, we'll do so the next! The enemy is, I think, feeling the strain of continuous fighting, and is not fighting so well. My troops on the other hand are in the best of spirits! and feel they are going to win. [21, p. 253]

The battle was based upon one tragically flawed assumption, namely that British artillery could destroy German wire. Unfortunately the British had neither the guns nor the right ammunition to achieve such a feat. Much is made of the fact that British soldiers were ordered to walk – not run – toward the German line. One Brigadier General observed:

> They advanced in line after line, dressed as if on parade, and not a man shirked going through the extremely heavy barrage, or facing the machine gun and rifle fire that finally wiped them out. ... [I] saw the lines which advanced in such order melting away under the fire. Yet not a man wavered, broke the ranks, or attempted to come back. [I have] never seen, indeed could never have imagined, such a magnificent display of gallantry, discipline and determination. ... hardly a man of ours got to the German front line. [114, p. 158]

Men who had rushed to the colours in 1914 walked to their death. The order seems idiotic, but makes sense when it is considered that most soldiers had no previous experience of battle. They were not well-equipped mentally for the chaos which would have resulted if each soldier had been allowed to determine his own pace. Running would not, in any case, have made much difference to the outcome or the number of casualties. It was undisturbed wire and monotonously effective machine guns that defeated the British; running would simply have brought Tommy Atkins to his appointment with Death that much more quickly.

On 15 September Haig tried to alter the course of the battle by introducing the newly invented tanks, but they were too unreliable, and the ground too rough, to have any measurable effect. Of the 49 tanks available, 13 broke down *en route* to the front lines, and 11 stalled in No Man's Land. The remaining number certainly struck fear in German hearts, but were too few in number to have a dramatic effect upon the battle's outcome. The Somme campaign, which began as a bold attempt to break through, ended many months later as a long campaign of attrition. 'It is not possible to say how near to the breaking point the enemy may be', Haig wrote on 7 October, 'but he has undoubtedly gone a long way towards it'. [21, p. 269] In fact, neither side was immune to the battle's corrosive power. One senior British commander rued 'the state of exhaustion to which the men are reduced'. [114, p. 186] Haig boasted that the damage he had caused the Germans was greater than that which the Germans had caused him. That was perhaps true, but only if one left French losses out of the equation. German casualties on the Somme totalled perhaps 500 000, while the British lost 400 000 and the French half that number. The historian Gerhard Ritter, who experienced the carnage, called it 'monotonous mutual mass murder'. Soldiers had been reduced to mere lumps of coal consumed in a giant blast furnace of battle.

Mutinies and mud – the battles of 1917

The fighting in 1917 began with efforts by the British around Arras and the French around Soissons and Champagne. General Robert Nivelle, a hero of Verdun, had replaced Joffre as the new French commander-in-chief. He boasted that he knew how to break the German line. The British Prime Minister David Lloyd George succumbed to his charms and agreed to put British forces under Nivelle's command. Haig protested that 'it would be madness to place the British forces under the French', but did not force his objection to the point of resignation. [21, p. 303]

Nivelle believed that artillery tactics learned at Verdun would provide the key to unlocking the trench stalemate. To this end, he amassed around 5000 guns on the front between Soissons and Reims and fired upon German lines for 14 days prior to sending his troops forward. The artillery effort was largely wasted, however, since the Germans were employing a 'defence in depth' which meant that French shells fell on forward lines only lightly manned. French troops attacked from 16 April to 19 May, with the deepest penetration less than ten kilometres. Their casualties exceeded 180 000, with German just over 160 000. A simultaneous British attack further north managed to capture Vimy Ridge, but the cost was high.

Nivelle had failed, but only in the sense that his gains did not equal his ambitious predictions. (He had promised a penetration of over 12 kilometres on the first day.) In relation to other offensives of this war, his achievements were not unimpressive. But French soldiers had been led to believe that Nivelle was their Messiah. When he failed to find a way out of the wilderness, they revolted. The mutinies severely weakened the French army, which was unable afterwards to mount a sustained offensive. Pétain replaced Nivelle on 15 May and, by carefully nurturing his army, managed to keep his country in the war.

Pétain appealed to Haig to attack the Germans relentlessly so as to relieve the pressure on French troops. Haig needed little encouragement. He had long dreamt of a massive campaign in Flanders that would turn the German flank and end the war. Two years of frustrating stalemate had not dented his conviction that a breakthrough was possible. Flanders proved attractive for a number of reasons. First, the flat land seemed to offer the best opportunity for quick movement, especially by cavalry. Second, Haig was convinced that great strategic advantage would accrue if the British were able to liberate the Belgian Channel ports. It was commonly assumed that these were used as submarine bases, when in fact their importance to the submarine campaign was greatly exaggerated. When Sir John Jellicoe, First Sea Lord, told the War Cabinet on 19 June that the British could not survive into 1918 unless the submarines were defeated, this added weight to Haig's argument. Third, an offensive in this area would allow him to conduct operations independent of the French, whom he despised. If a great victory were won, it would be singularly British.

Haig offered no new strategy to bolster his assertions that a breakthrough could be achieved. He intended instead to do everything he had done before, but in greater measure. The bombardment would be longer and heavier, the breadth of attack wider, the number of troops larger. In other words, Haig approached the problem like the man who, when confronted by a locked door, decides simply to push harder.

The relentless pushing terrified politicians at home, who warned Haig against 'incurring heavy losses with comparatively small gains'. [21, p. 321] Events in Russia made British leaders desperately afraid of the effect the war might have upon class relations in Britain. Numerous plots to remove Haig were launched, but all foundered for the simple reason that no individual of distinctly greater merit could be found. Lloyd George instead tried by subtle and not-so-subtle means to limit Haig's autonomy and the damage he might cause. But there was little that could actually be done to restrain Haig, who moved forward with the confidence of a man certain that God had chosen him to deliver victory. The French weakness acted in his favour since the need for sustained attack was self-evident.

The campaign in Flanders began well enough when a relatively small British force under General Herbert Plumer achieved a resounding victory in a set-piece action against the Messines Ridge. Central to his plan were the 20 mines dug under the German lines, which were filled with over a million pounds of explosives. A 17-day bombardment, consisting of some 3.5 million shells, preceded the attack. On 7 June, the mines were blown, the earth heaved, and the German lines virtually disappeared. Nine divisions surged forward, reinforced by 72 Mark IV tanks. A great British victory was achieved, but the cost was not cheap. British forces suffered around 25 000 casualties, 2000 more than the Germans. And, again, capitalizing upon the initial success proved impossible.

The Messines success paved the way for a massive offensive from the Ypres salient. Haig gave the task to Hubert Gough's Fifth Army, partially because Gough, a cavalryman, was a 'thruster' who could be trusted to approach the problem with ambition, optimism and drive. His force of 17 divisions, was supported on the right by 12 divisions of Plumer's Second Army, two divisions of General François Anthoine's French First Army, around 3000 guns and

136 tanks. Haig's confidence was bolstered by a steady stream of intelligence which reported 'a marked and unmistakable fall in the morale of the German troops'. [21, p. 328] But these revealed more about the delusion at British General Headquarters (GHQ) than the deterioration of will within the German trenches.

German defences were extremely well prepared, with many fortifications made of concrete. The rigid defence lines of the early part of the war had been replaced by a 'defence in depth' which relied on a zigzag series of pillboxes with interlocking fields of fire. The first line of defence was relatively lightly manned, with the defenders concentrated instead further back. This allowed the men to escape the worst effects of the preliminary bombardment and permitted counterattacks to be organized and deployed where they were most needed. The terrain also favoured the defenders. Though flat, the boggy ground rendered forward movement extremely difficult. The sustained bombardment, lasting fourteen days and using up over four million shells, destroyed many of the dikes and ditches which drained the soil. An extraordinarily wet summer further exacerbated the problem of mud. Crown Prince Rupprecht, who commanded German troops in the region, called the rain 'our most effective ally'. [45, p. 332]

Twelve divisions oozed forward on 31 July. The offensive was supposed to move north-eastward from Ypres toward Ghent, turning the German flank, liberating Belgium and leaving the German war effort in ruin. Haig fantasized about lunching on the banks of the Rhine. But dreams of relentless advance proved a cruel joke in the mud of Flanders. The British action was characterized by bursts of activity punctuated by periods of incessant rain. When his ambitious objectives were not immediately achieved, Haig continued to push, convinced that one more effort would force the Germans over the brink. Had he planned upon a campaign of attrition, his offensive might have been judged a modest success. But that was never his intent. Nowhere is it stated in his papers that the British army would fight from August to mid-November, lose 245 000 men and gain just eight kilometres of miserable mud. If the purpose of attrition is to inflict a heavier punishment upon the enemy than one suffers oneself, Haig had not succeeded, since German losses were probably around 230 000. Among the objectives of the first few days was the town of Passchendaele, cast as a minor prize in a drama of relentless movement. Instead it proved to be the limit of Haig's achievements, the final conquest after months of desperate fighting.

In order to relieve the pressure on the French army and to pursue his vision of victory, Haig had pushed his own force to the very limit. But he was not done. On 20 November, he launched an attack on Cambrai. The Germans were given an introduction to war of the future. Some 400 tanks bolstered the attack. In contrast to earlier experiments with the new weapon, this time they were deployed *en masse*, utilizing tactics designed to exploit their advantages. Instead of the usual prolonged bombardment, the 1000 guns were concentrated into a short but very intense barrage on the enemy front lines, before moving back to disrupt the movement of German reserves. This preserved an element of surprise. When troops and tanks went forward they briefly encountered a phenomenon hardly seen on the Western Front since August 1914, namely open countryside. By the end of the first day, the British had penetrated to a depth of eight kilometres in places. Church bells were rung at home, in celebration of the fact that the war seemed finally to have reached a turning point.

But the battle should never have been launched since Haig did not have sufficient reserves at his disposal to exploit the breakthrough he anticipated. The Germans, in contrast, did have additional men ready. A stream of reinforcements were brought to the theatre, allowing a massive counter-attack. In early December, Haig had to order a partial withdrawal to protect troops exposed in vulnerable salients. The Germans recovered most of the ground lost on the first day and, in places, made significant gains of their own. Haig blamed Lloyd George for the failure, arguing that the Prime Minister's preference for sideshows in the Mediterranean and Middle East had deprived him of troops. Lloyd George blamed Haig; specifically the way he had exhausted his available resources in three months of futile attack in Flanders. The Prime Minister, it must be said, had the better argument.

Postscript

Haig has received the lion's share of condemnation for the carnage on the Western Front. Some of the opprobrium seems deserved. Just seven years before the war, he claimed that bullets have 'little stopping power against a horse'. [21, p. 111] How, one wonders, could such a man ever possibly have understood the destructive power of modern weaponry? His apparent insensitivity to the suffering of his men was symbolized by his lavish headquarters, situated 40 kilometres from the front, where he led a life of unashamed luxury. And what should one make of a commander who thought himself chosen by God and who saw death in battle as merely 'a welcome change to another room'? [22, p. 271]

Falkenhayn, Ludendorff, Joffre and Nivelle all demonstrated a remarkable ability to squander the lives of their men, yet Haig alone has been accused of butchery. He *was* quite often wrong. His biggest mistake came in believing he could restore movement to this inevitably static war. Lives were needlessly lost because of this error. But his mistakes should be measured in thousands of dead not, as his detractors think, in hundreds of thousands. There was no cheap way to win this war.

Given the state of military technology, a war in Europe, involving massive armies fed with an endless supply of munitions, was always destined to kill millions. It was beyond any commander to avert this inevitability. There was little scope for genius on the battlegrounds of the Great War. In wars which preceded and followed it, mobility gave the commander much more power to impose his will upon the battlefield. Not so on the Western Front, where Haig was little more than an administrator, and the character of the contest was determined by forces larger than him.

An apparent catastrophe of the Great War's magnitude requires a scoundrel of proportionate ineptitude. Battles have always been synonymous with their commanders: Wellington, Montgomery and Schwartzkopf are praised; Lord Cardigan, Westmoreland and Haig derided. In our fantasy world, success arises when Great Men are present; disasters when they are absent. By such assumptions do human beings reassure themselves of their ability to direct their own fate. To believe that Haig was merely a petty operative in a war beyond the control of any man is to accept a very bleak picture of the world in which we live and the power which individuals hold. We cling desperately to the illusion that a Napoleon would have succeeded where Haig failed. It seems far better that thousands should have died because of one man's stupidity than because of the irresistible arithmetic of modern technological war.

3

The Eastern Front, 1914–17

In 1905, during the war with Japan, Russian soldiers waiting on the platform of Mukden station witnessed the astonishing spectacle of two of their commanders, Pavel Rennenkampf and Aleksandr Samsonov, at each other's throats in an unseemly brawl. Nine years later the two bitter rivals were assigned command of the First and Second Russian Armies which were preparing for battle in East Prussia. The events at Mukden station did not bode well for the Russian war effort on the Eastern Front.

The combatants

The Germans, as was discussed in the last chapter, mobilized a formidable force in 1914. Troops were deeply committed to the cause, enjoyed a wealth of modern weaponry and were commanded by dedicated and highly trained officers. But, though the German army was huge, it was overstretched. In divisional strength, the Entente outnumbered the Central Powers by around three to two. Germany addressed this problem through strategic manoeuvre, namely the Schlieffen Plan. Seven of her eight armies were placed in the West, the aim being to defeat France quickly, before Russia could cause too much mischief in the East. But this meant that Austria-Hungary would have to hold the Russians back for the first six weeks of the war. Any delay or setback in the West would leave Germany's eastern frontier dangerously exposed. [Map 3]

Austria-Hungary was not well-equipped for the role of damming the Russian flood. Though she had a population of 50 million from which to conscript, she could finance a standing army no bigger than 480 000 men. The Empire had proved singularly incompetent at raising an army: three in four potential conscripts managed to escape the government's clutches. Of the men who were called up,

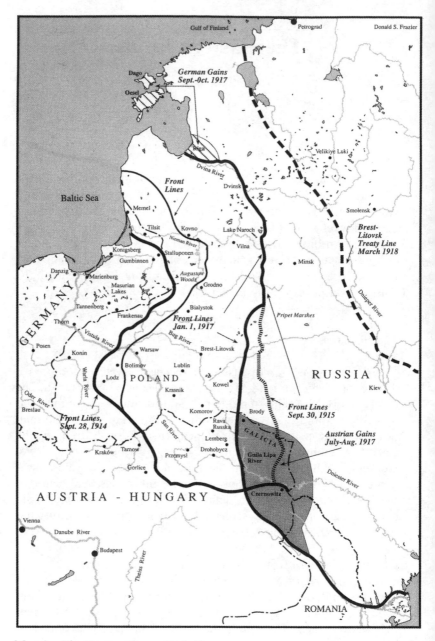

Map 3   *The Eastern Front, 1914–18*

less than a third received what might be regarded as full training. The supply of munitions and uniforms was perilously low. There was also virtually no reserve, which meant that any expansion of Hapsburg forces after the armistice would consist of completely raw recruits.

The ethnic problems that plagued the Dual Monarchy also plagued its army. A random sample of 100 soldiers in 1914 would have yielded 44 of Slavic descent, 28 Germans, 18 Hungarians, 8 Romanians and 2 Italians. It was impossible to build a cohesive force among so many different nationalities, many of whom were deeply suspicious of each other. The lack of a common language within some units made communicating orders extremely difficult. Morale and unit cohesion suffered because promotions and assignments were often decided on ethnic grounds rather than strictly military ones. Most of the officers were of German background, which made ordinary soldiers feel like footsoldiers in a colonial army. In ethnic terms, they often had more in common with their enemy than with the officer who ordered them forward.

There was also deep suspicion between the Dual Monarchy and its German ally. The Germans considered Austria-Hungary a bastard empire worthy of domination, while the Austrians still harboured resentment for their humiliation by the Prussian Army in 1866. In operational terms, this meant that very little effort had been devoted to establishing a structure for coordinating operations. Nor did the Hapsburgs take to the idea of placing themselves in the path of the Russian juggernaut while the Germans pursued foolish fantasies in the West. Conrad, the Austrian Chief of Staff, bombarded Moltke with memos warning him of the dangers of delaying too long the reinforcement of the Eastern Front.

A defensive war did not in any case suit Conrad, who worshipped only the god of attack. It was official policy, enshrined in a 1911 regulation, that the infantry could, 'without the support of other arms, even in inferior numbers, gain victory as long as [they are] tough and brave'. [56, p. 175] Austro-Hungarian strategy was formed around the premise that imperial survival required a policy of sustained aggression toward enemies who lay in every direction. But because there were so many contingencies to bear in mind (including German progress in the West, the speed and direction of Russian mobilization, the actions of Romania and Bulgaria, and Serbian behaviour), fixed plans were inappropriate. Conrad nevertheless went to war with a vague hope that he would soon be able to pinch off the salient of Russian Poland through a combined offensive by the Austrians from Galicia and the Germans from East Prussia.

Russia had a population of 167 million and, in theory, a standing army of 1.4 million men. The army was a microcosm of wider society, suffering the same class tensions, poverty, autocratic rule and backward technological development which plagued the nation as a whole. The enlisted man, like the peasant, was seen as sub-human, rendering him an easy target for revolutionary agitation. A high percentage could not read, a problem which was becoming increasingly serious given the rapid technological progress in warfare. But the Russian soldier made up in courage and determination what he lacked in training and intelligence. Because 80 per cent of soldiers came from peasant stock, they were used to hardship and adversity. They believed passionately in Mother Russia, even if they despised the Tsar and his government. They also felt a deep hatred of Austria, and were determined to avenge her cruelties toward the Slavic brotherhood.

These soldiers deserved better officers. At the top, senior commanders competed with each other for the Tsar's favour. Status and promotion were an acknowledgement not of proficiency but of loyalty to the ruler. A senior commander with real ability was simply a lucky coincidence. Lower down, junior officers were often corrupt, cruel, or simply stupid. Young men with money (and therefore education) were sent to the staff college and forever lost to regimental duty. Non-commissioned officers – the glue that holds any unit together – were in short supply. There was also little in the way of a supreme command or general staff, which meant that units in the various theatres were too often allowed to pursue their own idiosyncratic strategies. Supplies were perilously low and transport unreliable. But perhaps the most glaring fault in Russia's war machine was that her industry could not possibly cope with the demands of a huge army in a long and costly war.

The Russians had nevertheless made some progress since their humiliating defeat by Japan in 1905. The railway system had been improved, such that, between 1909 and 1914, the number of trains that could be sent to the front per day increased by one third. This is significant given that Schlieffen's plans had assumed a rather more primitive Russian rail network. On the eve of war, military spending exceeded that of Germany, though the money often went to the wrong sort of projects. Permanent fortifications were, for instance, well stocked with heavy artillery, while the mobile army was short on guns. The proportion of cavalry to infantry was excessive, given the impending obsolescence of the mounted arm. Troops could get to the front quite quickly by train, but had to rely on primitive transport once there. Though no country was able to predict the exact nature of this war, Russia was ill-equipped for the improvisation that would become necessary.

Russian strategists were torn between duty and instinct. In theory, helping the French meant attacking in East Prussia. But such a venture held little attraction, since the Russians did not actually covet that territory, nor did such a campaign strike at the main (and most hated) enemy – Austria-Hungary. An inadequate compromise resulted, with four armies devoted to the southern sector and two to the campaign in Eastern Prussia. Neither force was large enough to achieve its strategic purpose.

Battle begins

The French, who had to bear the brunt of German aggression in the West, depended on the Russians to foil the Schlieffen Plan by attacking in the East much more quickly than the Germans anticipated. To this end, French and Russian military representatives had agreed in 1910 that the Russians would 'undertake some offensive action on the sixteenth day [after mobilization] in the hope of tying down at least five or six German corps otherwise employable on the western front'. [56, p. 44] The plan called for an attack in East Prussia by two armies, one attacking north, the other west. The Russian mobilization was suitably quick, but organization and logistics suffered in consequence. In order to increase their speed, troops marched with light packs, which meant they were short of supplies when they arrived at their destination. Units were sent into combat immediately, without being allowed to organize themselves sufficiently. Coordination also suffered because of the acrimony between Rennenkampf, the First Army commander, and his nemesis, Samsonov, in charge of the Second Army.

The First Army advanced into East Prussia on 17 August, followed two days later by the Second. Each was larger than the total strength of the German Eighth Army, under General Max von Prittwitz. First blood went to the Russians at the battle of Gumbinnen on 20 August. General August von Mackensen's frontal assault upon Rennenkampf's force was easily rebuffed, with the Germans suffering over 14 000 casualties. Prittwitz, alarmed by Samsonov's approach from the South, immediately panicked, and advised a retirement behind the River Vistula. This angered Moltke, who promptly fired his timorous commander.

General Paul von Hindenburg, who had expected to spend the war in genteel retirement, was sent to the Eastern Front. Arriving on the same train was General Erich Ludendorff, the hero of the Battle of Liège, who became his Chief of Staff. A formidable partnership resulted. Hindenburg provided stability, authority and iron nerve, Ludendorff energy, imagination and occasional genius. Both were fired by a ruthless ambition and had egos the size of a howitzer.

Prior to their arrival, Lieutenant Colonel Max Hoffman, Prittwitz's Chief of Staff, had sketched out a plan for addressing the problem of the two advancing Russian armies. Hindenburg and Ludendorff gave force to Hoffman's plan and subsequently took credit for its success. A small cavalry force was left to guard Rennenkampf while the bulk of the Eighth Army moved south to meet Samsonov. The risk was great, but it helped that Rennenkampf moved like a turtle and the Second Army was in considerable disarray after its hasty mobilization. Spread out over a 100-kilometre front, it was advancing blind, without adequate reconnaissance. Since the Russians lacked trained coding staff they simply sent all wireless messages 'clear'. As a result, Hindenburg probably had a better idea of the disposition of the Russian Second Army than did Samsonov.

A classic envelopment took place near Grünfliess. By the 30th, the rout was complete. Two entire corps, a total of nearly 100 000 men, were forced to surrender. Another 50 000 Russians were killed or wounded, and 500 guns were lost. The cost to the Germans did not exceed 15 000 men. Upon learning of the fate of his army, a humiliated Samsonov crept into the darkness and shot himself. Since the name Grünfliess lacked heroic resonance, the battle was given the name of Tannenberg, and was quickly incorporated into German military mythology. Hindenburg was the war's first hero, a status he would milk for the rest of his life. The victory showed some genius, and a fair measure of daring, but owed more to Russian ineptitude than brilliant German command. Had Rennenkampf simply followed his victory at Gumbinnen with a determined march toward Samsonov, the German plan would have quickly unravelled.

Hindenburg then turned on Rennenkampf. Reinforced by two additional corps from the West, he attempted a second envelopment, with much less success. The two armies collided near the Masurian Lakes on 7 September. By the 10th, another Russian disaster threatened. But, displaying a determination heretofore well-hidden, Rennenkampf counter-attacked and then led his army in a rapid retreat back across the Niemen. The Germans gave chase, but could not make much headway against well-coordinated Russian defences. The battle was nevertheless an impressive German victory which cost the Russians 70 000 casualties, and another 30 000 captured. On the 13th Rennenkampf's army crossed back into Russia and Germany's eastern frontier was safe for the time being. A stalemate set in, which favoured the Germans since their losses had been light and they had not been banking on massive victories at this stage. 'Well, well, up to now, with inferior numbers, we have defeated about 15 Russian army corps and 8 cavalry divisions', Hoffman remarked with deserved pride. [28, pp. 57–8]

Further south, Hapsburg forces faced enemies in all directions. The war was supposed to strengthen the Empire by allowing it to assert its dominance over the upstart Balkan nations, chief among them Serbia. Given this goal, the temptation was to attack aggressively on a number of fronts. Yet moving massive armies in an area of rough terrain with only primitive modes of transport put a damper on even the most modest ambitions. Conrad proposed instead a joint offensive with the Germans, the aim being to crush Russians forces in the Polish salient within the first few weeks of the war. He thought he had Moltke's assurances that sufficient German troops would be made available.

But Conrad could not ignore the political need to 'slap Serbia'. Nearly half of Hapsburg forces (around 460 000 men) were therefore concentrated on that front, all expecting victory within a matter of days. But the Serbian army under Field Marshal Radomir Putnik, though smaller and less well-equipped than its enemy, had the advantage of fighting in terrain it knew well. Serbian troops had also undergone useful preparation during the two Balkan Wars.

On this front, fortunes swung like a pendulum. The Serbs first pushed the Austrians back into their own territory, then nearly lost Belgrade to a determined Hapsburg offensive. By the end of the year, no significant progress had been made, despite fierce and costly fighting. Given Austro-Hungarian expectations, the result has to be seen as a massive Serbian victory and a deep wound to Austrian pride. They suffered 200 000 casualties and left much valuable equipment on the battlefield, for which the Serbs were very grateful. [Map 4]

Further north, Austrian ambitions proved equally inappropriate. On 3 August Moltke informed Conrad that no German troops would be made available for the planned offensive against the Polish salient. Conrad, in a fit of pique, foolishly decided to go ahead regardless. The Russians had four armies in Galicia under General Nicholas Ivanov. Even after moving units from the Serbian front, Conrad could only manage to gather a numerically inferior force which was severely outgunned. The result might have been catastrophic, if not for the fact that the Russian bear was in truth a rather tame beast. The same poor communication and abysmal reconnaissance that thwarted operations further north plagued Ivanov. Conrad was therefore able to achieve some early successes in late August and early September, defeating the Russians in the battle of Kraśnik and then advancing toward Lublin.

By the first week of September, Russian forces began to gather momentum. There are few more frightening prospects in war than a massive Russian army on the move. With his two armies approaching from the east, the other two from the north, Ivanov pushed toward Lvov, forcing Conrad to withdraw. On 11 September he ordered a retreat to the River San but quickly found that even this line could not be held. By the beginning of October, Hapsburg forces had been pushed back to the River Dunajec. Conrad's losses were terrible, with around 400 000 casualties suffered in just six weeks of heavy fighting. Soldiers who managed to survive the battle had then to contend with an outbreak of cholera.

The Russians proved unable to exploit their success and concentrated instead on investing the fortress of Przemyśl, where 100 000 Austrian troops were garrisoned. The advance had fallen victim to its own logistical inadequacies. As was apparent on the Western Front, whenever an army lost momentum, stalemate quickly descended, as technological factors impeded forward movement. Though the mobility of all forces on the Eastern Front during the war stands in stark contrast to the situation in the West, the inability of either side to impose its dominance often led to a standoff, with trenches and fixed fortifications inevitably resulting.

The enormous cost and lack of success of the two campaigns had a highly corrosive effect upon the morale of the Hapsburg army. Its inherent instability rendered it ill-equipped for failure. Soldiers were easily tempted to switch sides, since ethnic ties to the enemy were often strong. Because officers and NCOs had suffered heavily, the job of restoring morale became all the more difficult. Huge stores of valuable equipment had been lost or used up, rendering any future campaigns even more precarious. Blame for the disasters must lay at Conrad's door. His ego, which greatly outweighed his ability, had blinded him to the disastrous predicaments into which he stubbornly marched. Never one to admit failure, he decided instead that fate had simply been unkind, and sheltered in self-pity: 'All reproaches over all that has not gone right in this gigantic struggle will be unloaded on to me. I will probably have to disappear from the scene like an outlaw'. [45, p. 96] Given the catastrophes he had already caused, it probably would have been better had he done so.

The Galician front had been stabilized only after German help had arrived. Conrad felt no qualms about receiving this help, since his 'secret foes' in Berlin were to blame for placing his army in such an invidious position in the first place. [99, p. 60] At one point he even suggested that a separate peace should be struck with the Russians. 'Why', he wondered, 'should Austria-Hungary bleed needlessly?' [45, p. 95] The deep resentment and distrust of the Germans which the first two months of war had inspired would poison future relations. Acrimony was likely to deepen, given that Austria-Hungary's losses rendered her more in need of German help. At the same time, Hapsburg dependence fuelled German contempt.

The 1915 campaigns

As the New Year approached, bitter argument divided the German command. The Schlieffen Plan had obviously failed. Falkenhayn, who had replaced Moltke as Chief of the General Staff, still believed that a decisive victory could be achieved in the West. But his argument was weakened by the fact that he could present no evidence to support his case since German forces seemed incapable of breaking the stalemate. In contrast, Hindenburg and Ludendorff could boast of impressive successes, achieved with meagre resources. When Ludendorff learned that four new reserve army corps were to be created, he demanded them for the Eastern theatre and promised that he could defeat Russia early in 1915. Falkenhayn accepted that

active operations in the East would have to continue, if only to keep
Austria-Hungary afloat, but ridiculed the suggestion that a quick
victory could be achieved.

In the end, the Kaiser fudged. The Eastern Front would receive
priority, but not to the extent of preventing an offensive in the West.
This essentially meant that both sides would be deprived of the forces
necessary to do anything decisive. Hindenburg and Ludendorff were
left in some doubt as to whether they were to strive for a complete victory over Russia, or merely conduct a holding operation.
Though they had managed to win priority for their theatre, relations with Falkenhayn continued to fester. Opportunities had been
lost, they felt, because of his 'criminal' waste of good troops in
senseless, unimaginative attacks. [99, p. 75] 'I can only hate and
love', Ludendorff confessed, 'and I hate General von Falkenhayn; it
is impossible for me to work together with him'. [45, p. 132]

Among Russian forces, the situation was precarious. Nearly one
third of soldiers lacked rifles. Some arrived at the front with only an
oak club and had to wait for a comrade to die before more
appropriate weaponry could be obtained. Draftees were often sent
into the line with only four weeks of training, very little of it
combat-orientated. Major-General Sir Alfred Knox, an observer
with the Russian army, found that the troops 'made a bad impression. Most of them seemed listless, of brutally stupid type, of poor
physique and stamina ... Not an inspiriting spectacle'. [61, vol. 1,
p. 255] The shell shortage which affected every army hit Russia
particularly hard. Artillery batteries were sometimes limited to four
rounds per gun per day. Munitions shortages were complicated by
the fact that weaponry had to be collected from any available
source; rifles of various calibre came from Mexico, Japan, or from
dead Austrians. Russia's allies were keen to help, but had their own
munitions problems and in any case could not find a way to get
large quantities of supplies eastward.

Given their predicament, it seems surprising that the Russians
still found reason for optimism in early 1915. They retained high
hopes that Austria-Hungary could be knocked out of the war
through a sustained offensive. This would remove Hapsburg influence from the Balkans, allowing the Russians to gain hegemony
there. But the Russians did not enjoy complete freedom to pursue
these objectives because, further north, a complete envelopment by
German forces threatened. Meeting that danger meant forgoing
more attractive opportunities in the South. Like the Germans, the

Russians fudged. Neither sector was given sufficient reinforcements to achieve its objectives.

The Central Powers effectively solved the Russian strategic dilemma by launching their own joint offensive, designed to stretch Russian resources to their limit. While the Germans attacked alone from Eastern Prussia, a joint German–Austrian operation was launched in the Carpathians. Troops were transferred from the West to bolster both sectors.

The offensive in Prussia was launched in terrible weather. Freezing temperatures neutralized the effects of poison gas, which the Germans used for the first time at the Battle of Bolimow. They at first dictated the pace of the conflict, enveloping the Russian Tenth Army near Grodno, and capturing 92 000 prisoners and 300 guns. Russian command and communication remained abysmal, suggesting that few lessons had been learned from the previous year. But German coordination was also lacking, causing significant opportunities to be squandered. When, on occasion, the Russians were able to establish local superiority, they pounded their enemy hard, inflicted horrible casualties and captured many prisoners. By the end of February, stalemate gripped the sector. 'We are stuck fast on the whole front', a disappointed Hoffman wrote. [28, p. 120]

Meanwhile, Conrad feared that the besieged garrison at Przemyśl would be forced to surrender if relief did not arrive before mid-March. He proposed an offensive in the Carpathians which would envelop Russian forces in Galicia. The attack was launched on 23 January, not a good time to hold a battle in that part of Europe. Both sides fought with a tenacity that defies description, especially given the terrible cold, poor communication and uncertain supplies. But, at times, conditions drove good soldiers on both sides to desertion or suicide. The fighting strength of the Austro-Hungarian Empire had once again suffered the effects of Conrad's ridiculous ambition. Failure did not, however, dent his ego.

In mid-March, General Aleksei Brusilov, commander of the Russian Eighth Army, unleashed a ferocious counter-offensive. He enjoyed a brief moment of triumph when Przemyśl fell. This was supposed to serve as a launching pad for further advance. Austro-Hungarian forces were indeed driven back, forcing Conrad to prepare plans for a retreat from Budapest to Vienna and on to Innsbruck. But those plans did not require implementation since Brusilov lacked the strength to build upon his victory.

The situation was nevertheless sufficiently alarming to convince Berlin that the eastern theatre required urgent attention. Troops were moved from the West, though argument raged over their deployment. Hindenburg wanted another attack from East Prussia, sweeping behind Warsaw. His ambitions frightened Falkenhayn, who still felt that victory could only be won on the Western Front. Operations in the East should instead aim at 'crippling ... [Russian] strength for an indefinite period'. [19, p. 173] He proposed another joint offensive in the Carpathians, to which the Kaiser granted approval. Meanwhile Hindenburg, who did not enjoy playing second fiddle, nursed his wounded ego.

Falkenhayn scraped together eight additional divisions, sufficient to establish a momentary superiority on the front between Gorlice and Tarnow. On 2 May, Austrians and Germans surged forward, annihilating Ivanov's Third Army. By the end of the third day, Russian defences were overwhelmed, and open countryside lay before the Germans and Austrians. After a month of fighting, Russian casualties exceeded 400 000. 'Their losses have been colossal', Knox reported. 'The army is now a harmless mob ... All realize the futility of sending men against the enemy'. [61, vol. 1, pp. 284, 287] Przemyśl was abandoned on 3 June, though the Russians did manage to leave with most of their supplies.

Mackenson, the Eleventh Army commander, pushed deeper into Galicia, capturing Lvov on 22 June. A week later German senior commanders met at Posen to take stock. Hindenburg wanted a huge encirclement of Russian armies from the north, but Falkenhayn felt that the idea, however attractive, could not be implemented with the troops at his disposal. He preferred a more cautious advance, the aim being to punish the Russians but at the same time to establish a front that could easily be defended over the winter.

The cautious advance turned quickly into a rout. The Germans stampeded through Eastern Europe, meeting success everywhere. Mackenson took Lublin on 30 July, then headed for Brest-Litovsk. Warsaw was abandoned on 5 August. The hugely successful campaign was, however, cut short due to the demands of other fronts. Action in the West and South had reached a critical stage. Falkenhayn, cognizant of the difficulties of supplying troops who were advancing so quickly, would not countenance a campaign in the winter. He advised the Kaiser:

One cannot hope to strike a comprehensive and deadly blow, by
means of an encircling movement, at an enemy who is numerically
stronger, who will stick at no sacrifices of territory and population,
and in addition has the expanse of Russia and good railways
behind him. [19, p. 185]

On this occasion, his caution was probably appropriate.

The dramatic victories of the summer had clearly been German,
even though Austrian soldiers had taken part. Each success eroded
Vienna's authority within the alliance. In late August, Conrad tried
to reassert himself with another bold offensive, this time toward
Rovno and Kiev. The operation went well at first, but then turned
to disaster as Austrian commanders indulged their own destructive
fantasies, with virtually no centralized direction. Once again, the
Germans had to ride to the rescue. An operation designed to restore
Austro-Hungarian prestige had the opposite effect.

By December, the front had stabilized along a virtually straight
line from the eastern end of the Carpathians to Riga on the
Baltic. A wide swath of Galicia, Poland, Lithuania, Latvia and
Byelorussia had changed hands. The Russians had lost some two
million men (half of them captured) and had allowed the Germans
to advance upwards of 500 kilometres in places. In Russian minds,
the Germans seemed invincible. In truth, poor strategic handling
of troops had transformed a containable offensive into a rout.
The Russians lacked the strategic flexibility and logistical apparatus to react effectively to a crisis. Disastrous command decisions and a fearsome enemy combined to erode the confidence of
Russian troops.

Italy joins the war

Despite their successes, the Germans still worried about the condition of their ally. It was widely understood that if the Italians
decided to enter the war on the side of the Entente Austria-Hungary
might find herself overwhelmed. Germany wanted desperately to
keep Italy at bay, but could only do so by offering the Italians
concessions detrimental to the Dual Monarchy. The Italians certainly coveted Hapsburg territory, since some 800 000 Italians lived
within the Empire. But for the Austrians, fighting the Italians

seemed preferable to buying them off with chunks of land, even if fighting them might prove suicidal. The Italians were inclined to sit quiet for the moment, waiting to see which side would make the best offer. Meanwhile, Austria-Hungary was forced to keep troops on the Italian frontier, depleting her strength in other sectors.

The issue was finally resolved on 26 April 1915, when Italy joined the Entente. True to her own interests, she declared war on Austria-Hungary only. The price of Italian alliance was high. Under the terms of the Treaty of London, large chunks of Hapsburg territory were promised to Italy, with the effect that, in the event of victory, 600 000 South Slavs and 230 000 Germans would find themselves under the rule of Rome. When these terms were leaked, they caused considerable annoyance among the Serbs, who were henceforth less inclined to cooperate with their Entente allies.

The Italians were unprepared for war. They had a standing army of 875 000 men, but munitions supplies were low. A narrow industrial base made it difficult to correct this deficiency. But these problems did not dent Italian resolve. Like all other belligerents, they entered the war determined upon attack. Unfortunately, offensive options were strictly limited. There was not much point in attacking toward the North-west (in the Alps), given the hostile terrain, the lack of suitable objectives and the need to defend the routes to Venice and the South. The only real scope for an offensive lay in the North-east, in the direction of Trieste, which would also open the possibility of linking with the Russians and Serbs. General Luigi Cadorna, the Italian commander, promised his political masters that he could take Trieste within a month, apparently ignoring the formidable barriers (both natural and man-made) in his way, including the stubborn fortresses of Gorizia and Tolmino. Half of the Italian troops were therefore dispatched to this 100-kilometre front along the Isonzo, while the other half were left to guard the Trentino.

The new war did not start well. Italian mobilization, which was to take 23 days, in fact took twice as long. Cadorna soon revealed himself an Italian version of Conrad – they rivalled each other in vanity, pigheadedness, and an inclination to ignore obstacles. For the next six months, the Italians launched four offensives on the Isonzo, always enjoying a two-to-one advantage in troop strength. Conditions were atrocious. Trenches had to be blasted out of solid granite and soldiers were regularly maimed or killed when artillery barrages let loose torrents of sharp rock. One Austrian subaltern recorded his horror:

The artillery fire became terribly intense during the night. I am done for, I thought, and prepared to die as a brave Christian. I am done for. An unparalleled butchery. A horrible bloodbath. Blood is running everywhere and all about are the dead and pieces of corpses ... [45, p. 153]

Elsewhere, barbed wire was strung across snowfields and soldiers froze to death. None of the offensives came near to threatening Trieste. Even Ludendorff was forced to admit that Austro-Hungarian soldiers seemed to improve in quality when fired by hatred of Italians. On paper the Italians were probably the victors, but their mastery of the battlefield was by no means clear. Though they had captured a considerable number of prisoners and equipment, losses of some 250 000 men exceeded those of their enemy. Nor did minuscule gains and horrible conditions do much for the morale of Italian troops, who had been led to expect a war of conquest.

The Italian war was as brutal as a cockfight and about as insignificant. The big players in Berlin, Paris and London were not overly concerned about what happened on the Isonzo. Italy's allies were quite happy that Hapsburg soldiers were being killed in yet another theatre, but did not place much store in Cadorna's grandiose promises. As for the Germans, they were not about to listen to Conrad's pleas for reinforcements to protect Trieste. The Prussian War Minister, Wild von Hohenborn, put it bluntly: 'Basically it does not matter a hoot to us whether Italy hacks another piece of the tail off the dying camel Austria'. [45, p. 153]

The 1916 campaigns

The bloodbath at Verdun had important repercussions in the East. Russia's allies urged her to relieve the pressure on the French by launching an offensive against the Germans. The Russians agreed, setting their sights on the area east of Vilna, where they enjoyed a considerable numerical superiority. The resultant battle at Lake Narocz ended disastrously, with Russian losses exceeding 100 000, five times those of the Germans. As far as relieving the pressure on the French was concerned, the operation had no effect at all. The bewilderment which had plagued Russian commanders throughout 1915 increased. It became enormously difficult to motivate junior officers and regular soldiers to fight an enemy who seemed invincible.

The British and French nevertheless continued to urge their ally to attack, even though the Russians seemed patently inept at doing so. The great exception was Brusilov, who demonstrated a strategic capacity and enthusiasm for the fight heretofore lacking among his colleagues. He was certain that the Austrians were vulnerable, and was confident that, if a well-coordinated attack could be launched, it would have positive repercussions for operations further north. This confidence was not unfounded since Austrian strength had been depleted by the transfer of units to the Italian front.

Brusilov settled upon an attack in two main sectors, the first opposite Lutsk and the second in the valleys of the Dniester and the Prut. Around 660 000 troops were concentrated along a 300-kilometre front. Having studied the situation, and past offensives, he concluded that the key to success was concealment and speed. A short preliminary bombardment would prevent the enemy from predicting where the blow would fall. Sapper trenches were dug to within 200 metres of the Austrian line, thus reducing the attacking force's exposure to enemy fire. Units were to probe for weak points in the Austrian line and then storm them with maximum force. Reserves were concentrated at the likely points of breakthrough, but were carefully concealed from the enemy in deep earthworks. All of this required meticulous preparation, an attribute heretofore lacking in Russian command.

The advance, launched on 4 June, justified Brusilov's confidence and demonstrated that Russian troops, if properly led, could perform well. All along the front, Austrian troops melted away whenever pressure was applied. By evening, a breach 30 kilometres wide and eight deep had been achieved. By the end of the month the Russians had stormed past Lutsk in the North and had burst through Bukovina in the South, along the way collecting 200 000 prisoners. Though there is no discounting the magnitude of Brusilov's achievement, the weakness of the Dual Monarchy's forces at this stage of the war cannot be ignored. They seem to have ignored lessons from the previous year, placing too many troops in the front line and concentrating reserves in such a way that they were easily overrun by an attack of any momentum. Austrian command was ineffectual, uninspired and at times plainly inept. Hapless soldiers had to suffer the effects of a sadly disorganized logistical system.

German divisions were hastily withdrawn from the Western Front to stabilize the situation in the East. The disaster underlined a fact apparent even before the war. The Germans were dependent upon the Austrians because they needed an ally. But in military terms, dependency went the other way. Austria-Hungary could not survive without German protection. Thus, the weaker ally had enormous bearing on German strategy, simply because of its weakness. The Austro-Hungarian tail wagged the German dog.

But Brusilov was the victim of his own success. In order to make as big an impact as possible, the bulk of his forces had been committed to the initial thrust, which meant that he was short of reserves to exploit early progress. His troops also advanced in some areas farther and faster than anticipated, creating huge supply problems. Knox observed: 'As so often happened in Russia, the Supreme Command ordered, but the railways decided'. [99, p. 151] In an effort to maintain the pressure, Brusilov tried to persuade General Aleksei Evert to attack the Germans around Vilna, but Evert had little enthusiasm for the task. When he finally moved in early July, valuable momentum had been lost and precious little was achieved. Brusilov then attacked again on 28 July, with limited success. Experienced troops able to implement Brusilov's complicated manoeuvres were by this stage in short supply, with the result that attacks reverted to the battering ram style of the previous year. Brusilov achieved some minor victories, advancing to the edge of the Carpathians, but was not able to duplicate his earlier success.

In October, the offensive ran out of steam. Around 400 000 Austro-Hungarian troops had been captured and more than 500 guns. Casualties may have been as high as 750 000. This enormously impressive victory undoubtedly relieved the pressure on the Western Front and destroyed the last shreds of Conrad's credibility. But it was frustratingly indecisive. Due in part to their tremendous losses in the previous year, the Russians were unable to muster sufficient strength to exploit their victories. They had discovered that they could inflict huge damage upon the Austro-Hungarian army, but lacked the killer punch to knock her out of the war. Russian troops had fought very hard and with great devotion for four months, yet in the end had little to show for their efforts. Though they were the clear winners, their losses exceeded one million. The strategic situation did not suggest further success, nor did the availability of troops. With the future again decidedly bleak, Russian morale imploded. By the onset of winter, one million troops had deserted.

On 17 August, another fence-sitter entered the war. The Romanians, who had waited for two years to see how things would develop, were suddenly sufficiently confident that the Entente would win. They declared war on Austria-Hungary, with the aim of securing the Romanian-speaking areas of Transylvania in Hungary. Around 625 000 new soldiers joined the cause, but they were poorly trained and badly supplied. They immediately thrust forward into Transylvania, only to be stopped in their tracks in September by an Austro-German force under Falkenhayn, whose errors at Verdun earned him this less glamorous appointment. Meanwhile, a combined force of Turks, Germans and Bulgarians took the Black Sea port of Costanza on 23 October, putting the safety of Romania in serious danger. The Allies had simply to sit aside, since they could do nothing to ease the plight of their new partner. On 27 November, Falkenhayn made contact with Mackensen outside Bucharest, which fell on 6 December. The Romanians withdrew their capital to Jássy, but the Germans did not follow them, deciding that a gentle approach might persuade the remnants of the Romanian army to switch sides. Assorted units did indeed do so, but most troops simply went home. In less than a month of combat, Romania lost 17 000 killed, another 56 000 wounded. Huge ammunition stocks and supplies of food and raw material were handed over to the Central Powers.

On the Italian front, progress remained slow, despite Cadorna's promises that 1916 would be his year. The fifth Battle of the Isonzo began in March, and went roughly the way of the previous four. The same destructive inconclusiveness typified the sixth, seventh, eighth and ninth battles, launched with impressive regularity but depressing results between the late spring and early autumn.

Even before the war, Conrad had dreamt of attacking Italy through the Trentino, in the process slicing off the northern part of the country. That aspiration had been enhanced by Italy's 'perfidious' treachery in joining the Entente. Falkenhayn had no desire to play along with the Austrian's fantasies, and refused all requests for troops. Conrad nevertheless went forward with his preparations, keeping his ally in the dark. In May, he decided that the time had come for 'my dream of beating these dago dogs [to] be fulfilled'. [45, p. 205] Plans for the offensive were devised as if the action would take place on a flat football pitch instead of rugged mountains. Daily advances of 20 kilometres were expected to bring the capture of Venice within a week. The thrust began on 15 May in deep snow. Supply trains failed to reach their destination and soldiers were buried by avalanches. The attack was nevertheless quite successful, though not as invincible as Conrad had planned. Arsiero and Asiago were captured by the end of the month, opening the Italian plains to the Austrian army. But, then snow turned to slush and roads to mud. On 6 June, the Italians launched a successful counter-attack and stalemate quickly descended. The Italians lost 147 000 men, Austria-Hungary 81 000. In a now typical manner, Conrad blamed his subordinate commanders for their failure to implement his brilliant plans.

Caporetto 1917

In the spring of 1917 the Italians attacked on the Isonzo – again. Weeks of heavy fighting left Austro-Hungarian troops in a surprisingly good position by early June. In response to this worrisome situation, Cadorna shifted his efforts to the mountains of the Trentino, an altogether unsuitable place to stage a battle. Troops used to dealing with pressure from the enemy now had to face rough terrain and thin air. After much suffering but little progress, Cadorna shifted to the Isonzo again in mid-August. The assault, heavier than in previous battles, achieved some success, pushing the Austrian line back more than eight kilometres. But a month of killing and 165 000 Italian casualties brought victory no closer. Morale plummeted.

Conrad had once again been agitating for a joint offensive on the Italian front, a proposal which the Germans greeted with less than polite indifference. But the condition of Austro-Hungarian troops after the August attack led to the conclusion that their war spirit was in need of buttressing if the Empire was to survive the winter. Seven German divisions were sent south, including a number of specially trained alpine troops. Some heavy artillery and air support were thrown in for good measure. It was a condition of the offer that future operations had to be commanded by a German, in this case General Otto von Below. Deciding that offence is the best defence, Below attacked on 24 October.

The attack itself did not surprise the Italians, but its intensity did. Cadorna had learned of enemy preparations from deserters, but remained confident that he could meet any blow. He assured the British that he would be able to withstand an attack on his front for five weeks without needing assistance from outside. But he failed to take into account the difference which fresh German troops and a capable German commander would make. Below's preparation was meticulous. A huge arsenal was gathered and troops were brought forward at night to well-camouflaged forward positions. A massive bombardment, complemented by gas, preceded the ferocious thrust.

Caporetto, the epicentre of the attack, was quickly added to the list of infamous place-names in the iconography of the Great War. Italian resistance rapidly melted. In places, the advance penetrated over 20 kilometres on the first day. Cadorna realized that his position was sticky, but was slow in reacting to it. He tried to hold the line on the Tagliamento River, but that goal quickly proved unrealistic. Before long, an orderly retreat disintegrated into total chaos. Troops fled in utter fear of the Germans. Soldiers and civilians mixed together in headlong flight, making the job of restoring order immensely difficult. Virtually overnight, the fighting strength of the Italian army was cut in half.

Cadorna was quick to blame the disaster on cowardly soldiers. But if any cowardice existed, it lay in his refusal to accept blame for the sorry state into which his army had plummeted. Stated simply, the Italian soldier had had enough. Relatively few had actually been beaten in a straight fight with the Germans. Some 40 000 were killed or wounded, but 300 000 were captured and 350 000 deserted. Futile offensives, cruel officers, idiotic command and erratic supplies had finally taken their toll. Thousands of soldiers decided that their war was over and went home.

But, as with so many dramatic battles on the Eastern Front, a great deal of sound and fury failed to produce a decisive victory. Despite widespread fears that the Italian army had completely collapsed, a semblance of order was restored on the line of the River Piave. On 9 November Cadorna told his troops: 'We have taken the inflexible decision to defend here the honour and life of Italy. Every soldier must know what is the cry and command issuing from the conscience of the whole Italian people: to die and not to yield'. [19, p. 464] Italian troops yielded no further. In defending their own country, they somehow managed to summon a spirit lacking in their earlier campaigns of conquest. Patience with Cadorna was nevertheless exhausted; on the day of the above dispatch he was replaced by General Armando Diaz, a man much more sensitive to the needs of his soldiers. Around the same time, eleven British and French divisions arrived, and immediately deployed behind the bedraggled Italians to restore order. This might still not have been enough, if not for the fact that the Austro-German logistical network could not cope with the problems of supplying a now distant army. The Germans had not expected to be so successful and therefore did not gather sufficient lorries to exploit the success. The battle did nevertheless lift Austro-Hungarian spirits sufficiently to keep the Empire in the war for one more year.

For the Entente, Caporetto had one positive effect. The fear of disaster prompted Entente leaders to agree upon a formal body for Allied cooperation. The Supreme War Council, formed when David Lloyd George, Paul Painlevé and Vittorio Orlando gathered at Rapallo, was composed of political and military representatives who were to meet regularly to discuss matters of common concern and to formulate a general strategy. The Council lacked the power to provide real coordination, but it was at least a step in the right direction. The Allied leaders, who had previously treated each other with nearly as much suspicion as they directed toward the enemy, were at least now gathering in the same room.

The Russian collapse – 1917

While Italy was struggling to stay in the war, the Russian will to fight evaporated. The war had had a profoundly disruptive effect upon the home front. Rapid industrialization, spurred by the need for munitions, caused a mass migration to the cities, which were transformed into pressure cookers of discontent. The transportation network did not respond well to the strains of war, causing widespread food shortages in the expanding urban areas. Added to these complaints was the flood tide of death caused by futile offensives and inept commanders. In February, the discontent reached critical mass. Workers in Petrograd downed their tools and took to the streets. They were joined by riotous soldiers who armed themselves with weapons stolen from the Liteinyi Arsenal. Activists formed themselves into the Petrograd Soviet of Soldiers' and Workers' Deputies, which directly challenged the authority of the Tsar. Attempts to restore order were feeble and ineffectual. The Duma, once the great hope for liberal reform, found it could not control the tide of discontent and was instead swept along by it. By 15 March a provisional government was formed by the Duma which had the backing of the Soviet. Realizing that events had overwhelmed him, the Tsar abdicated.

The Provisional Government could do little to resolve the practical problems which had contributed to the revolution in the first place. The people still starved and soldiers still died. Bolsheviks wanted an immediate cease-fire, which liberals feared would simply mean a punitive German peace. As a sop to the Soviets, the Provisional Government passed Order No. 1, which abolished many manifestations of rank and established political committees within each army unit to hear soldiers' grievances. The order undermined the system of discipline and authority essential to any army's effectiveness. It was also agreed that Russia would seek a peace without annexations and indemnities. But, until the other Great Powers were convinced of the logic of negotiation, the fighting would have to continue.

Alexander Kerensky, who took over as war minister of the Provisional Government in May, tried desperately to stave off military defeat and a Bolshevik uprising. Around this time, the government sanctioned the formation of the First Russian Women's Battalion of Death, an all-female unit. The women were employed not for their abilities on the battlefield, but specifically because it was hoped that they would serve as inspirational symbols for male soldiers. In fact, they probably had the opposite effect. When women appeared at the front, many men no longer understood what sort of society they were defending. Moreover, many were hostile to the women soldiers, who represented a desire to continue fighting when the majority of men wanted nothing else but to return home.

Russia's allies were desperate that she should remain in the war, and pressured Kerensky to launch new offensives. The Germans had been reluctant to attack after the revolution, on the grounds that there was no point in arousing an embattled reaction to an external enemy. It was instead felt that the Russians should be left to find their own path toward collapse. In a mood to stir things up, however, they did facilitate the return of Lenin and other Bolsheviks from Switzerland to Russia.

Kerensky ordered Brusilov to attack in Galicia, a desperate gamble designed to restore Russian populist pride, impress the allies and scupper the Bolsheviks. The plan was never likely to work, and Kerensky's willingness to sacrifice yet more Russian lives in such a dubious venture seems morally reprehensible. Brusilov, who had been made commander-in-chief in June, brought together three armies for a thrust toward Lvov, launched on 1 July. It was the last Russian offensive of the war. Some significant progress was initially achieved, but Brusilov could not muster the strength to capitalize on this success. On 19 July, the Germans and Austrians counter-attacked, causing Russian resistance to collapse like a soufflé. It is not necessary to narrate the last rounds of this pitiful struggle, since there was very little fight to it. Russian soldiers no longer saw a point to the war. The desire for individual survival had over-whelmed the fear of collective humiliation. Brusilov's forces were quickly ejected from all the territory they had captured in the previous year. In early September, the Germans captured Riga, a city of enormous symbolic importance to Russian pride. The war was effectively over.

Brusilov's offensive, which was designed in part to stave off a Bolshevik takeover, in fact made one more likely. A second revolution in November brought Lenin to power. He quickly entered into discussions with the Germans on 3 December. An armistice was agreed on the 15th, whereupon peace negotiations were begun at Brest-Litovsk. Deprived of her mighty ally, in the East, Romania also opted for an armistice.

For the Germans, the war had not gone according to plan. Victory in the West was to be achieved within two months of the declaration of war, so that they could concentrate their forces against the Russians in the East. Instead, the Western Front had evolved into a depressing stalemate, and a two-front war meant that troops had to be shuttled across the continent to put out fires in the East and the West. In fact, the war had three fronts: the persistent need to rescue the Austrians meant a steady drain on reserves and the curtailment of offensives in other theatres. But by the end of 1917, the Germans had achieved their long-sought aim of a one-front war. The Russians were defeated, and Austria-Hungary could be left to hold the fort in the East. German troops boarded trains for the climactic battles which would soon take place in the West.

4

The War at Sea

It is ironic that the Dreadnought class of battleship, a focus of passionate rivalry in the decade before 1914, was actually of little consequence to the outcome of the war. Instead, a much less obtrusive naval development had a more profound effect upon the nature of the war. It was the threat of the submarine, not the huge battleship, which came close to inflicting defeat upon the British Empire and the Entente.

Big ships and small

In the century before the war, the British saw the Royal Navy as their salvation. Its supremacy allowed deficiencies in the army to be tolerated. But the British understood that to maintain their naval dominance required effort, attention and money. From the end of the Boer War to August 1914, great energy was directed toward naval reform, in particular by Sir John 'Jacky' Fisher, who became First Sea Lord on 21 October 1904. He was responsible for improvements in officer training, the redirection of fleets to home waters, the scrapping of obsolete vessels and the creation of an active reserve. Fisher's characteristics read like a list of battleship names: indomitable, inflexible, ruthless, remorseless. Officers who opposed his policies saw their careers ruined.

Fisher's reforms were not at first directed toward the growing threat of Germany, being instead part of a periodic modernisation programme. In fact, until 1904, calculation of the navy's size did not take Germany into account; the two-power standard was instead measured in relation to France and Russia. (In simple terms, the 'two-power standard' meant that the British strove to maintain a navy larger than the combined size of the fleets of the next two largest naval powers.) But it gradually dawned on the British that the German naval bills of 1898 and 1900 were designed to give the

Kaiser a navy to rival the United Kingdom, even though he claimed that it was 'nonsensical and untrue' to make such an assumption. [87, p. 181] In February 1904, Lord Selborne, First Lord of the Admiralty, told the Cabinet that henceforth Germany would replace Russia in the calculation of the two-power standard. Fisher, who was something of a street fighter, delighted in the confrontation this implied. He spoke openly and belligerently about the possible need to destroy or cripple the German fleet before it could grow sufficiently large to threaten the Royal Navy.

Thus began the Anglo-German naval race. But that race was made more dramatic by the launching of H.M.S. *Dreadnought* on 10 February 1906. Because its size and gunnery theoretically rendered all other battleships obsolete, naval construction in Britain and Germany had to start again from square one. The contest itself was based on the uncritical assumption (derived from the writings of Captain Alfred Thayer Mahan) that political and economic hegemony was determined by sea power. Both the Germans and the British saw Mahan as a prophet. What is astonishing is the way his already suspect thesis was rendered even more absurd by a concentration on sheer numbers of big ships, without much attention to their effectiveness nor to the quality of men who sailed in them. Dreadnoughts were built because it was assumed that future naval encounters would follow the classical pattern of massed forces meeting in a set-piece battle like two grand masters sitting down to a game of chess. The humiliation of the Russian navy by the Japanese at the battles of Port Arthur (1904) and Tsushima (1905) had unfortunately reinforced this flawed notion. Behind it lay the same short war mentality that gripped European armies.

In fact, since the state of military technology militated against a short land war, a set-piece battle at sea was not very likely. No naval power (especially not an island nation) would risk the destruction of its entire fleet in one massive battle if the war was going to be long. Since big battles were unlikely, big ships were less important. In a long war, the navy's role is to maintain a blockade, keep shipping lanes open, transport troops, and protect merchant shipping, all of which are best performed by considerably smaller ships than those in the Dreadnought class. But this argument was beyond the ken of the British people, their government and indeed the Admiralty. They saw Germans eager for a race and sprinted off without bothering to check which direction to run. There was little the government could have done differently (even if it had understood the issues) given a rabid public fired by lurid invasion stories and newspapers shouting 'We want eight and we won't wait.'

The popular press delighted in an issue so perfectly suited to rouse jingoistic passion. But the naval race, though high on energy, was low on rancour. It was like a healthy rivalry between two closely matched schools and did not provoke a great deal of anti-German hatred. Rates of ship construction were presented in the newspapers like football league tables. This in fact alarmed some public officials, who felt that the German threat should be taken a great deal more seriously. Sir Charles Hardinge, Permanent Under-Secretary at the Foreign Office, complained as late as 1909 that 'Public opinion in England has not as yet grasped the danger to Europe of Germany's ambitious designs'. [20, p. 12]

It is entirely understandable that the British should have become so consumed by the naval race given that they are an island nation and did possess a huge maritime empire. The navy had always been the senior service – *the* focus of attention and pride. Unfortunately, an issue which so captivates popular imagination becomes easily divorced from reality. Public understanding was limited to the very simple notion of 'lots of big ships'. As a result, naval supremacy came to be judged by numbers and size, rather than more complicated qualitative measures. Few stopped to consider whether the Germans might have been doing other things, in the area of gunnery for instance, which might be relevant to the security equation.

'Nothing', wrote Arthur Pollen, the British gunnery expert, 'is more astounding than the extent to which Fisher perpetually assumed that guns had only to be fired to hit'. In 1906, he warned that 'If we went to war tomorrow, every gunnery lieutenant would be liable to be called upon to engage a fast moving target at a moment's notice, and this is a thing of which not a single one of them, nor any Captain, nor any Admiral has had any practical experience whatever'. [89, pp. 25, 51] As was the case in the army, naval commanders spent far too much time studying the battles of the Napoleonic War, without sufficient consideration of how new technology might alter strategy and tactics. Tradition clouded judgement; because the Royal Navy had been dominant for so long, it was blithely assumed that it would always remain dominant, as long as the number of British ships exceeded the combined total of the next two largest navies.

Britain had her Jacky Fisher, and Germany had Admiral Alfred von Tirpitz, another huge and deeply flawed personality. If Britain's naval expansion was divorced from reality, Germany's was cloud-cuckoo-land. One might reasonably ask why it was necessary to expend such huge sums of money and manpower, when Germany did not have much of a significant overseas empire to defend. Large Dreadnoughts were not going to do much to counter land-based threats, nor would they provide much security to Germany's ally, Austria-Hungary. The answer to this riddle is simple: rather like nuclear weapons in the post World War II era, ships provided prestige and were considered the measure of a great power, at least in the mind of the Kaiser, who was obsessed with image and size. Those inclined toward more pragmatic justification took solace in the fact that building ships put men to work, and quieted class antagonisms.

Britain won the race, for the simple reason that she began with a massive head start and did not have to finance a huge army at the same time. On the eve of the war, therefore, she had reason to feel confident. Her total fleet dwarfed all others. In 1914, she had 22 Dreadnoughts, 40 other battleships and 130 cruisers of various types, while Germany had 15, 22 and 45, respectively. If one adds Britain's allies into the equation, the margin of supremacy is even greater. Russia, forced to give the navy more attention after the defeat by Japan, had 10 battleships, though none were Dreadnoughts, and 12 cruisers. France had a fleet of 22 battleships and 28 cruisers, despite the fact that the lion's share of expenditure had gone to her army in the decades before the war. As for the Central Powers, Austria-Hungary had a fleet about the size of Russia, with Italy (still technically in the German camp) possessing a similar number of ships. Though the loyalties of the US and Japan had yet to be determined, both countries had undergone a dramatic programme of shipbuilding. (Figures of fleet sizes vary greatly, as each country built different ships which do not always fall into neat categories.) [41, pp. 1–20]

The numbers of ships is meaningless, unless their deployment is also taken into consideration. The agreements Britain signed before the First World War, with France, Russia and Japan, were designed to reduce the threat each of those countries posed to various outposts of the Empire and, in the process, to reduce the naval commitment that needed to be made. But this diplomatic effort had limited effect; though it allowed concentration of the fleet in European waters, it was still essential for the Royal Navy to sail all the world's oceans in order to keep the Empire protected and to reinforce the image of a dominant naval power. In other words, the Royal Navy was big because it had to be.

The Germans coveted a fleet capable of asserting similar power around the world, but any attempt at naval display in Asian or African ports inevitably reduced strength in the waters around Europe. The Russians reduced the effectiveness of their already substandard navy by failing to decide conclusively whether it should concentrate on the Baltic or the Black Sea. The other powers were much more parochial in their outlook, which meant that their small navies had a considerable impact in local waters. Italy and Austria-Hungary did not intend to drift far from the Adriatic, while the French saw their role as to patrol the Mediterranean. The Japanese and American navies were designed primarily to watch each other in the Pacific.

The naval war, like the naval race before it, would primarily be a contest between Britain and Germany. Although the two countries built ships which in theory were very similar, in practice there were distinct differences in matters other than the size of the respective fleets. Fisher was a gunnery expert who saw the Dreadnought as a gun platform which had to be protected by smaller ships providing a screen. Battle was simply a question of manoeuvring the fleet to an appropriate distance and then blasting away. The British therefore sought fast ships with powerful guns but protecting them from attack received low priority. Since the Germans could not match the British in numbers, they decided to outdo them in durability. Their strategy did not rely exclusively on big ships firing huge guns at great distance, but instead emphasised a more coordinated offensive by various types of ships. Thus, they worked hard to develop highly effective torpedoes and mines and to make their ships virtually unsinkable. To employ a boxing metaphor, the British had a long reach but only one good punch, while the Germans were good inside, wily, creative, unpredictable and very durable.

The Royal Navy's long years at the top had encouraged rigidity and a fear of change. It was a superbly organized and impressively disciplined force, but creativity had been bred out of the officer class. There was little scope for tactical imagination; battles were to be conducted by the book. Within the highly centralized system, initiative was not a prized attribute. (Admiral David Beatty was, perhaps, the exception to the rule. He encouraged individual initiative, which in part explains his difficulties with Jellicoe.) Ship commanders had always to await orders before acting and had to obey them implicitly. As with the army, the Royal Navy sought officers of high social rank, which meant that the pool from which potential commanders was drawn was rather shallow. There was no encouragement of strategic study, and no staff college system to analyse new developments in naval technology.

The great power and questionable defensive strength of British ships was a manifestation of the Royal Navy's offensive spirit. As was the case with the army, officers and men were trained to attack; to assume a defensive strategy was considered cowardly and unmanly. This in part explains why the idea of a naval staff, and indeed any organized system of strategic study, was seen as suspect. It was widely feared that thought would stifle emotion and that the navy would be saddled with a generation of commanders more inclined to deliberate than to take action.

The Germans, in contrast, had the qualities of an upstart. Since the navy had little tradition, precedent held little power. Bright, young and ambitious men saw real opportunities for social and professional advancement through service at sea. Men who demonstrated their intelligence through the study of naval strategy were rewarded with promotion. Technology was worshipped, not feared. As officers rose to high command, they did not forget how to learn, as was often the case with the British. Granted, in common with the Royal Navy, there were many German admirals whose position owed more to social status than to actual ability. But the decentralized system of command at least diminished their influence. Great trust was placed in individual officers to react to situations as they developed. Initiative was encouraged. Thus, if disaster threatened, the German naval officer was better equipped to improvise.

Strategies

Most British admirals were certain that the naval war would be won in the North Sea. As was the case in the army, a powerful group of 'Westerners' resisted attempts to utilize the navy elsewhere, such as in the ill-fated Dardanelles expedition. (The Dardanelles expedition is discussed in Chapter 5.) But a North Sea strategy could have been conducted in two ways. The first and more aggressive one was built on the assumption that since British naval mastery was invincible it should be used to obtain a decisive victory. Such a policy would have sought a confrontation with the German navy near its lair in the Heligoland Bight. It might also have involved taking control of the Baltic, thus cutting German trade routes to Sweden and depriving her of valuable raw materials. The successful pursuit of such a strategy might have led to a quick defeat of Germany. A considerable number of senior officers, raised on the gospel of attack, favoured this approach.

But utilization of the fleet in an aggressive capacity increased the likelihood of accident, in the form of mines, torpedoes or submarines. These dangers convinced some senior naval personnel, including Sir John Jellicoe, the commander-in-chief, that a conservative strategy, designed to maintain the fleet in being, was more sensible. Because the Royal Navy was in effect a deterrent (rather like a nuclear arsenal), it did not have to be used in order to be effective. As Winston Churchill, the First Lord, reflected during the war, even though the fleet had turned away from battle,

> they have enjoyed all the fruits of a complete victory. If Germany had never built a Dreadnought, or if all German Dreadnoughts had been sunk, the control and authority of the British navy could not have been more effective. ... There was no need for the British to seek battle at all. [89, pp. 159–60]

This was of course, a lot of nonsense, since the Royal Navy could have been a great deal more effective if it had denied the Germans access to the Baltic and to Belgian and Dutch ports. But to do so would have involved considerable risks which Jellicoe would not embrace. He was like the stockbroker who feels duty bound to protect his customers' interests by placing all their money in safe, low-interest bank accounts. They would not get rich but nor would they lose their money. He assumed, in other words, that Britain would win if she did not lose. She would avoid dramatic encounters and would not seek battle unless victory could be guaranteed. 'My contention is that when the Great Day comes it will be when the Enemy takes the initiative', he wrote in April 1916. [72, vol. II, p. 424] Until that day arrived, the Royal Navy would concentrate upon blockading Germany at great distance, in waters where it enjoyed distinct advantages.

Jellicoe's safe strategy placed the Germans in a strategic dilemma. His distant blockade did not require offensive action in order to be maintained. Yet the Germans could beat the blockade only by confronting it. Unfortunately, such a battle, in waters far removed from German ports against a numerically superior enemy, carried immense risk. Within Germany's ruling circle, there was marked disagreement over how to respond to this dilemma. When it became clear that the British would not lay on a close blockade nor seek a confrontation in Heligoland Bight, Tirpitz, whose gambler's instincts contrasted markedly with Jellicoe's accountant's mentality, advocated a proactive, aggressive response. A passive policy, he argued, would essentially 'embalm' the fleet and contribute nothing to Germany's quest for victory. His confidence rested in part on a belief that the German fleet had important technological advantages which counterbalanced its numerical inferiority.

Tirpitz did not, however, enjoy much support. A more cautious group, which included the Kaiser, favoured a *Kleinkrieg* – a protracted guerrilla campaign involving torpedo raids, mines, and submarine attacks designed eventually to reduce the overall strength of the Royal Navy to a point at which a full-scale confrontation might be contemplated. This strategy was adopted, even though it had little realistic hope of success, since the Royal Navy's distant blockade rendered it virtually invulnerable to guerrilla tactics.

Skirmishes

On land, the Great War was characterized by persistent stalemate in the main theatres, with more familiar mobile combat on peripheral battlefields. The same can be said for the naval war, where the truly dramatic encounters took place far removed from the main theatre of conflict. It was the battles in the Mediterranean, the Indian Ocean and the Pacific that provided the stuff of naval legend.

Perhaps the most important peripheral action involved the battle cruiser *Goeben* and light cruiser *Breslau* which managed to elude much more powerful British and French fleets in the Mediterranean during the first few days of war. The British commander Admiral Sir Archibald Berkeley Milne displayed in abundance the prized Royal Navy qualities of excessive prudence and barren mediocrity. Three separate opportunities to destroy the German cruisers were squandered because of his lack of initiative. Eventually the two ships arrived off Constantinople where their presence contributed to Turkey's decision to enter the war three months later. That decision led to the closure of the Dardanelles and the severing of supply routes to Russia through the Mediterranean. The costly and ultimately unsuccessful Dardanelles operation was eventually launched to resolve a predicament which a few well-aimed volleys might have prevented in the first place.

Another disaster quickly followed, this time in far distant waters. On 1 November 1914, the West Indies Station Squadron under the command of Vice-Admiral Sir Christopher Craddock met Admiral Maximilian Graf von Spee's East Asia Squadron off the coast of Chile. Spee had been sent on a mission of destruction to wreak havoc wherever and for however long he could. Craddock feared that Spee would attack the Argentine trade route, which was important to the Entente.

Spee had the firepower to feel confident in that corner of the world. He had at his disposal two heavy cruisers, the *Scharnhorst* and the *Gneisenau*, in addition to three light cruisers. In contrast, Craddock had two ageing heavy cruisers, the *Good Hope* and *Monmouth,* one light cruiser and an auxiliary cruiser made from a converted merchant ship. He requested additional help from the Admiralty, but only the elderly battleship *Canopus* could be spared. Though its guns were heavier than anything Spee could muster, the ship was dreadfully slow. Craddock feared that its presence would render it impossible for his fleet to chase down Spee's faster ships. On the other hand, without the *Canopus,* Craddock was seriously out-gunned.

Craddock decided to leave *Canopus* at Port Stanley while he went chasing Spee. After some preliminary manoeuvring, battle began late in the afternoon of 1 November. Spee cleverly exploited his clear advantage in long-range guns; every attempt by Craddock to close was rebuffed. After a short time, both the *Monmouth* and the *Good Hope* were sunk, with only five survivors from both ships. Craddock was among those killed. The result was a huge shock to a British nation accustomed to believing that its navy was invincible.

The Admiralty then sent a task force under Vice-Admiral Sir Frederick Sturdee to intercept Spee. He arrived in Port Stanley on 7 December 1914, where he assembled a squadron consisting of two modern battle cruisers (*Invincible* and *Inflexible*) and six other cruisers. Spee, unaware of Sturdee's arrival, decided to attack Port Stanley on the 8th. Sturdee confronted the situation with the confidence of a man who knows that his ships are faster and much better armed than those of his adversary. After a short chase, Spee ordered his light cruisers to escape, while the *Scharnhorst* and the *Gneisenau* assumed battle stations. Sturdee then dispatched his cruisers to chase Spee's escaping ships, confident that *Invincible* and *Inflexible* could handle the German heavy cruisers. Both the *Scharnhorst* and the *Gneisenau,* in addition to two of the German light cruisers, were sunk, with the loss of perhaps 2000 lives, including Spee and his two sons. The British ships suffered only minor damage and just 21 casualties.

By the end of the year the oceans were rid of Germans raiders. Since British command of the seas was now total, most German merchant ships in foreign ports simply remained there for the rest of the war. This first round in the naval war was won by Britain. It was not a dramatic victory, but it was significant, and did restore pride in the Royal Navy.

Jutland – 1916

Naval pundits had long expected that the German High Seas Fleet and the British Grand Fleet would eventually meet in dramatic battle, perhaps the greatest in the history of naval warfare. But, as has been discussed, Jellicoe felt no great blood lust. As the months passed, the anticipated encounter failed to materialize. When clashes did occur, as at Dogger Bank in January 1915, a studied caution prevailed, with only a few small and expendable ships taking part. In other words, in a situation not dissimilar to the Western Front, the proximity of two heavily armed sides within a confined space resulted in stalemate.

Early in 1916, however, the new commander of the High Seas Fleet, Admiral Reinhard Scheer, managed to convince those above him that the time had come to take the battle to the British. He hoped to engage Admiral David Beatty's cruiser fleet, stationed at Rosyth, and deal it a heavy blow before the Grand Fleet, head-quartered at Scapa Flow, could intervene. The long-anticipated encounter took place at Jutland on 31 May 1916. But the collision of these two mighty forces did not prove to be the decisive battle that had been expected. British losses totalled around 112 000 tons, or three battle cruisers, three armoured cruisers and eight destroyers. The Germans lost just under 63 000 tons, with one pre-Dreadnought battleship, one battle cruiser, four light cruisers and five destroyers sunk. The British dead totalled 6097, the German 2551.

Naval historians continue to argue over which side won the battle, an indication of just how inconclusive it was. German losses were less severe, but they left the scene when British supremacy was about to tell. The limited achievements were in part the result of the prevailing caution within British naval circles. Fear of disaster outweighed the attractions of dramatic victory. Thus, in the closing stages of the battle, Jellicoe did not give chase when the German fleet made to escape, since he feared he was being led into a trap. This response might have been predicted from a memo written in October 1914 in which he made it clear that 'if . . . the enemy were to turn away from an advancing fleet, I should assume the intention was to lead us over mines and submarines, and should decline to be so drawn'. Nor did he want to prolong the battle after nightfall, given the superiority of German searchlights. 'Nothing would make me fight a night action . . . in these days . . . of long-range torpedoes', he wrote. 'I might well lose the fight. It would be far too risky an affair'. [51, pp. 251, 262] The German withdrawal was, in his mind, sufficient demonstration of British supremacy.

While this caution undoubtedly disappointed those at home who craved another Trafalgar, Jellicoe's prudence made sense. Naval mastery did not have to be demonstrated in order to exist. As Churchill recognized, Jellicoe was the only man in Britain who could lose the war in an afternoon. On the other hand, his cautious strategy had limited results. Though British naval supremacy was reinforced by the battle, an opportunity to inflict a strategic defeat upon the German navy had not been exploited. Such a defeat would undoubtedly have shortened the war. It is easy to blame Jellicoe for the failure to exploit this opportunity, yet he, like Haig, was the product of a system which valued stability and caution more than creativity and initiative. It was not the British way to win wars dramatically.

Jutland nevertheless provided enough action to reveal that British naval supremacy had leaks below the waterline. 'There is something wrong with our ships', Beatty remarked with classic British under-statement. [51, p. 264] Three of his ships were destroyed when poorly designed magazines exploded after being hit. But the most glaring fault was that armour piercing shells did not actually pierce armour. It seems astonishing that this fault was not revealed in trials before the war, which leads to the conclusion that adequate trials did not take place. The Germans, in contrast, could be proud of the way their ships had performed. They absorbed a tremendous amount of punishment without sinking, and damage control procedures worked well. In addition, their shells proved a great deal better than those of the British, though gunnery technique was about equal. Given these deficiencies it seems that Jellicoe's caution was perhaps appropriate. Jutland revealed that the Royal Navy's supposed dominance was better left untested.

But, as one journalist remarked at the time, the German fleet had assaulted its jailer and was back in jail. It would remain there for the rest of the war. Thus, British naval mastery was demonstrated by default. As Scheer advised the Kaiser shortly after the battle:

> With a favourable succession of operations the enemy may be made to suffer severely, although there can be no doubt that even the most successful result from a high sea battle will not compel England to make peace. ... A victorious end to the war at not too distant a date can only be looked for by the crushing of English economic life through U-boat action against English commerce. [40, pp. 328–9]

The British blockade

At the beginning of the war, Britain's 'Business as Usual' strategy held that the Royal Navy would blockade Germany, while the French and Russians made the major contribution on land. While this strategy proved unworkable once war came, the naval aspects of it did endure. The navy was still given the remit of starving the German people into submission. British confidence in the viability of such a strategy was built on some rather hasty and ill-founded assumptions about German dependence upon overseas trade for food and raw materials. The British blockade did cause widespread hardship, forcing the Germans to make do with ever more un-palatable *ersatz* commodities like coffee made from roasted corn and bread laced with sand. But it was never within the power of the British to win the war by starving Germans.

The matter of a blockade was complicated by the Treaty of London of 1909, which prevented belligerents from interfering with commodities entering a neutral country. In order for a blockade to work, Britain had to stop goods entering Germany not only directly, but also through a neutral nation such as Holland. The use of Dutch ports as a conduit to Germany became evident in the first few months of the war when imports of tobacco into Holland increased ten-fold. (Either that or the Dutch had suddenly taken to smoking in a big way.) But, fortunately for the British, the treaty was signed but not ratified, a legal nicety that allowed them to interfere with trade carried in neutral ships or bound for neutral ports.

The British could not simply ignore the treaty, since to do so would anger neutral states who traded with Germany. Annoying the Dutch was not a problem, but annoying the Americans was another matter entirely. The Americans asserted their right to trade freely with all belligerents. The issue proved a sore point in Anglo-American relations, with the British pushing American tolerance just about as far as it would stretch. In February 1916, they instituted a system of *ad hoc* rationing of goods entering Germany, based on pre-war levels of trade between the countries concerned. Anything beyond stipulated levels was considered war contraband and was confiscated. This system did not exactly satisfy the Americans, but the British case was at least helped by the fact that the Germans were proving a great deal more adept at annoying the US, through their submarine attacks on merchant ships. In the scale of war crimes, sinking 'innocent' merchant ships was considered more heinous than simply stopping them and preventing the delivery of cargo. (The effect of the blockade upon Germany is discussed in Chapter 7.)

The submarine war

It is commonly assumed that the British completely ignored the potential of submarines before the war, an explanation for why she was nearly defeated by them during it. True, there were doubters aplenty and some who questioned the morality of fighting underwater. In 1902, for instance, Admiral of the Fleet Sir Arthur Wilson described the submarine as 'underhand, unfair, and damned unEnglish'. [72, vol. 1, p. 332] But, at the outbreak of war, France and Britain each had over twice as many submarines as Germany. Mere numbers are, however, misleading. The Germans had an advantage in that, from 1907, they began to think of submarines in terms of ocean-going operations, not simply coastal ones. The British, in contrast, were much slower to widen their perception of the U-boat's utility. Furthermore, progress in submarine technology (in the engines used, range, torpedoes, periscope design, and so on) was occurring so fast that, when war broke out, all the belligerents started on a virtually even keel, since all fleets were technically obsolete. Mastery of the submarine war would go to the country that managed to build the greatest number of new vessels in the shortest time. Germany won this race hands down.

Though most British admirals recognized the enormous potential of the submarine, they did not see it as an immediate threat. This was in part because that threat was minimal without an effective weapons system – namely torpedoes – and effective torpedoes posed little danger if the method of delivering them, the submarine, could not stay under water for long, or travel great distances. Developments under the water were like a very effective pincer movement: great strides in submarine design occurred simultaneously with rapid progress in torpedo construction. Since most planners did not anticipate that both problems would be solved in time to pose a serious threat in a forthcoming war, most failed to take on board the possibility that the submarine might permanently alter the shape of naval warfare.

But those who doubted the potential of the submarine received a rude awakening before the war was two months old. On 22 September a single U-boat sunk the British cruisers *Aboukir*, *Hogue* and *Cressy*, with the loss of 1600 lives. That disaster explains in part the subsequent British reluctance to seek battle with the German surface fleet, since Jellicoe could never be sure about what hazards lurked beneath the surface. But his fears were probably exaggerated. The Royal Navy knew how to protect its own vessels. Dreadnoughts could be screened by destroyers and were, in any case, capable of greater speed than submarines, thus minimizing the latter's threat. No Dreadnought was ever sunk by a U-boat during the war.

But submarines did play a role not quite anticipated. Since the British seemed to be stretching the legal definition of acceptable interference with international trade, the Germans concluded that two could play at that game. They decided to impose their own blockade on Britain by a cordon of submarines. But U-boats posed a problem that no expert in international law nor naval strategist quite anticipated. Ordinary blockades worked on the principle that ships would be turned back or would have their cargoes confiscated, while the ship itself and the crew would be left unharmed. But the submarine could only be effective as an agent of blockade if it sank the ships in question. Its lethality was based on the fact that it could not be seen. When it surfaced, it was rendered virtually impotent. Therefore a conventional blockade, free of civilian casualties, could not very well be accomplished by U-boats.

The Germans decided to ignore these complications. On 4 February 1915 they issued the following declaration:

> All the waters surrounding Great Britain and Ireland, including the whole of the English Channel, are hereby declared a war zone. ... Every enemy merchant ship found within this war zone will be destroyed without it always being possible to avoid danger to the crews and passengers. ... It is impossible to avoid attacks being made on neutral vessels in mistake for those of the enemy. [27, p. 153]

The US naturally protested, with some vehemence. Germany softened her policy, but not sufficiently to prevent the sinking of the *Lusitania,* a British liner, in May. Included among the dead were 128 Americans. It is a measure of just how determined the US was to stay out of this war that the tragedy did not rouse them from their neutrality. Nor did another controversial sinking, of the *Arabic* in August, push the Americans much closer to intervention.

The sinkings nevertheless aroused sufficient anger among the American people to convince the Germans that greater care needed to be exercised in the selection of targets. The Chancellor Bethmann-Hollweg prevailed upon the navy to assume a more cautious approach, much to the frustration of the U-boat commanders. One recalled:

> So many [restrictions] were issued that it was impossible ... to learn them all, and many a time it was necessary for the helmsman or some other trusty support to bring the orders to the conning tower and hastily run through the mass to find out whether or not a certain vessel could be torpedoed. [40, p. 304]

It was not that Germany refused to countenance war with the US but rather that she recognized that such an eventuality would have to come at a time when American participation could not be significant. In other words, it was better to wait until an end to the war was in sight before angering the US. So far, events on the battlefield did not provide the Germans with the confidence to treat the Americans with disdain.

Even a restricted approach to the submarine war caused an enormous amount of damage. In 1915, some 750 000 tons of shipping were sent to the bottom. Meanwhile German yards were producing new submarines at a prodigious rate, while the Royal Navy searched in vain for an effective response to the threat. The Entente managed to destroy less than 50 submarines in the first two years of the war, a tiny figure in comparison to the number of new vessels produced. By the autumn of 1916, losses were steadily increasing, with 150 000 tons of shipping sunk in October alone. But this was still restricted warfare, designed to keep America tottering on the brink of war without falling over the edge. Hawks within the German war establishment argued that a restricted campaign was not working, and would never do so. The submarines might cause some discomfort, but were far short of destroying the British capacity to wage war. Despite shipping losses, the British were still eating better than any other belligerent.

On 22 December 1916 Admiral Henning von Holtzendorff, Chief of the Admiralty Staff, submitted a memo to the Chancellor in which he stated that 'The war demands a decision by autumn 1917 if it is not to end ... disastrously for us'. [45, p. 312] Since Germany could not win a protracted war, the submarine seemed the only salvation. Civilian advisers, carefully studying British shipping tables and rates of consumption, calculated that if sinkings exceeded 600 000 tons per month for six months, British imports would reduce by 39 per cent, a fatal level of loss. If the campaign was launched in February, defeat would come before the August 1917 harvest. Such a campaign would inevitably provoke the US into declaring war, but that eventuality did not frighten senior military figures, since America could not possibly mobilize effectively within six months. Admiral Eduard von Capelle, who succeeded Tirpitz at the Navy Office, claimed that the danger posed by the US was 'zero'. Hindenburg likewise assured the politicians that American help to the Entente would be 'minimal, in any case not decisive'. [45, p. 315]

Bethmann-Hollweg remained sceptical, frequently expressing his disdain for the reckless assumptions of his military advisers. He had eventually to bow to the weight of opinion, but decided to time the new strategy to coincide with a peace initiative. Approaches were made to Paris, London and Moscow, but the proposed terms were too insulting to inspire anything other than an immediate rejection. This reaction nevertheless allowed Bethmann-Hollweg to assume the moral high ground and to argue that the subsequent escalation of the submarine war had been forced upon Germany. He also hoped that the new strategy would lift German morale at a time when food shortages were causing rumblings of discontent. The people might renew their commitment to the war if they believed it would be over in just six months.

The Germans therefore imposed unrestricted warfare from 1 February 1917. The strategy nearly worked. Between February and July, losses averaged just over 600 000 tons per month. In April alone, submarines sunk 169 British and 204 allied or neutral vessels – a total of 866 000 tons, or one-quarter of the tonnage bound for British harbours. The effects upon the food supply were considerable; from February to June 1917, 85 000 tons of sugar were lost, at one point reducing Britain to four days' supply. Huge stocks of meat also went down. Panic set in at the Admiralty, with Jellicoe, the new First Sea Lord, telling the War Cabinet on 19 June that the naval situation was essentially hopeless. 'There is no good discussing plans for next Spring', he said, 'we cannot go on'. [21, p. 327]

Impending disaster focused minds on a solution. The Royal Navy understood how to protect its own valuable ships, namely by surrounding them with a cordon of destroyers which would act as a screen for torpedoes and participate in anti-submarine warfare. But senior Admiralty officers did not consider it practical to apply the same protection to merchant ships, given the scale and complexity of the operation. The crisis forced them to reconsider.

On 10 May the first convoy of 17 ships left Gibraltar. All arrived safely in Britain twelve days later. This small success spelt defeat for the submarine campaign. Losses declined steadily for the rest of the year, as ever more ships were convoyed. Before the introduction of convoys, losses caused by submarines averaged 10 per cent of the tonnage leaving port, rising to 25 per cent in April 1917. After convoys became the norm, this figure dropped to just one per cent. At the same time, destruction of German submarines increased steadily. Eventually the system was applied to other sea-lanes in the Atlantic and the Mediterranean, providing much relief to the Italians, who had suffered terribly from the ravages of the U-boat. The number of escort ships greatly increased with America's mobilization. Each passing month put a nail into the German coffin since Britain was not starving and the American contribution to the war steadily expanded.

Britain also responded to the U-boat with better coordination of shipping. The Ministry of Shipping, with Sir Joseph Maclay at its head, was a welcome if tardy response to a dangerously disorganized industry. The Ministry assumed powers to requisition shipping at fixed rates, to allocate space on vessels and to coordinate docks and railways in order to relieve congestion. Maclay, no respecter of established trading relationships, further directed importers to secure goods from the closest supplier in order to reduce shipping times. The reforms were sometimes ridiculously simple: for instance, casting aside traditional practice, the Ministry ruled that American wheat should be shipped as flour, rather than unmilled, thus reducing shipping space.

In the end, the submarines caused a huge scare, but could not sink merchant ships in sufficient number and with sufficient speed to cripple the Allied war effort, or even to create real hardship within Britain. Wishful thinking and poor strategic calculation inspired a campaign that had little hope of success and carried grave dangers. German experts completely miscalculated the ability of the British farmer to adjust to the crisis. Grain production, for instance, increased by 31 per cent due in part to the conversion of pasture to arable land (though the impressive increase can also be explained by the fact that the 1916 harvest had been poor). In addition, huge grain reserves from North and South America were made available.

During the war a total of 391 U-boats were commissioned, which were responsible for sinking 6394 Entente and neutral ships totalling 11.9 million tons. The Germans lost 178 vessels, either to enemy action or to malfunction. Though their destructive potential was immense, there were simply not enough of them to make the submarine a war winner on its own. Naval strategists had calculated in 1914 that at least 222 submarines would be needed to make a blockade effective. When the unrestricted campaign was launched, just 107 were available. Since one-third were always en route to the war zone, and another one third returning for refitting, that left just 35 submarines available at any given time. Though an energetic programme of new construction was instituted, it could only just keep pace with the Entente's increased proficiency at sinking vessels. The U-boat fleet expanded by a net total of just 25 during the course of 1917. As in the land war, the Germans had demonstrated that they possessed the capacity to make significant short term gains but could not deliver a knockout blow.

The submarines, a weapon given little attention before the war, made a great impact during it. In contrast, the Dreadnoughts, which captured the pre-war imagination, proved little more than a herd of very expensive white elephants. Their expense lay not only in their construction, but also in the fact that, once constructed, they had to be kept battle-ready – a tremendous drain on manpower and resources. For the British, they provided a deterrent –a demonstration of naval supremacy – but one which could not easily be used, given the risk of loss. As a result, the deck of a Dreadnought proved a pretty safe place to spend the war, but also a terribly frustrating one.

5

Sideshows and Imperial Struggles

The Great War began as a rather small disagreement in the Balkans. Britain, Germany, France and Russia joined the fight because that disagreement seemed crucial to the European balance of power. Other countries, including Romania, Bulgaria, Italy and Greece, entered the war for the gains they thought might come their way. A European war was transformed into a world war because the belligerents saw an opportunity to expand their respective empires. Thus, an assassination in Sarajevo led to fighting in Kut-el-Amara, Jerusalem, Tsingtao, Port Stanley and the Marshall Islands. White men from Europe died fighting for miserable bits of territory in Africa, while Africans and Asians drowned in the mud of Flanders.

The Eastern and Western Fronts provided the deaths in this war, but the outlying theatres provided the real drama. On small battlefields hastily improvised armies, often poorly armed, fought with extreme ferocity and consummate bravery. The tyranny of technology, which imposed a demoralizing stalemate on the fighting in France, was less evident away from the European vortex. In the Middle East and Africa, armies still advanced; cavalry still conquered. The issues that drove men to fight in these theatres might seem minuscule in comparison to the gargantuan struggle for European hegemony, but to the participants they were crucially important. In any case, a bullet in Togoland could be just as deadly as at Verdun.

Gallipoli – 1915

The war between Australians and Turks began not in Asia Minor, but near Broken Hill, in New South Wales. On New Year's Day 1915, two Turkish militants fired on a picnic train, killing four and wounding seven. The police arrived, a gun battle ensued, and both assailants were wounded, one mortally. Afterwards, an angry crowd, lacking anything obviously Turkish to attack, settled with burning down the local German Club. On the following Sunday, the Archbishop of Sydney preached forgiveness of one's enemies, but also warned that the Empire was in danger. It was Australia's duty to respond. Broken Hill would be avenged on the rocky slopes of Gallipoli.

By early 1915, stalemate gripped the Western Front and Russia seemed on the verge of collapse. The British War Council decided that the best way to aid Russia and defeat Germany was to attack Turkey. [Map 4] A force of 75 000 men, one-third of them Australians and New Zealanders, was dispatched to the eastern Mediterranean.

> And the band played Waltzing Matilda
> As the ship sailed away from the quay,
> Midst the songs and the cheers,
> Flag-waving and tears,
> We sailed off for Gallipoli.

'Australians were not makers of their own history', the maverick historian C. Manning Clark later complained. [16, vol. 5, p. 397] He was right, but the cohesiveness of the British Empire can nevertheless be measured by the willingness of colonial subjects to fight for England in every rotten corner of the globe.

By forcing the Dardanelles Straits, the Entente hoped to destroy the Ottoman Empire and capture the exotic prize of Constantinople. Winston Churchill, chief architect of the plan, argued that the operation would open a passage to Russia and expose the soft underbelly of Germany. It would also allow Britain to dominate the carve-up of the Ottoman Empire that would inevitably follow the war.

Life imitated myth. Fighting in the land of Troy appealed to Englishmen raised on Thucydides and Homer. It also offered the chance to escape the tactical morass of Western Europe, where machine dominated man. The tyranny of the spade would be broken: Allied troops would cleave Turkish lines like Moses parting the waters. Real war and real heroes would be rediscovered in the ancient world. By their participation in this drama Anzac troops were transformed from crude colonials to Homeric heroes. 'There

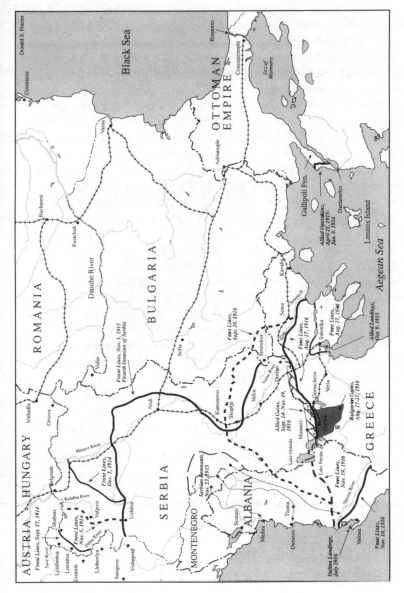

Map 4   *The Balkans, 1914–18*

was not one of these glorious young men', Compton Mackenzie recalled, 'who might not himself have been Ajax or Diomed, Hector or Achilles'. [74, p. 193] Yet these were the same soldiers whose rude behaviour in Cairo had earlier caused George V to complain to the Australian Governor-General.

The British effort was based upon what one commander called 'the fundamental and inherent superiority of the European as a fighting man over the Asiatic'. [53, p. 359] This assumption encouraged a perfunctory approach. Thus, the campaign that was supposed to change the course of the war was from the start starved of men, weapons, ships and supplies. Water was always short. Soldiers had to make their own grenades and trench periscopes. Junior commanders, deprived of maps, bought Baedeker's guides at secondhand book-shops in Cairo. The British had not the foggiest idea how many Turkish troops faced them. As it turned out, the Turks, fearing a rout, had packed the peninsula with 350 000 troops, leaving just 150 000 to guard the Russian frontier.

The campaign was doomed even before the first salvo was fired. It required audacious egotism to assume that the Royal Navy could conquer a corridor as well-defended as the Dardanelles. The bombardment of the outer defences, which began on 19 February, went reasonably well. The commander of the operation, Admiral Sackville Carden, signalled London that he would reach Con-stantinople within two weeks. But he then found that the guns of his battleships were ineffective against the inner forts. The fire from those forts prevented the minesweepers from doing their job, and, unless the mines were cleared, the big ships of the flotilla could not proceed further. Carden wanted troops landed in order to over-run the inner forts, but London was opposed to a land campaign, unless the naval operation failed.

And fail it did. Churchill assured the War Council that the ships could get through, and pressed Carden to proceed. The seemingly inevitable disaster which beckoned caused Carden's nerve to snap; on 16 March he was replaced by Admiral John de Robeck. Two days later the fleet attempted to force the Narrows. At first, the ships appeared to be holding their own against the shore batteries. But then the French battleship *Bouvet* exploded after one of its magazines took a direct hit. Heavy fire forced the minesweepers to pull back without completing their task. The battle cruiser *Inflexible* and the battleship *Irresistible* were both quickly disabled by mines. Then chaos descended. The *Irresistible* and the *Ocean* virtually disappeared when they ran into the same belt of mines. A storm blew in, and the advance was halted. On the 19th, Whitehall ordered a second thrust, and promised five more battleships. De Robeck, who had gathered together a huge armada of minesweepers, at first felt optimistic, but then abruptly changed his mind. The War Council supported his decision to abort the operation. As a result of the action on the 16th, the British and French had lost three battleships, had two others seriously damaged, and suffered losses to a number of other ships. Some 700 sailors were killed. The Turks celebrated the humiliation of the mighty Royal Navy.

After the naval operation failed, troops were landed on 25 April. Instead of quickly bisecting the peninsula (as the script read), they secured miserably small beachheads at prodigious cost. Another push in June was no more successful. Thereafter, stalemate settled upon the battlefield. The Allies had recreated the deadlock of the Western Front and in the process proved that a Turk with a machine gun has the same murderous potential as a German. Finally, in December, they withdrew – rather more successfully than they ever attacked.

'Nothing in the world is as loathsome as the sight of human beings who have forgotten they are human beings', wrote one Anzac soldier of his encounter with Johnny Turk. 'We caught one another by the throat. We rolled about the dirt locked in death grips. We used stones, knives, bayonets, clubs, even fists, hurled ourselves upon one another in fiendish bestiality such as the battlefield rarely sees'. Noble battle had disintegrated into savage brawl. 'And in all that effort of pain and blood and sweat and wasted gallantry we gained not a single position of any tactical or strategical importance'. [139]

The campaign still tortures romantics. Because it was so poorly planned and ineffectually executed, there are those who fantasize what better leadership and good preparation might have accomplished. A coordinated land and sea operation, it is argued, would have smashed the Turks, crippled Germany and saved Russia. There would have been no revolution, no communism, no Cold War. But much more important than these flights of fancy are the actual consequences of the campaign. It was, arguably, the worst defeat suffered by the British Empire since Yorktown. Britain's hold upon her empire was based upon the assumed superiority of the white man over the coloured races – a superiority generally accepted by both sides in the equation, but one which Gallipoli fundamentally undermined.

For Manning Clark, the war in general, but Gallipoli in particular, was one great swindle. The Australian dream of paradise was, he felt, crushed by a tidal wave of belligerent jingoism. As colonial subjects fighting for colonialism, Anzac soldiers suffered the irony of Empire. They were 'a spearhead for the preservation of bourgeois society in Russia ... and the world at large ... There was no mention of the dream of Australia as a place free from Old World race dissensions, free from Old World errors and wrongs and lies'. [16, vol. 5, p. 403] Thus, for Manning Clark, Gallipoli was a watershed. Volume 5 of his six-volume history of Australia ends with the evacuation of Anzac troops. His last volume examines a country in which idealism was replaced by the worship of 'heroic deeds which held out no hope for the future'. [16, vol. 6, p. 12]

Manning Clark was perhaps too pessimistic. It was he who wrote that 'Men make their history more wisely when they know what that history has been about'. [16, vol. 4, p. 427] Republicans like Paul Keating grew wiser on Clark's history. And, every year on 25 April, Australians and New Zealanders observe Anzac Day, ostensibly a celebration of imperial honour, but in truth a ritual of Antipodean identity. 'In the war we found our national spirit' concluded the New Zealand official historian. [119, p. 300] Rupert Brooke was confident that, if he should die in battle, there would be 'some corner of a foreign field that is forever England'. But he died at sea, on the way to Gallipoli. After that battle, one Australian veteran referred to Anzac cove as 'the most sacred corner of *Australian* soil'. [16, vol. 5, p. 425]

The Russians ironically proved able to do for themselves what the British had tried to do, namely defeat the Turks. Frightened by the failure at Gallipoli, General Yudenich launched an expedition against Turkey in January 1916, mainly designed to forestall the possibility of victorious Turkish troops appearing on the Russian frontier. By mid-February, the Turks had been driven from Erzerum, and another thrust led to the capture of Trebizond. By the summer, the Russians controlled Turkish Armenia.

Salonika, 1915–17

The Dardanelles fiasco resulted in large part from a Western European hubris, an assumption that civilized folk of French or British stock would always defeat Johnny Turk, no matter how ill-prepared the campaign. Out of this reasoning grew the assumption that there was an easy way to win the war, a back door to Berlin. The same pride and fantasy shaped the Allied campaign in Salonika.

The campaign grew out of the troubled state of Balkan politics, made more desperate by the failure of the Allies to tame the Turks. [Map 4] Had the Gallipoli operation succeeded, it is likely that the Balkan states would have been lining up to join the Entente. When it failed, the resolution of the war grew more uncertain, and they sat back to weigh their options. After months of deliberation, Bulgaria, courted by both sides, finally decided that her best interests lay with the Central Powers. The decision was not made on ideological grounds, but on purely pragmatic ones: Germany and her friends seemed at that point most likely to win.

Falkenhayn had pushed his armies across the Danube and Sava rivers in early October 1915 with a view to defeating Serbia and keeping the line of communication open to Turkey. The Bulgarians were enticed into the venture by a promise of Macedonia as the spoils of victory. The Allies had wanted to make a similar offer, which was somewhat justified on ethnic grounds, but the Serbs vetoed the idea. The Germans further promised that if Romania joined the Allies, Bulgaria would receive the additional reward of the Dobrudja and, if Greece entered the equation, the Kavalla region would be added as a bonus.

The Serbs, who had struggled so valiantly against assaults by Austria-Hungary in the autumn of 1914, were alarmed by the rumblings of a new offensive. They appealed to Britain and France, and also sought help from the Greeks who were bound by a 1913 treaty to send help to the tune of 150 000 troops if the Serbs were attacked. The Greek Prime Minister Eleutherios Venizelos decided, without much consultation, to strike a bargain with the Entente. In a rather bold attempt at blackmail, he argued that since Britain and France could not afford to let Serbia fall, they should provide the troops that his country was duty bound to supply under the terms of the treaty. The Entente Powers reluctantly agreed. Much to the dismay of his countrymen, Venizelos allowed French and British troops to land a force in Salonika, in preparation for a mission to save Serbia.

The campaign made some strategic sense, but then so did Gallipoli. Missing in both campaigns was the tactical planning and logistical preparation to make the strategy work. It might also have helped had the British and French deployed enough troops to make a real impact. By the end of October, the British had managed to send only one division, the French a meagre three. The Greeks, as it turned out, were unwilling to contribute any more. In the midst of the British and French deployment, Venizelos was forced to resign on 5 October. King Constantine refused to take his country into the war, but, for the moment, allowed Allied troops to remain in their lonely outpost, where they were unable to affect the course of the war.

The offensive by the Central Powers was planned and executed with a great deal more expertise and foresight than was evident on the Allied side. Bulgaria, invading from the south-east, supplied four divisions, Germany and Austria-Hungary six each. Belgrade fell within two days. The Serbs were forced to retreat in a south-westerly direction, unable to avail themselves of the assistance General Maurice Sarrail, commander of Allied forces in Salonika, had hoped to provide. The Serb link to Salonika was cut on 22 October. Serbia itself was overrun, but the Serb Army managed to escape complete destruction. They took refuge in Albania, eventually making it to Durrës on the coast, where the remnants (just 75 000 men from an original force of 300 000) were evacuated by British, French and Italian ships to Corfu.

The Allied plan for the Balkans lay in tatters, though their dubious occupation of Salonika was maintained. Sarrail, grasping at straws, argued that his small force was necessary to maintain a presence in the Balkans, and because it would tie up a much larger enemy force. Aristide Briand, who became French premier in October 1915, somehow managed to persuade Kitchener to buy that argument, which meant that the British force was permitted to stay. Greece meanwhile declared herself a 'benevolent neutral', a legal nicety which allowed the Allies to remain in Salonika, but, it was hoped, would enable the Greek people to avoid the worst ravages of the war. 'Benevolent', in this case, carried a certain irony, since the Greeks were anything but kind to their guests. Keen to keep the Central Powers at bay, they did their best to make life miserable for the French and British in Salonika.

Sarrail fumed, growing increasingly frustrated with the half measures of the Entente. Meanwhile the Greeks found it increasingly difficult to stand aside while bitter enemies, Turkey and Bulgaria, had their way in the Balkans. But the Greek government remained deeply divided. Constantine, who still feared the Entente more than the Central Powers, hung on to a neutrality that grew more illogical with each passing day. Behind the scenes, Venizelos stubbornly argued that the only sensible course was to join the Entente. The British and French did their best to foment discord by accusing Constantine of pro-German sympathies, a not altogether inaccurate accusation. When the King allowed a Bulgarian–German force to occupy Fort Ruppel in Greek Macedonia, he argued that it was merely quid pro quo for the fact that the Allies remained in Salonika. In June 1916 Allied tactics shifted from persuasion to force. A blockade was placed on Greek ports which, it was made clear, would be lifted only if the Greeks mobilized their armies and formed a new (more friendly) government.

The rehabilitated remnants of the Serbian army in Corfu were sent to Salonika in late June 1916. When some reinforcements from the Western Front were added, the force numbered around 250 000. It went into action at the Battle of Doiran in early August. After some initial success, it was eventually driven back by a German and Bulgarian counter-attack. The Fourth Greek Army also came under pressure, but did not respond to it, instead deciding to surrender Drama and Kavalla in mid-September. This did, however, give Venizelos the additional impetus to establish a pro-Entente movement. His provisional government, set up in Crete, declared war on Bulgaria and Germany on 23 November.

The Allies meanwhile stepped up the pressure on the official Greek government. The easy surrender of Kavalla was interpreted as a hostile act, prompting the demand that Constantine should surrender his navy. He complied on 11 October, but further demands were rejected. Their options exhausted, the French and British invaded on 29 November. Landing parties went ashore at Piraeus, but, after encountering stiff Greek resistance, promptly withdrew. The blockade was instead intensified, and the Venizelos government recognized. Further Allied action in the area achieved some local successes but had little effect upon the overall picture. The Germans, pleased with the way Allied troops were tied down in 'the greatest internment camp in the world' were in no hurry to force a decision. [117, p. 153]

Briand's exit in March 1917 brought in a new premier, Alexander Ribot, who increased the pressure upon the Greeks. On 11 June, Ribot presented Constantine with an ultimatum demanding his abdication. Entente troops at the same time advanced through Thessaly and a French force occupied the Isthmus of Corinth. The pressure proved too much. Constantine abdicated on 12 June, giving way to his second son Alexander, who was much more amenable to the Anglo-French cause (or much more clear-sighted). He appointed Venizelos Prime Minister, and the latter declared war on Germany and Bulgaria on 2 July. But that long-awaited action did not change affairs on the battlefield. The British and French could not quite figure out what to do with the Salonika garrison, though Lloyd George occasionally entertained daft notions that it might prove the key to unlocking the German back door. Salonika remained a relatively peaceful place for some soldiers to sit out the war. They greeted with dismay any suggestion that they might actually have to fight.

Africa

The war provided the British an opportunity to take over German colonies in Africa. They did not necessarily want new territories but did enjoy seizing them from the Germans. The principle of African neutrality, enshrined in agreements made at the 1885 Berlin Conference, was conveniently swept aside by the British. The Germans, who were sorely stretched in Africa, would have benefited from strict observance of the Berlin accords. But their attack upon Belgian vessels on Lake Tanganyika called into question their commitment to neutrality.

On paper, the British and French should have been able to do as they wished in Africa, given their numerical superiority and their well-established military and political presence. But mutual distrust proved a stumbling block. The Anglo-French Entente, after all, had originally been designed to forestall colonial rivalries in Africa, a goal only partially achieved. French suspicions rendered British efforts toward conquering German Africa rather haphazard. That aim was also slowed by natural elements: poor communications, inadequate transport, uncertain supplies, disease, and so on. In places, insects proved a more formidable enemy than the Germans.

The one exception was the campaign in Togoland, which was a model of good preparation and inter-allied cooperation. The colony was strategically important because a German radio station played an important part in coordinating the German naval effort. On 7 August 1914, four companies of native troops, led by British officers, and reinforced by Senegalese troops loyal to France, invaded the colony. The move surprised the British government, which had not actually sanctioned the campaign. But surprise turned to delight when Togoland fell nineteen days later.

Elsewhere, the situation was much more difficult. In the Cameroons, a British, French and Belgian force (which, in truth, consisted mainly of native troops), struggled through hostile territory and a ruthless climate. The British invaded from Nigeria on 7 September 1914, the French and Belgians from the south and east. But stiff German resistance was maintained until February 1916, when the colony finally fell, at a cost of some 6500 Allied casualties. Far more men fell to disease than to enemy bullets.

In South Africa, the Empire was defended by troops who had, only fifteen years earlier, been its bitterest enemies. When war broke out, Louis Botha informed London that his troops could be counted upon to defend that corner of the Empire. The British, grateful for this support, then instructed the newly formed South African Defence Force (SADF) to move against the Germans in South West Africa (Namibia). Botha complied, no doubt aware that cooperation carried its own long-term benefits. His decision nevertheless caused bitterness at home, with radical Boer elements arguing that the withdrawal of British troops should be used as an opportunity to assert independence. SADF troops had first to quell a revolt by some 12 000 Boers in the Orange River Colony and the Transvaal before they could embark upon their campaign into German South West Africa.

With the Boer threat neutralized, Botha led a force of 50 000 into the German colony on 14 January 1915. By mid-July the campaign had achieved its goal, at relatively low cost. With the Germans vanquished, South African troops were sent either to the Western Front or to the altogether more challenging campaign in German East Africa, where the enemy commander was the redoubtable Lieutenant-Colonel Paul von Lettow-Vorbeck. Though he commanded a force which never numbered more than 3000 Europeans and 11 000 Askaris, his troops were well prepared for a highly mobile insurgency campaign and were deeply committed to their commander. In August 1914 Lettow-Vorbeck took the bold step of invading Kenya, the aim being to tie down as many troops as possible, thus preventing them from joining the cause in Western Europe.

In November 1914 he trounced an Indian force bent on capturing the port of Tanga. The British then settled on a more methodical approach, which finally gained them control of Lake Tanganyika in

November 1915. A force of Belgian, Portuguese, British, Indian and South African troops finally captured Tanga the following July. Dar-es-Salaam and Tabor fell in September, but Lettow-Vorbeck then took the Allies on wild goose chase, invading Mozambique. He continued his marauding for the rest of the war, causing the British and their allies considerable embarrassment. They were not only unable to defeat the German commander, most of the time they could not even find him. In late 1917, he re-entered German East Africa, before invading Northern Rhodesia in November 1918. Throughout the war, he displayed a remarkable ability to mount a sustained campaign virtually without a stable source of supplies, relying instead on the booty he could capture, buy, or steal on the way. He was able to live off the land in part because he treated his native troops with considerable respect, an unusual approach among European commanders in Africa.

The fate of Germany did not rest upon the outcome of the East Africa campaign, but that campaign did provide opportunities for considerable valour. Lettow-Vorbeck demonstrated that there were still some theatres of war in which human qualities remained paramount and good command could make a difference. His army was never defeated and, as he would no doubt have argued, the troops mustered to chase him were prevented from making a contribution on the Western Front.

The Pacific and Far East

The British also coveted German outposts in the Pacific, among them Samoa, and New Guinea. Again, imperial troops figured large, in this case being drawn from Australia and New Zealand. In August 1914 a weakly defended German Samoa fell to troops of the British Empire, transported by French and Australian cruisers. New Guinea fell shortly afterwards, at similarly low cost to the victors.

Japan was keen to exploit the opportunity to expand its overseas possessions at the expense of Germany. She quickly took the northern Marianas, the Carolines and the Marshall Islands in the autumn of 1914. Eager to keep Japan friendly, Britain struck a deal with her in 1917, assigning her the former German Pacific colonies north of the equator, with Australia getting those south of the equator. The latter objected to the deal, but could not make much of her objection. As it turned out, the Paris Peace Conference overruled this treaty, though Australia nevertheless benefited to nearly the same degree under the Mandate system. (see p. 191)

Japan also wanted to rid China of German influence, the better to exert her own. Of particular concern was the port of Tsingtao, which the Germans had wrested from the Chinese on a 99-year lease in 1897. The fortress covered the entrance to Kaiochow Bay, where the German Navy's East Asia Squadron was stationed. Given the money and effort the Germans had invested in strengthening the fortress and improving the port, this was indeed a major prize.

The Japanese siege began on 25 August 1914. Though the fortifications seemed impressive on paper, the German Empire was woefully overstretched, with little ammunition to feed the massive array of guns. The Japanese mustered a naval assault force of four battleships, two cruisers and fifteen destroyers, which was further reinforced by a British pre-Dreadnought battleship. They also landed an assault force which eventually numbered around 50 000 men (heavily out-numbering the Germans), fortified with over 100 large guns and howitzers. The beleaguered garrison withered under a relentless bombardment, eventually falling on 7 November, though not without some ruthless hand to hand combat. The Japanese paid dearly for their prize, suffering around 6650 casualties, ten times as many as the Germans.

Japan went on to exert additional pressure on China, with a view to complete control. In January 1915, the Yuan Shikai regime was confronted with the infamous 'Twenty-One Demands' which, if accepted, meant that Japan would essentially govern China. The Chinese appealed to the West for help, but the Entente Powers, preoccupied elsewhere, were not particularly bothered by China's predicament. The latter therefore secretly agreed to most of the demands, though stopped short of surrendering her government to the Japanese. Hopes were raised when the Americans declared war in April 1917, since the Chinese assumed that Wilson's interest in self-determination would apply to them. The Chinese declared war on Germany and Austria-Hungary in August 1917 in order to gain favour with the Americans. This, it was thought, would have the added benefit of gaining China a seat at the peace conference where she might present her case for release from the Japanese yoke. This hope proved ill-founded. The war brought to an end German exploitation of China, but replaced it with Japanese rapaciousness.

The British Empire at war

In August 1914, just after the British ultimatum to Germany had expired, Prime Minister Herbert Asquith received a telegram which read: 'Do not worry, England, Barbados is behind you'. [139]

These were no idle words of encouragement. Within days of the outbreak of war, recruitment of a black West Indian regiment had begun. Eventually, 15 000 men would leave the Caribbean to join the war. This response was duplicated throughout the Empire. India contributed 1.4 million soldiers, Canada 630 000, Australia 430 000 and South Africa another 136 000. Nor do these figures include the millions of non-combatant labourers – Africans, Chinese, Maori, Indians and Egyptians – who worked for the war. Britain could, in theory, call upon a combined population of 425 million people and a vast imperial store of food, raw materials, money and the paraphernalia of war. Though many in Britain likened their struggle to David confronting a German Goliath, in truth the British Empire was the giant in this war.

J. D. Burns, a sensitive young man from Melbourne who fancied himself a poet, described in 1914 the call to arms which drew him to Europe:

The bugles of England are blowing o'er the sea,
Calling out across the years, calling now to me.
They woke me from dreaming in the dawning of the day,
The bugles of England: and how could I stay? [83, pp. 158–9]

'The war is ours in the sense that all we are, and all that we hope to be, are staked upon the issue', went the tortured prose of the New Zealand correspondent to *The Times*. [140, 22 May 1915] National identity, if it existed at all, was quickly subsumed by devotion to Empire. Nellie Melba, Australia's Queen of Song, included not a single identifiably Australian tune in her Patriotic Concert held at the Melbourne Auditorium on 10 September 1914. 'Remember we are Britons', the Australian Prime Minister told his troops before sending them off to fight the Turk. [139] Granted, this sense of devotion was not universal. Irish nationalists saw Britain's predicament as their opportunity, as did Afrikaners. Minor insurrections also occurred in Egypt, India, and black Africa. But by far the most common response was unconditional fealty. If empires are by definition exploitative, one wonders at this extraordinary willingness to come to the aid of the exploiters. After all, most colonial subjects knew almost nothing of Britain. Gurkha units, informed that they were to fight in Europe, sharpened their kukris when their train drew into Calcutta – they assumed they were nearing the battlefront.

Propaganda played its part. Recruits in Nyasaland were told that the Germans would come and take their land. Keith Fallis, a Canadian volunteer, admitted after the war that he 'never questioned that what we were doing was right and that the Germans were all wrong and that we were fighting to make the world safe for democracy'. [53, p. 368] The threat of German encroachment was taken seriously even in the Antipodes. Defeating the Hun would, it was argued, 'make New Zealand a sweeter place for little children'. [139] But in many cases the colonial soldier's motivation was similar to that of his British counterpart: war offered a bit of excitement and the chance to be a hero, not to mention a steady wage, wholesome food and sturdy boots. Even some ardent separatists considered British rule worth upholding if the alternative was German hegemony. Some were driven by opportunism: war offered a chance to gain British respect, which would prove useful after the war. After his release from prison, Bal Gangadhar Tilak, who had once incited fellow Indians to murder British officials, joined Mohandas Gandhi in recruiting men for the imperial war effort. 'The gateway to our freedom is situated on French soil', Gandhi told his followers, 'If we could but crowd the battlefields of France with an indomitable army of Home Rulers fighting for victory for the cause of the allies, it would also be a fight for our own cause'. [63, p. 65]

Relying upon the manpower resources of the Empire created problems, some of them unforeseen. Blacks from the West Indies and Africa were keen to fight, but the Colonial Office was determined that they should only fight other blacks. To encourage a black man to kill a white, even if the latter was German, undermined the principle of white supremacy upon which the Empire was built. In any case, it was widely held that 'the black man generally has an unholy fear of the gun'. [86, p. 198] Blacks, when they were sent to Europe, were therefore mainly employed in labour battalions. Even so, many whites were appalled at the prospect of white nurses treating black (or Indian) men. The British felt some sympathy with German prisoners of war who complained bitterly when they were guarded by Indian or black soldiers. Nor were cultural prejudices merely a matter of colour. It was widely feared, among British commanders, that the impudent pride of the Australian soldier and the democratic inclinations of his officers would infect the British army, eroding its sacred discipline. Field Marshal Douglas Haig was convinced that the notorious misbehaviour of the Australians arose because their army had foolishly outlawed the death penalty. He also found it hard to accept that soldiers from the dominions considered themselves allies of Britain and showed little allegiance to him as commander-in-chief.

Though the Great War was fundamentally a struggle for continental hegemony, Britain could not ignore its imperial ramifications. If, during the war, Britain lost any colonies, she would be able to get them back if she won in Europe. If, however, she lost in Europe but won elsewhere, she would still lose her colonies – either as the price of peace with Germany, or because of her inability to continue to defend them. This suggested that all efforts should be concentrated upon defeating the German army in France and Belgium. But that did not mean that the colonies could be neglected until the business of subduing Germany was completed. Defending imperial interests became a dangerous juggling act: men taken from a colony to fight in Europe endangered the security of that colony. Natives could be enlisted to defend themselves, as was the case in India, but because of the ever-present danger of nationalist insurrection, no colony could be left entirely alone. Just how precarious the situation became is revealed by the fact that during the war the British garrison in India dwindled to a low of just 15 000 troops, 23 000 fewer than were present on the eve of the Indian Mutiny. 'I want every white soldier in India I can get', a panicked Viceroy Lord Hardinge wrote to Kitchener in March 1915. [53, p. 360]

Before 1914, Britain did not covet German imperial possessions. But, once war broke out, the rules of the imperial game changed. 'Now everything becomes fluid, we can redraw the map of the world', says the protagonist in H. G. Wells's 1917 novel *Mr Britling Sees It Through*. [120, p. 197] To the victor would go the spoils, including some that the victor had not previously wanted. The war also provided irresistible opportunities for expansion into new areas. Thus, though the British did not enter the war bent on conquest, they found themselves drawn in that direction.

Attention was directed specifically toward the Ottoman Empire, Germany's ally. Prior to August 1914, the British were not inclined to upset the status quo in the Middle East: the Ottoman Empire seemed strong enough to maintain a semblance of order in the area, but too weak to threaten British interests. Friendliness toward the

Empire protected the Suez Canal and the passage to India. With the coming of war, the prospect of Turks as enemies raised new dangers, but also new opportunities.

The Sultan of Turkey assumed that Britain's preoccupation with the German threat would leave a power vacuum in Asia. As Caliph of the Faithful, he commanded the spiritual allegiance of Suni Muslims, some 57 million of whom were Indian. In November 1914, he proclaimed a *jihad*, or holy war, calling upon Muslims to cast out the British infidel. For the British, *jihad* was an ever-present nightmare made worse by the fact that now the Turks were supplied with modern weaponry and skilful commanders, courtesy of the Germans. And, since Muslims constituted the main source of recruits for the Indian Army, *jihad* threatened Britain's tenuous hold upon her imperial jewel.

Jihad, in fact, never materialized. There were too many influential Muslims scattered throughout the Middle East and India who perceived it in their best interest to remain loyal to Britain. But, damp squib or not, the threat of *jihad* motivated the British to take proactive steps to protect her interests, namely the Suez Canal and India. As was so often the case in the past, Britain responded to danger by embarking upon conquest.

Of immediate concern was access to Persian oil. It was pumped from the oilfields to Abadan, an island situated opposite the Turkish-ruled port of Basra. Aware that the Turks could immobilize the Royal Navy if they seized Abadan, the British decided upon a pre-emptive strike. By taking Basra, they hoped to seal off the Gulf. Units of the Indian Army accomplished this rather easily in November 1914. But, as in the past, each new conquest, secured to protect previous conquests, required further conquest to protect it. Also, waging war in a region so ancient – the land of Babylon and Nineveh and, legend has it, of the Garden of Eden – had a mesmeric attraction to officers raised on the classics at Harrow, Eton or Winchester. Only the faint-hearted considered stopping at Basra. 'So far as we can see, all advantages, political and strategical, point to as early a move on Baghdad as possible', advised the Indian General Staff. [83, p. 163]

An expedition was mounted under the command of Major-General Charles Townshend, a vain publicity hound more lucky than brilliant. His first objective was Amara, which he bluffed his way into on 3 June with a minuscule force of 100 men. It was the wrong kind of victory for a man of Townshend's ego. 'How much

I enjoyed the whole thing', he wrote to his wife. His troops, he felt sure, would 'storm the gates of hell if I told them to'. [83, p. 166]

Hell was where he next took them. The British government, sufficiently distracted by events in France and desperate for any sort of victory, approved a further advance on Baghdad. Never mind that 30 000 high quality Turkish troops were lurking in the area. Townshend's capture of the miserable river town of Kut-el-Amara in September swelled his already dangerously distended pride. Driving relentlessly on, his force ran out of steam at Ctesiphon, just 29 kilometres from Baghdad. Townshend withdrew to Kut to regroup, but within a week was besieged. Some 13 000 British and Indian troops endured five months of hunger, bombardment and disease in a squalid little town where logic suggested they did not belong. Feeble attempts at rescue failed miserably. On 29 April 1916 came the inevitable surrender. The prisoners were marched to Turkey, where they sat out the rest of the war in foetid, pestilential prison camps. Less than half survived their ordeal. Meanwhile Townshend enjoyed a comfortable imprisonment at an island villa near Constantinople – a captivity more appropriate to an earlier war. Less than a year after the Kut débâcle, a much better equipped force under the considerably more stable General Sir Stanley Maude captured Baghdad. Over the course of the war, the Mesopotamia campaign cost the British Empire 92 500 casualties, with nearly 16 000 dead in battle and 13 000 the victim of disease. For that price British ships were kept well supplied with oil and Britain obtained control of a troublesome piece of real estate.

The British campaign in Palestine and Syria contrasted sharply with the blunders in Mesopotamia. Led by General Sir Edmund Allenby, it secured Jerusalem in December 1917 and overran Palestine and Syria the following year. The expedition was truly imperial, with soldiers from Britain, Australia, South Africa, New Zealand, India, Singapore, Hong Kong, and the West Indies taking part. Three battalions of Jews (including men from the US, Argentina, and Canada) enlisted in the Royal Fusiliers, among them David Ben Gurion, future Prime Minister of Israel.

But the crucial ingredient in this campaign was the participation of Arabs who were enticed into what they thought was a nationalist rebellion against Turkish rule. A letter from Sir Henry MacMahon, the Egyptian High Commissioner, to Hussain, Sharif of Mecca in October 1915 promised that the British would 'recognise and support the independence of the Arabs'. [91, p. 243] While the letter was studiously vague, most Arabs felt that they had been promised the land previously occupied by the Turks, including Palestine. Unfortunately, the British also counted upon French help. Assurances made to them under the Sykes-Picot treaty of April 1916 contradicted MacMahon's promises to the Arabs. But the scheming did not end there. A bargain was also struck with the Zionists, motivated mainly by the British desire for a Zionist nation in the Middle East which would feel indebted to the Empire. Thus, the Balfour Declaration of November 1917 pledged British support for 'the establishment in Palestine of a national home for the Jewish people'. [71, p. 159] According to its author, the declaration was 'extremely useful propaganda' which would impress Russian and American Jews. [91, p. 245] As long as these contradictory agreements were kept secret they served their purpose: Britain's carefully constructed coalition of forces proved sufficient to turn out the Turk. But, out of expediency, there grew the betrayals and bitterness of the post-war period.

Militarily, the Palestine Campaign was brilliant, thanks primarily to the imagination, leadership and drive of Allenby. It is a pity that his prowess will forever be overshadowed by the escapades of one of his officers, the devious deviant T. E. Lawrence. The romance of Lawrence's exploits has effectively camouflaged the egotism and trickery of the man. An intelligence officer by training, he possessed in abundance the cynicism of that profession. But 80 years after his campaign, his carefully constructed legend shines brighter than the sordid reality. Of the promises he made to the Arabs who trusted him, Lawrence wrote: 'I risked the fraud, on my conviction that Arab help was necessary to our cheap and speedy victory in the East, and that better we win and break our word than lose'. [64, p. 24] An imperialist swindler who masquerades in Arab garb is still a swindler.

The Empire expanded because of the war, but the days of imperial glory were over. The mandated territories would bring more grief than gain. And, because of the war, the ties holding the imperial edifice together grew horribly frayed. Before 1914, most ardent imperialists argued that Indian self-government was far too remote to be worthy of discussion. But the war had turned the colony into what Edwin Montagu, the Secretary of State, described as 'a seething, boiling political flood'. [81, p. 66] In August 1918 the Montagu-Chelmsford Report recommended a system of 'dyarchy'. As Montagu explained to the Commons, the government sought 'the gradual development of self-governing institutions, with a view to the progressive realisation of responsible government in India'. [63, p. 65] Self-government, once unmentionable, had become the policy of the pragmatists who recognized that the only way to keep India out of the hands of discontented radicals was to reward those who remained loyal.

The *Lagos Weekly Record* argued in 1917 that victory for the Allies must usher in an era of 'democracy for all peoples, regardless of race, creed or colour'. Openly calling for an end to white exploitation, the paper argued: 'The pretence that the superior have a right to impose their authority upon the inferior is a mere euphemism for the vicious idea that the stronger has a moral right to subjugate the weaker'. [86, p. 88] The mere fact that the British had been so dependent on the help of their colonies eroded the notion of white supremacy. Thanks in part to Johnny Turk, the white man seemed a great deal less competent and supreme than he had before 1914. Black Africans who worked the Liverpool docks were astonished to find white men working alongside them. Whites, they had been told, did not perform menial labour.

The breadth of the imperial war effort can be measured by the solemn memorials dotted around the old Empire: in Alice Springs, Auckland, Lagos, Cape Town, Delhi and Vancouver. Roughly speaking, the war killed 62 000 Indians, 60 000 Australians, 56 000 Canadians, 17 000 New Zealanders, 7000 South Africans and another 3000 men from the black colonies of Africa. At home, there was widespread realization that the Empire's sacrifice had been Britain's salvation. *The Times* commented: 'Never while men speak our tongue, can the blood spent by the Canadians at Ypres and by the Australians and New Zealanders at Anzac be forgotten. That rich tribute of love and loyalty to the highest ideals of our race has not been wasted'. [83, p. 199] In 1915, the Over-Seas Club offered £5 to the person who came up with the best synonym for 'colonial', which now seemed too demeaning. The club was so inundated with responses (including Britonial, Imperialist, Co-Briton, Out-Briton, MacBriton and Albionian) that it felt unable to declare a winner. [140, 9 August, 1915] Nearly every Empire Day during the war, *The Times* reminded its readers that it was no longer appropriate to think of people from the colonies as inferior human beings. (Whether this applied equally to coloured peoples was not discussed.)

Some, including the redoubtable Lord Milner, saw the imperial war effort as proof that a twentieth-century version of *Pax*

Britannica could be established. Britain would retreat within a cocoon of imperial preference and snub her nose at sordid Europe. 'No one pretends that we have made the most, in the past, of our vast Imperial resources', *The Times* commented in 1916. [140, 24 May 1916] But out in the colonies, few wanted to turn the clock back. Their performance in the war furthered a sense of independent national identity. The heroism of their troops was incorporated into a distinct national folklore which was not British, not imperial, but their own. And, as the Great War patently demonstrated: no matter how friendly, cooperative and bountiful her empire might be, Britain could not avoid becoming embroiled in power politics closer to home. She might enjoy the adventures and glory of empire, but she had to live in Europe.

On 9 January 1918, Lloyd George bet his War Minister, Lord Derby, 100 cigars that the war would not be over by the end of the year. Haig, who witnessed the wager, thought Derby the likely winner. He thought the war would be won within the year because of the 'internal state of Germany', and did not think the Russian defeat would make any difference, since 'even after the Germans brought over all their reserves from Russia they would still have too small a superiority over the French and British to ensure a decisive victory'. There was, in other words, 'no cause for anxiety'.

Haig correctly estimated that the Germans would be able to bring over 32 divisions from the Eastern Front, at a rate of about ten per month. This suggested that they would be ready to attack in March. He did not, however, believe that they would risk everything on a massive attack because if they failed '[their] position would become critical in view of the increasing forces of the allies in August'. [21, p. 356] As will be seen, he paid dearly for his confidence.

America joins the war

According to Haig's calculations, if the Allies could hold on until August 1918 Germany would be defeated soon thereafter. August was critical because at that point the gathering strength of American forces would begin to tell. The United States had entered the war in April 1917, but did not materially affect the fighting until over a year later.

American anger was a slow-burning fuse. They had preferred neutrality for a number of reasons. First, they did not want to embroil themselves in sordid European affairs, and saw no clear-cut issue around which to rally. Second, the way the belligerents used the war to expand their empires appalled those Americans who found colonialism abhorrent. Third, many American businessmen sensed that they could do just fine out of the war by loaning money and selling arms to both sides. They feared that profits would fall sharply if the US actually entered the war. Fourth, ethnic loyalties divided Americans. Those of French, British or Italian ancestry sided with the Entente, but those of German or Irish descent were neutral or favoured Germany. Even those who supported Britain and France often had severe misgivings about the alliance with Russia. Aware of the fervent anti-war mood, President Woodrow Wilson campaigned for re-election in 1916 on a platform promising to keep the US out of the war.

America would have stayed out of the war if German U-boats had not forced her into it. In addition, a rather stupid German overture to Mexico, under which she was promised land in the American South-west in exchange for entering the war on the German side, exhausted American patience. Once in the war, they cast themselves as crusaders who would save Europe and make the world safe for democracy. But by this time, all the other belligerents had jettisoned noble ideals in favour of a hard-bitten cynicism. Virtue and honour were three years out of fashion. This profound difference in attitude encouraged a calculated aloofness on the part of the Americans. They would help defeat the Germans, but would not support the war aims of the Entente. Their semi-detached status was expressed in their insistence that they were an 'associated power', or a 'co-belligerent', but definitely not an ally. (Nevertheless, for the purposes of simplicity, 'the Allies' will henceforth be taken to mean Britain, France *and* the United States.)

'America on the eve of World War I', writes David Woodward, 'aspired to have its world influence match its unquestioned economic power without assuming the inevitable international responsibilities that would ensue and without developing the military means necessary to support a global policy.' Existing stocks of field artillery ammunition in the US were sufficient for a bombardment of only a few minutes duration. The US had no flamethrowers, hand grenades, trench mortars, tanks, or suitable aircraft. In terms of size, the army was ranked seventeenth in the world. But these inadequacies caused surprisingly little concern, since most Americans optimistically assumed that their mere presence would be decisive. Colonel Edward House, the President's close adviser, thought that the threat of American mobilization alone would 'break [the Germans'] morale and bring the war to an earlier close'. [135, pp. 7, 20, 43]

American troops arrived with rather too much swagger in their step. They insisted upon being treated as partners of equal weight from the beginning, and seemed reluctant to learn from their allies' considerable experience. George G. Moore, a businessman who had visited the front on a number of occasions, expressed a common American view that 'political urgency and the personal ambition of commanders have caused a hideous wastage of the man-power of England and France in attacks from which there was no intelligent hope of success'. [135, p. 56] General John Pershing, commander of the American Expeditionary Force, was of the opinion that his troops had nothing useful to learn from the French or British. In practical terms, this meant that he insisted that foreign commanders should not have control over his men. Instead, American units were to be inserted into the line intact, and could not be broken up to patch weak points in the line. Relations with the British and French were, therefore, strained from the very beginning.

Cold charity

When the Supreme War Council met at Versailles on 29 January 1918, Haig was decidedly less sanguine than he had been three weeks earlier. He sought to 'bring home to our Prime Minister's mind the seriousness of our present position and to cause him to call up more men while there is yet time to train them'. If the Germans did attack in force, he warned, British losses might exceed half a million men, or an overall reduction of 30 divisions by autumn. Pétain presented an equally dismal scenario, predicting a reduction of 25 French divisions by normal wastage alone. Lloyd George was not moved by the argument, having heard Haig whistle a different tune a few weeks before. Maurice Hankey, the Cabinet Secretary, thought that Haig and Pétain 'made asses of themselves by absurd panicky statements'. [21, pp. 361–2]

Leaving the manpower problem aside for the moment, Allied representatives discussed strategic plans. A defensive strategy was agreed upon for the short term, though the various commanders-in-chief were allowed to consider offensive projects 'suitable for the forces at their disposal'. Approval was also given to Lloyd George's proposal for an offensive against the Turks, much to Haig's dismay. An extension of the British line by about twenty kilometres was left for Haig and Pétain to work out among themselves. Haig was confident that Pétain ('a grand old man, full of go and determination') would see reason on that issue.

The most significant, and ominous, decision reached at Versailles pertained to the formation of a General Reserve. Haig doubted its necessity, since 'Pétain and I get on very well'. [21, p. 362] He opposed the plan primarily because of the command issues implied, a sensitive topic after the Nivelle affair of the previous year. When he learned that the General Reserve would be under the control of the Supreme War Council, in which General Ferdinand Foch was the senior representative, unease turned to alarm. He did not trust the British representative, General Sir Henry Wilson, to keep the best interests of the British Expeditionary Force (BEF) in mind. When pressed in late February to contribute troops to the Reserve, Haig refused. Wilson reminded him that the Reserve had been formed to benefit all commanders, and warned Haig that if ever he had to 'live on Pétain's charity ... he would find that very cold charity'. [21, p. 369] Lloyd George tried to persuade Haig to cooperate during a meeting on 14 March, but the latter remained characteristically stubborn. Keen to avoid another embarrassing row with his commander, the Prime Minister gave way. It was decided that implementation of the General Reserve would wait until the arrival of the Americans in greater numbers. Haig celebrated his victory, apparently unconcerned that his future security rested solely on a personal agreement he thought he had with Pétain.

Playing the last card

Ludendorff, his ego further swelled by triumph in the East, used his prestige to consolidate control over the political and military direction of the war. The Chancellor, Bethmann-Hollweg, whose occasional pessimism had exhausted Ludendorff's patience, was the immediate victim, being forced out on 13 July 1917. In his place came Georg Michaelis, a poodle who could be trusted not to interfere with important issues of governance. There were henceforth few checks on Ludendorff's gargantuan power. 'The German *Volk* [people] now stands higher with me than the person of the Kaiser', he boasted. [45, p. 381] He had no doubt that he spoke for, and understood, the *Volk*. Megalomania became official German policy.

But Bethmann-Hollweg's pessimism had solid foundation. Within Germany hunger was rife, with potatoes precious and sausages bearing little resemblance to their pre-war form. The hungry, cold and war-weary population reacted predictably, namely by taking to the streets in protest. Though the strikes and riots had political overtones, they were in the main a collective hunger pang by a people whose food consumption had been cut in half since the beginning of the war. According to some estimates, 750 000 German civilians starved to death during the war. Government reaction was also predictable. Strike leaders were imprisoned, riots were brutally repressed, and all problems were blamed on traitors or foreign subversives. The unrest did not, however, deflect Ludendorff from his course. He was certain that discontent would disappear when a new offensive brought dramatic victory.

Victory in the East did allow a huge transfer of troops to the Western Front. It also allowed Germany to strip conquered Russian territory of valuable industrial plant and natural resources. But with the captured territory came a troublesome population which required a huge army to police. Enforcing the peace in the Ukraine was complicated by the inevitable ripples of revolution emanating from Moscow. The net benefit of Ludendorff's conquests was therefore negligible – one million troops were left in the East, where they probably consumed more food and raw materials than they managed to gather and send west.

Ludendorff wanted to strike a massive blow in the West in order to win the war before the Americans could mobilize sufficiently. Operation Michael, in preparation since November 1917 and formally approved on 21 January, would strike first at the point of juncture of the French and British armies, between Arras and Laon. This would cleave the front in two, causing the British and French to draw away from each other in order to protect themselves. The British would presumably retreat toward the channel ports, their essential link with home, while the French would move in the opposite direction in order to protect Paris. The ambitious plan depended upon the German ability to achieve a breakthrough on a front where advances had heretofore been minuscule. Continued stalemate would not suffice.

The plan was pure Ludendorff – superbly organized but strategically flawed. It was based on an assumption that brilliant tactics alone could win the war. 'I object to the word "operation"',', Ludendorff confessed before the offensive. 'We will punch a hole into [their line]. For the rest, we shall see. We also did it this way in Russia.' As the Official History would later state, 'the tactical breakthrough was and remained the initial goal'. [45, p. 400] What Ludendorff had in mind was little more than a bareknuckle fight of uncertain duration in which victory would go to the last man standing. His plan rested on the assumption that the Germans could 'keep our nerves for ten minutes longer than the enemy'. [45, pp. 392–3] Quite a few senior commanders (among them Hoffman) doubted that Germany had the resources to fight such an offensive in 1918. But their doubts were bulldozed by Ludendorff's stubborn belief that a miracle victory could be achieved.

Victory would be achieved not by clever strategy, but by brutal force. The plan was derived from the successes at Riga and Caporetto. Instead of the customary prolonged bombardment, Ludendorff devised a short, vicious artillery attack, which would not necessarily destroy enemy defences but would leave them in temporary disarray. The infantry would then move forward, not in one great slow wave, but in small groups at great speed, probing for areas of weakness. Reserves would continually move forward like cogs on an assembly line, ensuring that there would be no loss of attack momentum. Troops were instructed to penetrate as far as they could, leaving pockets of resistance to be mopped up by those following behind. Like hundreds of termites attacking a single block of wood, they would weaken the structure sufficient to cause its collapse, but would not consume it entirely.

Attack forces were organized and trained for the specific purpose they were to perform. Forty-four 'mobile' divisions with full-strength battalions were to be the cutting edge of the offensive. Drawn from the freshest and most healthy (youngest) men available, these units were generously armed with machine guns, trench mortars and flamethrowers and were provided with solid logistical support. Behind them came 30 'attack' divisions, similarly armed but designed specifically as a second wave to consolidate advances and prepare for counter-attacks. Another 100 'trench' divisions were composed of soldiers in the poorest physical or mental condition, who were provided only the bare essentials. They were to hold trenches after advances had been consolidated.

Punching a hole in the line meant bringing as much force as possible to bear on a single point. In the month before the offensive, nearly 10 500 full-length trains brought men and supplies to the front. But even this mammoth effort fell far short of Ludendorff's hopes. Each regiment was to have been supplied with 30 heavy and 72 light machine guns, but production difficulties often meant that only half of the required number actually materialized. The largest offensive of the war was in fact woefully ill-equipped for the objectives it was designed to achieve.

Awaiting the blow

While the Germans planned, the British bickered. Lloyd George had decided that, since he could not remove Haig, the only alternative was to prevent further costly offensives by refusing the troops he requested. The Prime Minister was confident that a future German offensive would fail like all previous ones had, and become mired in stalemate. Haig had, after all, encouraged just such an under-estimation of German capabilities. Thus, when Haig asked for half a million additional men, Lloyd George refused. Since the British had been forced to take over a considerable length of the front in order to relieve the bedraggled French, Haig's demand had merit. British strength on the Western Front in 1918 was about 70 000 troops lower than in the previous year.

But a reduction in numbers need not have meant a decline in strength. The Germans had convincingly demonstrated that divisions could be reduced in size without diminishing their capability, as long as they were given greater firepower. This was a concept that Lloyd George, Ludendorff and Foch understood, but Haig did not. Nor was he entirely innocent in this affair: if the British line was ill-equipped to meet the German thrust, some blame must rest with him. His intelligence officer, Brigadier General John Charteris, had warned as early as December that the Germans were likely to attack in the spring on the St. Quentin sector, covered by General Hubert Gough's Fifth Army. When Haig visited Gough on 16 February, he concluded that 'Everything seemed carefully thought out ... if we only have another month in which to work, this sector ought to be very strong.' In early March he told his Army commanders that he 'was only afraid that the enemy would find our front so very strong that he will hesitate to commit his army to the attack with the almost certainty of losing very heavily'. [21, p. 367]

On the eve of the offensive, Haig recorded that Gough's sector was very well defended. In truth, it was a disaster waiting to happen. Though the British had tried to copy the German 'defence in depth', theirs was a poor imitation. Far too many men were concentrated in the front line. Haig furthermore thought that the main German attack would eventually move in the direction of Calais and Boulogne, in other words that Flanders would hold the same attraction for them as it did for him. This area was therefore heavily reinforced, at the expense of Gough's sector. Along the entire British front, the German advantage was six to four. In the Fifth Army sector it was five to one. Gough had to defend the longest part of the line with the fewest number of troops. He repeatedly warned GHQ about this weakness, but each time was politely told to quit complaining.

Haig wanted the extra troops for another offensive in Flanders. He did not anticipate that they would be needed for defence, since his defence seemed solid. Haig simply could not accept that the Germans would be able to break through his lines since he had never been able to break through theirs. It is a measure of his confidence that he approved leave for over 80 000 men on the eve of the German offensive. He assured the War Office that he would be able to withstand an attack on any part of his front for at least 18 days with the forces at his disposal. For this reason, the government felt comfortable retaining a reserve of 120 000 men at home instead of releasing it to Haig.

The problem was further complicated by the failure of the Allied commanders to agree to any coherent system of support. All were suspicious of cast-iron agreements that might tie their hands in the event of a crisis and all abhorred any suggestion of unified command. Pétain and Haig did manage to agree to share reserves if circumstances merited it, but this agreement had little substance, which perhaps explains why it was acceptable to both men. Haig was confident that he could work with Pétain because he thought he could control him. He did not envisage circumstances in which he would need Pétain's help, and felt sufficiently dominant to refuse to provide assistance to the French if a claim was pressed.

The German spring offensive

On 21 March, the Germans began their attack on a 100-kilometre front. [Map 5] In a five-hour hurricane bombardment, 6600 guns and 3500 trench mortars threw forth a torrent of fire which shredded British front-line trenches. Seventy-six German divisions pressed forward at 9:40 a.m., supported by over 1000 aeroplanes.

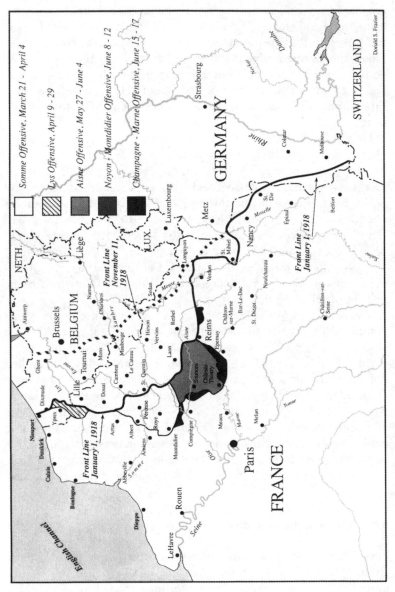

Map 5   *The German offensives, 1918*

Gough's line quickly collapsed, and German troops rushed forward into open countryside. When the attack began, Haig was at first delighted, since he feared that his men would otherwise become 'stale from expecting and preparing so long'. By the end of the day, the British were forced to retreat along a significant portion of the line, yet Haig still described the result as 'highly creditable to ... British troops'. [45, p. 371] By the fifth day, however, penetration measured 65 kilometres in some places, with Amiens under serious threat. Meanwhile, the Germans were experiencing similar success in the French sector, advancing as far as Noyon.

Haig did not waste time in apportioning blame. The chief culprit was naturally Lloyd George, who had supposedly left the BEF dangerously weak. In time, Haig would also sacrifice Gough, despite his effusive praise of the commander before the attack. But, according to Tim Travers,

> One does ... have to look far to explain the German success ... This was not primarily due to the German superiority in divisions, nor to the reduction in infantry battalions in the BEF, nor to the divisions sent to Italy. *Rather it was due to a defensive system that was not understood, did not work and did not properly exist at all.* This was primarily the fault of GHQ, which lacked a sense of urgency in preparing defences ... and which did not ensure the BEF's comprehension, coordination and compliance with its defensive concept.

According to one senior officer, there was great suspicion of the 'defence in depth' idea. Corps, division and brigade staff 'either mistrusted this doctrine or insisted on the exact opposite'. [113, p. 65] In other words, Gough deserves condemnation for his failure to implement a coherent defensive strategy. But so too does Haig.

Dramatic as the advance seemed, it did not live up to Ludendorff's ambitions. Some units had penetrated deeply, but consistency was lacking. In many places, troops found themselves bogged down, far short of their first day's objectives. This uneven penetration made it difficult to capitalize on the dramatic breakthrough, and left the most successful units in vulnerable salients. Ludendorff had also failed to anticipate the British capacity for orderly retreat, something he had not encountered while fighting the Russians on the Eastern Front. He had hoped for another Tannenberg – a massive pincer movement which would trap the Third and Fifth Armies in the Cambrai salient. But the result fell far short of that objective. Though the number of British prisoners was high, it was not disastrous. Perhaps the most worrying aspect of the offensive was the fact that the Germans had failed to win the artillery duel. Despite the huge bombardment, only one in six Allied guns were put out of action.

But these limitations were not immediately apparent to those at the sharp end of German aggression. From the British perspective, the Germans suddenly seemed capable of unrestrained advance. Haig eventually began to worry that his troops might be 'rounded up and driven into the sea'. [21, p. 372] On 24 March he found himself in a predicament he thought he would never have to encounter, namely that of having to ask Pétain for help. Haig pleaded for 20 French divisions to be moved into the critical area, but Pétain, as Wilson had warned, provided cold charity. Only two divisions were promised. Haig then reminded the Frenchman of their mutual support agreement, whereupon Pétain argued that the main German thrust had yet to fall. Since, he thought, it was likely to fall in the French sector, he needed his reserves to protect Paris.

There followed an exchange which remains hazy to this day. According to Haig, Pétain suggested that, if the German advance continued, the French Reserve Army Group, located on the British right, would retreat south-westward to cover Beauvais. This implied that French and British forces would become separated, an implication Pétain did not deny. In other words, he seemed willing to allow the British army to be destroyed. But Pétain claims that it was Haig who first suggested a break with the French, made necessary because the BEF was on the verge of collapse and the route to the channel ports had to be protected. The disagreement over what was actually said is understandable because the implications were so embarrassing. But more important were the consequences of this meeting. Haig, whether alarmed by Pétain's attitude or by the imminent risk to his own forces, summoned Wilson to France. The immediate need for an Allied supreme commander was agreed by both men. Haig then suggested Pétain, a surprising choice given his supposed loss of confidence in him. Wilson nevertheless vetoed the idea, eventually persuading Haig to accept the appointment of Foch.

When Allied representatives met at Doullens on the 26th, the atmosphere was thick with acrimony. Because unified command had never been established during times of quiet, implementing it during a crisis was enormously difficult. But Foch rose to the occasion, proving himself one of the few commanders willing to fight in coordinated partnership with his allies and aware of how best to do so. He immediately reversed Pétain's panicked hoarding of troops for the defence of Paris and instead distributed them at weak points in the line. It was decided that the Amiens railway junction had to be defended at all costs. Within days, Haig noticed a change in the mood at the front: 'Foch has brought great energy to bear on the present situation'. [21, p. 373] The crisis had another positive effect since Pershing abandoned his stubborn insistence that American troops could not serve under foreign commanders.

The mechanism had thus been created for the swift transfer of troops in the event of crisis. French troops were indeed shifted to the British sector, ironically at a point when they were no longer needed. The eye of the storm had already passed. The British Fourth Army replaced the shattered Fifth, and the line quickly stabilized. This left Ludendorff at a loss as to where to strike next. He opted for a number of small attacks against both the French and the British which yielded some some minor gains, but had no strategic coherence. In early April, another attack toward Amiens stalled, though some significant gains were made. The Germans had proved that they could restore mobility to this war, but they still had not discovered how to achieve a decisive victory. Their gargantuan efforts and massive losses had resulted in nothing more than a longer front to defend, and a lengthier line of communication to maintain.

The cost to the Germans was huge. Half of the available reserve divisions had been committed by the third day of the battle. The deeper the advance, the more complicated became the problems of keeping attackers supplied. By the time Operation Michael ended on 5 April, German losses stood at around 240 000, roughly equal to the combined losses of the British and French. But, by this stage, the Allies could bear the losses much better. German troops had been encouraged to believe that this offensive would end the war. When it did not do so, their morale plummeted. It is commonly held that the German spirit broke because they discovered, during their advance, how well supplied Allied soldiers were, evidence in stark contrast to the official propaganda. Another popular myth holds that the advance stalled because German soldiers availed themselves rather too eagerly of enemy alcohol. The entire subject has, in truth, received much more attention than it deserves. The offensive failed because it ran out of steam and could not be supplied with reinforcements of men and weaponry, not because troops were drunk or depressed.

But Ludendorff was in no mood to throw in the towel. He still thought he could achieve a stunning victory that would alter the course of the war. His next move came in Flanders, north of the La Bassée canal, where the British were reinforced by a small Portuguese force. Before the attack, Haig appealed to Foch for help, but the latter felt that the situation did not merit assistance. Again, the initial thrust on 9 April was frighteningly effective. Within British staff rooms panic percolated. The faint-hearted began to talk about evacuating Calais. Haig issued his famous 'backs to the wall' despatch which made great newspaper copy but probably had little effect on troops who were already painfully familiar with their own predicament. But, before long, the battle assumed a familiar pattern. British resistance stiffened and the German attack slowed, due to the problems of bringing forward reinforcements of men and weaponry. The pile of rubble called Ypres remained in British hands. All along the German line discontent fermented. Additional military police had to be brought in to deal with worsening problems of insubordination and desertion. By late April, attacks dissipated because troops simply refused to go forward. Ludendorff had gone to the well too many times.

He nevertheless took solace in the fact that the British and French had suffered heavily. Thus softened, they might collapse with one more blow – or one more after that. On 27 May, German troops surged forward on the Chemin des Dames, crossing the Aisne and sweeping frightened French units before them. Within three days they penetrated some 48 kilometres and reached the Marne, just 64 kilometres from Paris. One million Parisiens left the city in panic. This time, Foch appealed to Haig for help. Haig undoubtedly derived some dark delight from replying that this was not the main German thrust, which would inevitably fall on his front. He could not believe that Ludendorff would waste much effort attacking the French, who would surely make peace if the British were knocked out of the war.

Haig was technically right. The German attack was not supposed to be the main thrust, but was instead designed to draw reserves toward Paris, prior to another massive assault in Flanders. But Ludendorff could hardly ignore the fact that good fortune had brought him so close to the French capital. To terminate an attack so successful seemed madness, therefore he continued to push. But, once again, he found it impossible to sustain his success of the first three days. French troops, reinforced by American units, repulsed wave after wave of Germans who tried to cross the Marne.

After their success on the Marne, the Americans stopped another German thrust at Château-Thierry. Their growing presence was ominous for the Germans. In June, some 275 000 troops were despatched from the US, the highest monthly total so far. Haig had five American divisions under him, Foch had fourteen. Though Ludendorff still insisted that the Americans were not a serious threat, even he realized that time was not on his side.

Ludendorff had painted himself into a corner. The attack on the Aisne and Marne had created a highly vulnerable salient that could not easily be abandoned. But defending it required troops earmarked for the Flanders assault. According to Ludendorff's warped sense of logic, the only way to improve the situation was to attack again. German troops therefore pushed forward on 9 June, in the direction of Compiègne. Again, the initial thrust was successful, penetrating to a depth of around 16 kilometres. But by this stage the French were fully prepared, and dramatic break-throughs were no longer possible. Troops under General Charles Mangin, reinforced by Americans, blunted every assault, at great cost to the Germans. Heavy losses, at this stage in the war, made sense only if they brought impressive advantage. Wasting bodies for no gain was sheer madness. But like a drunk gambler who has lost his fortune, Ludendorff continued to roll the dice. In the Reichstag on 24 June the State Secretary for Foreign Affairs bravely suggested that 'an end to the war can hardly be expected ... by purely military decisions alone without diplomatic negotiations'. [99, p. 263] He was rewarded for his honesty by being sacked.

The attack did render Haig slightly more sympathetic to Foch's predicament. When the two commanders met on 28 June, the atmosphere was more amicable than it had been for weeks. Despite the incessant German pressure, there seemed a noticeable difference in the quality of enemy attacks. Foch and Haig both decided that the turning-point was imminent, and that, when it came, they had to be ready to counter-attack. The counter-offensive was tentatively scheduled for August.

Ludendorff had not yet abandoned his plans for a massive thrust in Flanders. But that goal remained difficult to implement due to the situation around Paris. In desperation, he decided to launch another assault, this time against Reims. But, as with the attack of

9 June, French defenders had solid advance intelligence, and knew quite well how to absorb German thrusts. The Marne was nevertheless crossed, causing considerable panic in Paris. But most of the German 'progress' was in truth the calculated elasticity of French defences. Allied commanders had learned that the dramatic breakthroughs of the spring had resulted in part because their first line of trenches were too rigidly defended by troops who had been wrongly instructed to hold the line at all costs.

Ludendorff refused to accept that his grand plan had failed, and refused to countenance the possibility that his Flanders offensive might never be launched. For his troops, weakened by flu and wracked by doubt, the future seemed much clearer. The promised *Friedensturm* (last push for peace) had not materialized. They began to question the wisdom of sacrificing themselves for a madman's fantasies.

Counter-attack

On 18 July the Allies made apparent what Ludendorff refused to see. In the Second Battle of the Marne, 19 French and 4 American divisions surged forward, supported by 750 tanks, 2100 guns and over 1000 aeroplanes, wiping out the salient on the Marne. The Americans, now collected into Pershing's dream of an autonomous First American Army, performed without brilliance, but also without serious misfortune. Just weeks before, the Entente had seemed in terminal disarray. Now, the Germans were stunned by the ferocity, discipline and determination of the offensive. They nevertheless managed to withdraw from their salient in impressive order. The difficult re-crossing of the Marne was achieved under enormous pressure, with a new fortified line established on the River Vesle. But German morale had suffered severely. New troops arriving at the front were denounced by hardened veterans for prolonging the war. The desertion rate sky-rocketed, with, in some cases, 20 per cent of a unit's strength simply disappearing on the way to the front. Alarmed by the situation, General Fritz von Losberg proposed a carefully executed strategic withdrawal to fortified positions, thus shortening the dangerously attenuated line. Ludendorff recognized the logic of the suggestion, but could not bring himself to implement it. He refused to accept what had become obvious to all but his most sycophantic subordinates. His mind was closed to the morale problem, to the debilitating flu epidemic, to the shortage of supplies, and, especially, to the imminent prospect of defeat.

When Foch met Haig on the 24th, both agreed that German forces were 'breaking up'. They decided that the time had come for 'regaining the initiative and passing to the offensive'. On 8 August, French, American and British troops, reinforced by tanks and aircraft, combined in a massive offensive designed to reduce the salient at Amiens. The battle seems in retrospect out of place – more appropriate to the mobile offensives of the Second World War. The Germans could not possibly withstand the fatal combination of Allied numbers, superior weaponry and a seemingly endless supply of fresh American troops. Ludendorff subsequently called it 'the black day' of the German army in the war. With his army in disarray and his plans awry, he suffered a severe nervous collapse. His orders, which previously lacked logic, now lacked coherence.

For one brief moment, a ray of reality broke through Ludendorff's hazy delusion. He advised the Kaiser that it might be best to settle for a negotiated peace. At a Crown Council in Spa on 14 August, it was decided that diplomatic overtures should be made 'after the next success in the west'. [99, p. 287] The decision is an indication of Ludendorff's unbalanced mind, since he obviously believed that he could still engineer a success similar to those achieved in March and April. He was torn between his increasingly bizarre fantasies and the hard evidence of failure emanating from the front. By early September, the once great Teutonic knight had been transformed into a gibbering wreck who required the frequent attention of a 'nerve specialist'.

Foch, recognizing that the situation had changed radically, decided that the time had come to give the Germans some of their own medicine:

> In the presence of the resistance offered by the enemy, we must not try to reach him by pushing forward simultaneously along the whole front. ... Instead of this, we must make concentrated and powerful attacks against the important points of the region ... against those whose capture by us will increase the disorganization in the enemy's ranks, and more especially jeopardize his lines of communication.

The Allies had put static warfare behind them. Foch wanted attacks 'executed with such rapidity as to inflict on the enemy a succession of blows'. On 21 August the Allies struck again with even greater ferocity. Like a film played in reverse, the Germans eventually found themselves back at the Hindenburg Line, where they had begun five months before. As if to underline the inevitable, the Americans in mid-September launched their very own offensive, eliminating the St Mihiel salient in four days. 'It is good war', Rawlinson wrote, 'Under Foch's tuition and the lessons of four years of war, we are really learning and the sychronization of the various attacks has been admirable'. [113, pp. 131–2]

The Germans were defeated by the factors Ludendorff had so stubbornly underestimated. He had refused to put much effort into tank construction, with the result that his troops were overrun by a weapon they had been told to treat with disdain. Because the tank was not supposed to matter, an effective anti-tank weapon had not been developed. Ludendorff also refused to believe that the Americans would be able to make a telling contribution to the war in 1918. In fact, by mid-summer, he found himself facing 25 divisions of healthy, fresh and confident American doughboys (the nickname for American infantrymen). Most of all, he underestimated the resilience of the British and the French and the ability of troops from both countries to recover from seemingly devastating blows. He did not think his enemies could fight like Germans, but they demonstrated that they could.

The counter-offensive had defied all expectations, but many still doubted that the tide of war had turned. Most politicians were still planning for a 1919 campaign. The Hindenburg Line seemed impregnable. Lloyd George, for one, was deeply uneasy about allowing Haig hundreds of thousands of troops to attack it. In Whitehall, British strategists devised Plan 1919, a mobile offensive to be launched in the spring, which placed the emphasis on machines not men. The British contingent on the Western Front would grow proportionately smaller as a greater burden was assumed by the Americans.

Haig and Foch had other ideas. Both were concerned that to call a halt to the offensive would squander the initiative. 'I hope everything will be done to *maintain* the army at full strength in order to beat the enemy as soon as possible', Haig wrote on 3 October. 'If we allow him any breathing time at all, much of the work of "wearing him out" will have to be started afresh'. [113, p. 169] Foch agreed, deciding to go all out for victory despite the meagre resources at his disposal. Though he did not think he could force the Germans to surrender, he did hope to cause them sufficient damage to provoke a disorderly retreat into Germany. Thus, he settled upon a giant pincer movement, which had the French and British attacking in the North, the French and Americans in the South.

On 26 September, Franco-American forces attacked toward Mézières and Sedan. On the following day, the British, reinforced by French, Belgian and Canadian units, attacked in Flanders. Despite excellent cooperation between the various units, progress was not uniformly impressive, with the Americans in particular achieving much less than expected. But the Flanders operation did accomplish the symbolically important objective of piercing the Hindenburg Line, which pessimists in London had assumed was impossible. Haig argued that the enemy was on the verge of collapse and that one more push would do the trick. For his critics, the claims seemed ominous echoes of the arguments made in 1916 and 1917. This time, however, Haig's confidence was warranted. German morale had reached rock bottom.

Ludendorff realized his army could last the winter. In the early spring the Germans would be able to mount a more determined defence when an additional 637 000 men from the 1900 pool would join the ranks. But to take this route would only delay the inevitable. Prolonging the war into 1919 could never bring victory. Try as he might, Ludendorff could not close his eyes to the formidable triumvirate of a rejuvenated French force, a triumphant British, and an American army yet to reach its full strength. His own rapidly disintegrating army had no hope against such overwhelming power. On 1 October he told the General Staff that the German army was finished and that 'final defeat was probably inescapably at hand'. [45, p. 425] The new goal was to avoid complete defeat and an ignominious settlement.

The Germans therefore notified President Wilson on 6 October that they were willing to negotiate peace on the basis of his Fourteen Points. By so doing, they hoped to be allowed to hang on to some of their conquered territories in the East and to German-speaking areas of Alsace and Lorraine. The request caught Britain and France unprepared. To grant an armistice before peace terms were agreed was dangerous, since continued military action was the best way to guarantee the kind of peace they desired. There was also considerable suspicion of Wilson, whose peace plan had never been adopted as Allied policy. Georges Clemenceau, the French Prime

Minister, feared that the President's ideas might preclude the possibility of forcing Germany to atone for the war through reparations and surrender of territory. Cynical Europeans had little tolerance for his sermons about a peace that would be the 'moral climax of the final war for human liberty'. [99, p. 292] Wilson found British and French aims distasteful; he wanted to make the world safe for democracy and had no desire to facilitate their ambitions.

Keen to get a jump on the President, Clemenceau asked Foch to draw up terms for an armistice. Foch concocted a set of demands designed to render it impossible for the Germans to resume hostilities at a later date. They would evacuate all captured territory within two weeks, including Alsace and Lorraine. Within four weeks they would have to evacuate the right bank of the Rhine to a depth of 10 kilometres and would surrender control of the bridgeheads to the Allies. The demand for haste was cleverly calculated to render units in a disorganized state. In addition, a vast collection of military hardware (including 5000 artillery pieces, 25 000 machine guns and 1700 aircraft) would be surrendered, plus 5000 locomotives, 150 000 railway cars and 5000 lorries. Admiral Beatty weighed in with his own demands, namely that Germany had to be reduced to a second-rate naval power, surrendering all of her submarines and the bulk of her surface navy. The demands were calculated to be acceptable only to an enemy who acknowledged utter defeat. For this reason, few realistically expected that Germany would agree to them before the end of the year.

By the end of October, the US, Britain and France settled upon terms roughly similar to those proposed by Foch. The Fourteen Points were generally accepted because they offered wide interpretation, though the clause about freedom of the seas was deleted and a right to demand reparations was added. While these discussions were going on, Wilson made it clear to the Germans that they should expect a harsh peace. In a series of notes, he effectively dashed all hopes that something might be salvaged from the rubble of defeat. The Germans were to consider themselves militarily defeated and safeguards would be implemented to ensure that hostilities could not be resumed. They should also expect punishment for their submarine warfare and their destruction of France and Belgium. Wilson further insisted that he would deal only with the elected representatives of the German people, not with the Kaiser. For Ludendorff, this amounted to a demand of unconditional surrender.

Ludendorff had once again fatally misjudged his enemy. Realising his mistake, he demanded that the German government cease all armistice negotiations, warning the Vice-Chancellor, Friedrich von Payer, that, if the talks continued, 'within a few weeks you will have Bolshevism in the army and at home'. [14, p. 62] Meanwhile, Hindenburg appealed to his army: 'Wilson's answer demands military capitulation. Thus for us soldiers it is unacceptable. ... Wilson's answer can only amount to a challenge to continue to resist to the utmost of our capabilities'. [45, pp. 428–9] But the rallying cry was shouted into a vacuum. The two commanders who had once led an army of millions to victory in the East now stood alone in defeat.

Few expected that Germany would accept the harsh armistice terms because few understood that the German state was in terminal meltdown. Once the possibility of an armistice was raised, there was no further hope of rousing the people to continue the war. On 8 November a German delegation headed by Matthias Erzberger met Foch and his entourage in a railway carriage outside the village of Compiègne. The terms were then read out, sending Erzberger and his colleagues into a state of shock. However, after some adjustment of relatively minor points, the terms were accepted, and it was agreed that the armistice would take effect at 11:00 a.m. on 11 November. Troops would stop fighting at the appointed hour.

Germany's allies crumble

The German spring offensive had been dependent upon the assumption that German troops would no longer have to come to the rescue of Austria-Hungary. In fact, Ludendorff assumed that, with the Russians out of the war, Germany's allies would sweep through south-eastern Europe and end the war there quickly, perhaps in time for Austro-Hungarian troops to join the final offensive in the West. These assumptions, of course, proved preposterous.

Austria-Hungary only barely made it through the winter. Coal supplies were desperately low, crippling industry, paralysing the transportation network and leaving the population miserable and cold. Food riots at home spread resentment and impaired production. The effect of the riots was nevertheless limited by the fact that many of the discontented did not have the energy to protest. But out of disaster, some found opportunity. One thousand extra censors were hired to keep the public ignorant of the dire situation at the front. The Hapsburg Empire had reached the point where patriots could serve it better with a pair of scissors than with a rifle.

The army's manpower pool was down to dregs – unhealthy or otherwise unsuitable men who had evaded every previous combing out. Established troops suffered terribly from food shortages, with malnutrition quite common in the ranks. The meat ration was just 100 grams per day, one-quarter of the 1914 standard. The supply of potatoes – the usual balm to empty stomachs – was due to run out in May. Horses suffered even worse than men, with some 70 000 dying of starvation over the winter. Uniforms were in short supply, with new ones being of atrociously poor quality. Men were issued paper underwear and wounds were dressed with paper bandages. In an excellent example of official understatement, one report outlined how the desperate situation had led to 'unfortunate incidents of human weaknesses and moral lapses'. [45, p. 355] Some 28 300 military police were needed to hunt down deserters. Nor did the return of prisoners of war (POWs) from Russia provide much benefit. Of the two million captured, perhaps 500 000 had died in captivity. Most of the rest returned home in a sorry physical and mental state. The home front was ill-equipped to handle this flood tide of human misery. To make matters worse, a great many of the returnees had embraced revolutionary politics and were keen to spread the word at home.

Conrad reacted to the desperate situation by, predictably, deciding to attack. Preparations for an offensive in Venetia were set in train. Missing from these preparations was any careful calculation of the needs of an attacking army, nor how those needs were to be transported to the front if the rail network was close to complete collapse. On the eve of the battle, approximately two million rounds of artillery were still stockpiled in distant depots, awaiting transport to the front. Valuable manpower was deployed in hauling supplies, as men took the place of horses.

On 15 June Conrad's bedraggled Eleventh Army attacked on a 80-kilometre front between Astico and the River Piave. The terrain had been rendered impassable by weeks of incessant rain. Nine days later the attack ground to a halt, with no significant gain. Some Hapsburg units managed to force their way across the Piave, but were then driven back by a fierce Italian counter-attack, reinforced by French and British units. The Austro-Hungarian army suffered more than 140 000 casualties, with Allied losses just under 85 000.

Once again, Conrad's vain ambition had taken precedence over good judgement. He reacted as before, blaming everyone but himself. But his woeful lament had been told once too often. On 15 July he was dismissed. In reward for his efficient slaughter of his countrymen, he was made a count.

After the disaster on the Piave, the Austro-Hungarian army rapidly disintegrated. Desertion reduced the force on the Italian front by nearly 50 per cent in just three months. Diaz, the Italian commander, quietly watched while his enemy melted away. He realised he could be patient, since reliable rumours suggested that the political demise of Austria-Hungary was imminent. He finally attacked with 57 divisions (including some Americans) on 24 October. Hapsburg forces initially fought with surprising stubbornness, but at the end of the month the collapse came, with some 500 000 prisoners taken. The victory brought the war in that theatre to an end, with an armistice signed on 4 November.

Meanwhile, General Franchet d'Espérey, the new commander of Allied forces in Greece, pushed northward with a Franco-Serb force on 15 September, an attack timed to coincide with operations on the Western Front. The Bulgarians were quickly routed and French cavalry advanced as much as 160 km in two weeks, lending credence to those who had always argued that the Salonika theatre deserved more attention. But this was not a case of knocking out the props, or of finding the soft underbelly of Germany. The offensive succeeded because the only real prop, Germany herself, was on the verge of defeat elsewhere. The force that d'Espérey led northward had been in place for over three years, but achieved nothing of note until the issue had become virtually immaterial.

Further east, the British capture of Jerusalem was not followed, as some expected, by a relentless romp through the old Ottoman Empire. Allenby's force had been drastically pruned to satisfy the needs of Haig in the West. Nevertheless, in the spring, some progress was made, with Lawrence managing to cut the Hejaz railway and isolate Medina. But the real breakthrough came in the early autumn. Victory at Megiddo was followed in quick succession by the capture of Damascus, Beirut and Aleppo. The strains of having to move so quickly through difficult countryside had a more profound effect upon the British and Arab force than did the pressures exerted by the enemy. At the end of October an armistice was signed between Turkey and Britain, though local skirmishes continued. Ethnic animosities which had plagued the region for centuries, and would continue to do so up to the present day, could not be solved by a world war.

The last battle of the war was a German victory. In East Africa, Lettow-Vorbeck captured a small British outpost in Northern Rhodesia on 13 November. He may have been unaware of larger events in Europe, or simply determined to ignore them.

7

Home Fronts

In 1917, a baker in Edinburgh was arrested for selling jam tarts on a day designated by the government as 'sweet-free'. The British were prohibited from throwing rice at weddings and building bonfires on Guy Fawkes Night. In Austria-Hungary, shortages of copper forced the government to confiscate church bells, lightning rods, kitchen pots and door handles. Volunteers scoured caves for bat guano to replace conventional fertilizers. In all countries, mothers busily knitted for soldier sons. Since a good many of the women should not have been allowed near a knitting needle, millions of homemade socks went unworn. Clearly, the war touched the lives of those not remotely connected to the fighting. But, though it affected nearly everyone, a great gulf developed between those at the front and those at home. When Vera Brittain visited her parents after serving as a Voluntary Aid Detachment nurse in France, she found them obsessed by the shortage of good chocolate. It is perhaps no wonder that soldiers often felt more in common with their enemies than with their own families.

Civilians worked for the war, starved for the war and suffered deep emotional strain because of the war. Fundamental freedoms were sacrificed for the greater good of victory. It was virtually impossible for a citizen of one of the combatant nations of Europe to avoid losing a relative or close acquaintance. Beyond the direct experience of loss, war also fundamentally changed work patterns, diet, health, entertainment, and the availability of goods and services. Victory went to those nations best able to mobilize the people and keep them believing in the war.

Industrial policy and the state

All combatants expected a short war. This expectation was based on two premises: (1) that war itself had not fundamentally changed

135

despite the advance of military technology and the expansion of European armies and (2) that modern industrialized economies would not be able to withstand a prolonged war. Before 1914, economists and political theorists had argued that a pan-European war would cause severe economic dislocation, forcing combatants to opt for a negotiated peace if military victory did not come quickly. Strategic plans were formed according to this assumption. Count Graf von Schlieffen, author of the plan to defeat France within six weeks, argued that long wars 'are impossible at a time when a nation's existence is founded on the uninterrupted continuance of its trade and industry; indeed a rapid decision is essential ... A strategy based on attrition is unworkable'. [43, p. 55] Thus, existing stockpiles of ammunition and supplies were considered sufficient to preclude a massive shift to a war economy. Existing munitions factories would cope with demand merely by working at peak production. There was little recognition of the need for special measures to finance the war, or of the possibility that precious resources might need to be stockpiled.

Both France and Germany planned for a land campaign of strictly limited duration, in other words, a conflict like the Franco-Prussian War (1870–71), not like the long American Civil War (1861–65). Germany, for instance, did not anticipate that armaments consumption would *increase* as the war progressed, therefore no steps were taken to convert factories outside the armaments industry to munitions production. Russia and Austria-Hungary, also wedded to short-war preconceptions, were nevertheless unprepared even for a limited contest, due to weaknesses in their economies. Britain, her eyes open to opportunity, devised a strategy of 'business as usual' under which her army would make a minimal contribution to the fighting, while the Royal Navy applied an economic blockade upon the Central Powers. Meanwhile, Britain would make money out of the war by being the arsenal and financier of the Entente, and her businessmen would commandeer German export markets disrupted by the blockade.

Hindsight tells us that twentieth-century total wars produce full employment, full production and inflation caused by increased demand for scarce goods. Yet faith in the logic of a short war meant that the combatants were preoccupied by worries over recession and unemployment due to a trade slump, a fall in demand and uncertainty in the stock markets. They therefore anticipated that the government would have to intervene to reassure the business community, and to guard against social unrest. Thus, in Britain, steps were taken to prevent a run on gold and to protect food supply and distribution. Likewise, in Germany, new laws anticipated a currency crisis, not a munitions crisis. These preparations were not entirely unwarranted. At least initially, war's disruption did cause unemployment to rise, in Germany as high as 20 per cent in the first months of the war. A similar pattern occurred elsewhere. In fact, male unemployment explains in part the enthusiasm for military enlistment. The great number of unemployed males made it difficult for jobless females to find work. Thousands of women were made redundant because traditional sectors of female employment, like confectionery, millinery and fish-processing, were adversely affected by the war.

But before governments could sufficiently mobilize to deal with these problems, the war solved them. Ubiquitous death meant that dole queues quickly disappeared. The failure of the Schlieffen Plan, the French Plan XVII and the Russian invasion of Central Europe made a long and costly war inevitable. The belligerent nations proved more adaptable than pessimistic economists had predicted. To varying degrees, they began to address the problem of how to balance the needs of the military (in munitions and men) against those of civilian society and industrial production. This meant an expanded role for the state in the economy – the state would (or should) plan, coordinate and oversee management of the war. The extent and nature of government intervention differed from country to country, depending as it did on levels of preparation, degrees of crisis, willingness (or ability) of politicians to assume autocratic control and the strength of countervailing ideologies. But nowhere was state expansion fuelled by an ideological shift in attitudes toward government and the economy. The growth of the state was accepted only as a pragmatic response to the war crisis.

Every state has a maximum level beyond which its military forces cannot grow. This level is determined not only by population size but also by industrial configuration, balance of trade, access to raw materials, wealth (or ability to borrow), access to surplus labour, willingness of citizens to make sacrifices for the war effort, and by competing commitments. A country cannot, much as it might wish, allow unrestricted military expansion, for eventually the requirements of its gargantuan force will no longer be able to be met by the productive capacity of its ever-shrinking civilian population nor by its ability to purchase commodities abroad. Britain mobilized 12.5 per cent of her men for the forces, Germany 15.4 per cent and France 16.9 per cent. Yet these figures should not be taken as a relative measure of each nation's commitment to the war. The differences are explained by the interplay of capabilities and commitments within each country. Each mobilized an army (and navy) near to its maximum potential size. But each arrived at this level of commitment not through careful planning and adjustment but through blind groping in the dark.

Some countries mobilized armies of a size beyond the capacity of the home front, with disaster the inevitable consequence. For instance, Russia's industrial infrastructure was not equal to the task of keeping its huge army supplied. In Germany, the military's needs were for too long given priority over those of the civilian sector, with the effect that civilian morale eventually collapsed under the weight of endless sacrifice. As for Austria-Hungary, there is no reason why an empire of 51 million inhabitants, with a solid industrial base, should not have been able to place in the field five million soldiers and keep them fed and supplied. But to do so would have required placing the country on a total war footing, which was beyond the capacity of the weak, decentralized Hapsburg government. The lack of unity among the population is apparent from the tendency of provinces or villages to impose trade barriers against each other whenever scarcities arose. Hungary, relatively well-endowed with food, actually cut grain exports to Austria in 1915 by over 80 per cent in order to maintain domestic harmony. Thus, the Hapsburg Empire was over-mobilized – not in the sense that she fielded an army larger than her infrastructure could support, but because she could not psychologically mobilize her people to support the war.

No country knew its own capabilities until it exceeded them. Thus, the shift to a war economy was in no sense smooth; problems were attacked on an ad hoc basis according to the principle of the squeaky wheel. For instance, France did not immediately build huge, specially constructed and highly efficient munitions factories once her shortage of armaments became apparent. Instead, the government at first tried to make do by converting existing factories, paying little attention to economies of scale. Eventually, larger projects, with greater specialization and division of labour, were encouraged. When this did not solve the shortages, the French reluctantly accepted the inevitable necessity of large purpose-built, government-run factories. As the war escalated, so too did the pace of government intervention and mobilization. Escalation matched escalation as each nation squeezed the last man and the last gun from civilian society. For example, the Hindenburg Programme of 1917 was Germany's response to the prodigious British shell production revealed on the Somme in 1916. Yet British firepower on the Somme was a response to the frustrations experienced in 1915 against superior German defences.

Since it was impossible to nationalize all factories, war put the state at the mercy of private enterprise. Industrialists delighted at the opportunity to be both patriotic and rich. If the goods were delivered on time, no one seemed to care if the workers were exploited or prices rose too high. Any worker who complained was deemed unpatriotic. There were few factory owners able to resist the temptation of taking advantage of cheap, unskilled labour. Women, for instance, were often paid one-third to one-half the male rate of pay, a proportion which did not accurately reflect their actual productivity.

'Profiteering' understandably annoyed the working class, for whom war meant sacrifice, not good fortune. In fact, the word profiteer entered common usage in Britain during the war, to describe a social ill which did not exist before it. The extent to which businesses were controlled depended on the authority and assertiveness of the state and its sensitivity to the workers. General Wilhelm Groener, who tried to persuade Ludendorff to include a system for limiting profits in the Hindenburg Programme, paid for his sense of justice by being sacked. In Russia and Italy, a phenomenal level of corruption existed: businessmen landed huge advances for supplies often never delivered. Britain, more sensitive to the image of profiteering, did introduce an excess profits duty early in the war. But clever accountants usually found ways to bypass the rules. Germany waited until 1918, when the workers were already dangerously restless. One does not need to be a Marxist to notice that the cooperation of business was won with a carrot, that of the workers with a stick.

Since the first priority was the survival of the nation, armies usually got the first call on manpower. The belligerent nations rushed headlong toward economic catastrophe by forcing every available man into uniform. They were aided in this effort by the willingness of the population to serve. At least during its first year, this was a popular war, and a sense of duty ran deep, as was evident in the British response to War Minister Herbert Kitchener's call for volunteers. Unfortunately, the more successful Kitchener was at raising an army, the more of a failure he was, by implication, at equipping it. The shell shortage of May 1915 arose in part because the government failed to pay sufficient attention to the industrial implications of a large citizen army.

But every combatant nation experienced a shell shortage for the simple reason that the need for shells defied all predictions. This was a *Materialschlacht*, a conflict of machines, not just men. During the Battle of the Marne of September 1914 (a contest tiny compared to those which followed), more artillery shells were used than during the entire Franco-Prussian War. Before 1914, France planned for a munitions output of 10–12 000 shells per day. She eventually had to produce 200 000 per day. Germany's gunpowder needs increased five-fold in the first six months of the war. Even industrially backward Russia produced 150 000 shells a day.

In both France and Germany munitions crises arose during the first months of the war. France's industrial capacity was seriously depleted by the loss of industrially important areas to the Germans. The captured territory represented 16.3 per cent of her industrial capacity and 21.1 per cent of her industrial labour force. The Longwy-Briey area alone was responsible for 64 per cent of France's pig iron production, 58 per cent of steel and 40 per cent of coal. Germany likewise found herself in desperate straits when the Allied blockade cut supplies of essential raw materials like nitrogen. She consequently established the *Kriegsrohstoffabteilung* (War Raw Materials Department), or KRA, within the War Ministry, which oversaw procurement and distribution of raw materials and encouraged the development of substitutes. This included a massive campaign to persuade citizens to surrender raw materials. 'It is an interesting sight', one observer remarked, 'to see cartloads of old pots and kettles and candlesticks, door-handles, chandeliers, etc., being driven along the street, and a poor woman or schoolboy carrying a copper kettle or brass lamp to the collecting offices to be weighed and paid for'. [45, p. 256]

The problem of manpower

More often than not, supply problems were essentially manpower problems. If coal was scarce, it was because miners left pits to join the army. If farmers became soldiers, fields went untilled and food supplies dwindled. Mobilizing the reserves (as in France, Germany,

Russia and Austria-Hungary) or calling for volunteers (as in Britain) meant removing men from civilian production. The economy could not long withstand this drain upon human resources. Steel production in Austria-Hungary fell by 73 per cent in 1914 because the government did not think to exempt skilled workers from conscription. Most were sent immediately to Galicia and Serbia where many were promptly killed. The situation was so critical in France that in September 1914 the armaments industry was given a higher labour priority than the armed forces. But by that time it was too late, since so many skilled workers were already in uniform. By the end of 1915, over 500 000 skilled men had to be called back into industry. Germany, likewise, recalled 1.2 million workers in September 1916 and 1.9 million the following July.

There was some flexibility within the economy: luxury goods did not need to be made, services could be cut back and bureaucracies culled of labour. But eventually, everywhere, shortages of labour began to develop in industries essential to the war effort: raw materials, food production, and especially munitions. Shortages of labour were all the more acute because of the unexpectedly massive losses on the fighting fronts. The war, like some ruthlessly efficient blast furnace, consumed men (essentially a non-renewable resource) at a prodigious rate. In the first four months of the war, France lost 455 000 men killed or missing, another 400 000 wounded.

There were three principal ways to attack labour shortages: first, by managing output; second, by transforming production processes and labour practices so as to make more efficient use of workers; third, by tapping sources of surplus labour. These three methods were used to varying degrees in all the combatant countries.

Controlling output meant determining what could be produced in what quantities. It also meant controlling imports and exports in a manner most suited to economic efficiency and the needs of the war. In other words, market forces would no longer determine what was produced or imported. Early in the war, shoemakers might have made gentlemen's fine riding boots if a market existed, even if that meant fewer boots for the infantry. Governments gradually asserted control over industries deemed non-essential. Under the Hindenburg Programme, these industries were not technically shut down, but they were allowed to wither on the vine, being deprived of labour and raw materials. But, while in theory it was possible for a government to control the type and quantity of goods produced, in practice manifold difficulties arose. Governments often lacked the expertise, confidence or will to intervene, especially since those with power (the industrial oligarchy) often stood most to lose from expanded state authority and were most inclined to resist it. In managing output, governments usually appealed first for voluntary restraint, then turned to polite cajoling and only reluctantly resorted to regulating producers.

Production could be made more efficient through scientific improvements that increased output per labourer. Across Europe, war inspired modernization. Assembly lines were introduced, standardization was imposed, labour grew more specialized, and electrification spread. Huge, purpose-built factories allowed combatants to exploit economies of scale. Improvements in the transportation network also reduced inefficiencies caused by transit delays. In Britain, productivity improvements brought about by various means meant that an 18-pounder-high explosive shell cost the government 32 shillings in January 1915, and just 12 shillings and sixpence a year later. Much of the technology already existed before the war (as with Bessemer converters for the steel industry), but the motivation to introduce it had not. This was particularly true in Britain where supposedly secure imperial markets had encouraged inefficiency. Improved productivity can be gauged by the fact that while production increased massively during the war, the industrial labour force actually declined in Germany and increased by just 100 000 in Britain.

But science could achieve only so much. By far the greatest manpower savings were achieved through radical changes in the management of labour. In the half-century before the war, trade unions had amassed significant power for the worker by carving out small monopolies for individual trades. Agreements with employers regarding which skilled labourers could perform which specific tasks protected workers from being undercut by non-union labour, but in the process introduced massive complexity and inefficiency into production processes. Relaxation of these agreements paved the way for dilution, by which unions accepted (or were forced to accept) that previously skilled trades could be performed by semi-skilled or non-skilled labour. This did not mean that skilled men were suddenly made redundant and sent to the front, but rather that production processes were reorganized so that the skilled worker only performed tasks which genuinely required skill. The rest of his duties were either mechanized or performed by those less skilled.

Governments sought not only to manage but also to control labour. Since the worker is most powerful when labour is scarce, manpower shortages played into the hands of the unions and should have increased their power. But government intervened by introducing new laws limiting the unions' ability to exploit the situation. Both Britain and Germany passed laws restricting the worker's right to change jobs. The Auxiliary Service Law in Germany was the most comprehensive measure of worker control introduced by any nation during the war. It required all males aged between 18 and 60 to accept essential war jobs, if they were not already in military service. Universities were closed down, the Sunday holiday was abandoned and women encouraged into war work. 'The entire German people should live only in the service of the Fatherland', Hindenburg stressed. [45, p. 264] Soldiers' wives (those without children) and prostitutes were deemed parasites who sucked vital resources from the state.

Under the terms of the Munitions of War Act of 1915, the British government assumed similarly wide powers to control labour, in the process restricting the worker's freedoms. Wartime governments also introduced compulsory bargaining legislation and prohibitions on the right to strike. Conscription was occasionally used to rid workplaces of troublesome agitators. These rulings played into the hands of the employers, contributing to a rise in working-class consciousness and antagonism between classes. Coercive laws nevertheless could not stop determined workers from striking. In all the combatant countries industrial action increased during the war, as the initial mood of cooperation evaporated.

Conscription was in theory a means by which to manage labour. It was not simply about moving men into the trenches, but also allowed governments to select those men whose removal from the workforce would be least detrimental to war production. Unfortunately, these powers were seldom used well – as revealed by the frequent need to recall skilled men from the front. Industrial conscription, acting in tandem with military conscription, might have allowed a better management of labour and a balancing of civilian and military requirements. But attempts to introduce industrial conscription in Britain and Germany ran aground because of doctrinal objections and fears of working-class rebellion. Austria-Hungary introduced some of the elements of industrial conscription, but mainly out of desperation, not as part of a logical programme of labour management. Workers who avoided military service because they were essential to industry were paid the soldier's rate of pay and those found guilty of fomenting industrial unrest were quickly transferred to the front, with a consequent loss of civilian benefits. Factories with a history of unrest were taken over by the military and some industrial areas came under military law with curfews imposed and prohibitions on the right of assembly introduced.

The unions sacrificed much, but also made gains. The Auxiliary Service Law recognized the trade unions and confirmed the workers' rights of association. Thus, an authoritarian law ironically empowered those heretofore somewhat impotent. In Britain, unions were brought into the management process, for instance in determining which workers should be 'badged' – reserved for civilian work. Governments also made promises about an eventual return to pre-war practices. Greater and more comprehensive government control reduced the power of labour but at the same time made the workers more cohesive as a group. Divisions between various crafts and between the skilled and less skilled were reduced. Though the workers felt somewhat emasculated by the war, at the end of it they presented a more united front. In Germany, Russia, Austria-Hungary and Italy, adversity encouraged solidarity.

Dilution and the various laws controlling labour paved the way for the introduction of substitute workers, many of them unskilled itinerant male labourers who suddenly found themselves in secure, relatively well-paid employment. Workers in non-essential industries were either directed by their governments into war work, or enticed by higher pay. Combatants also turned to juveniles, the disabled, the retired and returned servicemen for manpower. In Austria-Hungary, it was not unusual for children as young as eight to be employed in war factories. Germany even tried to force men from occupied areas in Belgium and Poland into war industries, a programme more controversial than successful. Ludendorff, hoping to tap into the 600 000 unemployed males in Belgium, demanded that 20 000 per week be transferred to Germany. He soon found, however, that German industries were not geared up to absorb them and, more often than not, it was counter-productive to force men to perform skilled labour. By early 1917, the plan had been quietly ditched.

The most significant new source of labour was women, who proved especially efficient at the exacting processes involved in munitions making. 'If the women working in the factories stopped for twenty minutes', the French General Joseph Joffre once remarked, 'France would lose the war'. [31, p. 292] Contrary to myth, the women who entered industry were almost all working class, and most already had jobs, or at least were not without job experience. In other words, waged labour was nothing new for them; the female labour force did not increase to the extent often carelessly presumed. What was different was the *type of jobs* women performed. The proportion of women to men in German industry was 22 per cent in 1913, and 35 per cent in 1918. The corresponding figures for Britain are 26 and 35 per cent. Most of these women would have worked (or expected to work) in traditionally female employment (domestic service, food processing, millinery, light industry) which was disrupted by the war. Most found better pay and more secure employment in war industry. German women, for instance, saw their average earnings rise by 158 per cent during the war, compared to 112 per cent for men. But the conditions were hard and sometimes dangerous and the work by its very nature temporary. Though these women gained some status and self-esteem through participation in the war effort, real progress was strictly limited since nearly everyone accepted that after the war they would give up their jobs to returning soldiers and would return to pre-war patterns of employment.

The improvisation of a war machine was everywhere chaotic. Government intervention, lacking plan or direction, could be misdirected and contradictory. But there is no doubting the industrial expansion that each country underwent in order to meet the voracious appetite for munitions. British defence spending expanded from £91 million in 1913 to £1.956 billion in 1918, the latter figure being 80 per cent of all government expenditure. In 1914, 91 artillery pieces and 300 machine guns were produced. In 1918, the figures were 8039 and 120 900 respectively. But the most impressive achievement was perhaps that of France, given her loss of industrially important territory in 1914. Starting from a much higher base than Britain, France still managed to increase her rifle production 290-fold and machine gun production 170-fold. One has to conclude that the war inspired in France an industrial surge that should have occurred forty years earlier.

Mobilizing minds:

Since civilians were involved in the war effort as never before, their energies had somehow to be inspired and channelled. Propaganda designed to encourage ever greater effort was improvised by governments and concerned individuals. Civilians were constantly reminded of their relationship to the war: thus it became patriotic to use less fuel, waste less food, refuse to go on strike, collect scrap metal, be optimistic, arrive at work on time and, of course, volunteer for the forces. Millions of posters reminded citizens of correct wartime behaviour.

At the same time, civilians had to be persuaded that their country's cause was just and that the war was going well – in other words that the sacrifices were justified. Mythic images were frequently used to remind citizens of the purpose of their struggle. These, of course, bore little relation to reality: British posters idealized a green and pleasant land which seemed foreign to those more familiar with dark satanic mills. The evil German on a British poster was usually fat, had a handlebar moustache and (for ease of identification) had a string of sausages dangling from his pocket. The Americans went further, depicting him as a giant ape who raped innocent women and imposed '*Kultur*' on conquered lands. Convincing the population of the nobility of their cause also meant reminding the people of the enemy's evil. The German people were told that the war was Russia's fault, the French that it was Germany's. German invaders were accused of atrocities by Belgian, French and British propagandists, while the Germans claimed that the British blockade killed the infirm, the old and babies. Tales of raped nuns, women with their breasts cut off and babies impaled on bayonets were told in every language, and bore a remarkable similarity to stories from previous wars.

The two main objects of propaganda often worked against each other. Reports that the war was going well acted against pleas for redoubled effort. The problem was all the more acute because the combatants had so little experience in mobilizing minds. Efforts were often crude, counter-productive, disorganized and ad hoc. Private propaganda organized by concerned patriots often worked against the efforts of official agencies. It is difficult, in the end, to assess the effectiveness of propaganda campaigns. The Germans claimed that British propaganda was instrumental in their defeat. But, since this allegation dovetails nicely with the 'stab in the back' thesis popularized by Adolf Hitler, one needs to be wary of according it much credibility. Much propaganda was based on a poor understanding of the civilian mind. It is well to remember that the poet Rupert Brooke, out of fashion on the eve of war, gained in popularity because he articulated the British sense of heroic mission. The war inspired a collective craving for bad patriotic poetry and sugary, sentimental songs. For every Wilfred Owen there were ten romantic rhymers who have deservedly been forgotten.

War encourages citizens to believe the best about their country; patriotism rises in direct relation to a perceived threat. Both British and German workers declared an industrial truce at the start of the war, without government persuasion. Atrocity stories were invented and spread without government encouragement. In Britain, the most impressive surge in support for the war came not as a result of any propaganda campaign, but because of the startling success of the German offensive of spring 1918. This suggests, in turn, that censorship – the other tool of those assigned to manipulate public opinion – has dubious utility, based as it is on the misguided assumption that the public cannot be trusted with bad news. Yet all governments assumed sweeping powers over the press.

The cinema, which had experienced a massive surge in popularity in the decade before the war, was an important tool in the manipulation of morale. Films and newsreels could keep the public informed, encourage greater effort, and keep people entertained and happy. There was also a gradual recognition that concerts, dance-halls, pubs and clubs were useful in keeping the people content when they were not working. But many sporting contests, because they drew fit men away from the forces, were curtailed. Licensing hours and the potency of beer were also limited. Fearful of grain shortages, the German government outlawed the consumption of spirits, but beer (or what passed for beer) continued to be produced. Full prohibition might have meant a more sober population and even a better fed one (since grain used for beer would make more bread) but the resulting discontent would have been counter-productive.

Because the First World War was not truly total in the sense that civilians did not (with few exceptions) come under attack, a chasm of experience developed between the home front and the fighting front. Soldiers felt deep antagonism toward civilians who, they felt, could never understand the horror of the trenches.

> You smug-faced crowds with kindling eye
> Who cheer when soldier lads march by
> Sneak home and pray you'll never know
> The hell where youth and laughter go. [33, p. 283]

This chasm was both an advantage and a disadvantage for those who had to mobilize minds. When it came to the soldiers' suffering, ignorance was perhaps bliss. But, as the Second World War would demonstrate, sacrifices shared tend to be more easily endured. It was impossible to establish a truly cooperative war effort if the worst experience of war – death and injury – remained a forbidden zone for most civilians.

The development of state bureaucracies and advancing technologies of mass communication made it easier for states to keep tabs on and control over populations during the war. But, at the same time, mass involvement in the political process (more developed in some countries than in others) made citizens more resistant to and suspicious of state control. Though it is commonly held that it is easier to wage war in a dictatorship than in a democracy, the Great War suggests that the opposite is true. The more representative the political system, the more effective was the mobilization of the population. In Britain and France, a collective spirit (which needed little encouragement from the state) proved resilient to most of the strains of war. When Britain and France occasionally resorted to heavy-handed techniques, as with the imprisonment of pacifists, these measures often backfired, giving the accused more publicity than they could achieve on their own. Louis-Jean Malvy, the French Minister of the Interior in 1917, recognized that wartime discipline was most effective if it was 'freely consented'. [50, p. 198] In contrast, in Germany, Austria-Hungary and Russia, the state relied on increasingly repressive measures to keep the population mobilized. As commitment flagged, controls grew ever more stringent, with diminishing returns. Oppressive laws inspired doubts about the purpose of the war. Since most discontent was caused by war-weariness rather than by subversive politics, bureaucratic repression usually exacerbated problems by making the people even more weary and distrustful.

Repressive states were caught in a vicious circle. As the war went on, civilian morale plummeted, prompting harsher measures, which in turn further damaged morale. The only solution to this problem was usually unacceptable: regenerating consensus could only be achieved by encouraging liberal reforms and allowing greater participation in the political process. But that undermined the authoritarian power of the state and, specifically, the privileged role of the military.

Housing, food and health

Total war is supposed to be unhealthy. While soldiers are killed, civilians starve. Those most vulnerable – the poor, elderly and very young – are the most common victims. These assumptions, though generally valid, need careful qualification. During the First World War, deprivation was not universal. Improvements in living standards were not uncommon. Some people emerged from the war healthier than they entered it.

That said, in the area of housing, decline was the rule. Towns caught in the path of opposing armies were often completely destroyed, with a resultant tide of refugees. France lost 290 000 houses in the battle areas, and absorbed over 900 000 refugees, 150 000 from Belgium. But far more important was the effect of war on housing in areas untouched by combat. The need for labour meant that the construction industry virtually ground to a halt. Since working-class housing was already in a poor state before the war, the situation became even more appalling during four years of forced neglect. At the same time, a housing shortage developed in areas affected by the wartime industrial boom. Workers left towns and villages, converging on cities where the housing shortage was already acute. Rampant overcrowding resulted, with a consequent rise in diseases associated with poor housing – tuberculosis, bronchitis, rheumatic fever, etc. Governments, preoccupied with winning the war, could do little to alleviate poor conditions beyond making hollow promises of improvement when victory came.

The food supply was everywhere severely restricted. Before the war, France was nearly self-sufficient in most commodities and was a net exporter of food, as was Italy. Germany produced 90 per cent of the food she consumed. Austrian industry and Hungarian farms had a symbiotic relationship which rendered the Dual Monarchy virtually self-sufficient. Russia was the largest exporter of agricultural products in the world. Yet all these countries suffered drastic food shortages during the war. In Germany, conditions deteriorated to such an extent that civilians were allotted rations well below subsistence levels. The cereal ration was 64 per cent of pre-war consumption, that of meat 18 per cent, and fats just 12 per cent. Austria's agricultural production was 41 per cent of pre-war levels, Hungary's 57 per cent. The country to fare best was ironically Britain, where, before the war, the population could feed itself from home production only 125 days out of a year. Her salvation was her navy, which insured a reasonably steady flow of food imports. Yet, for a short period, Britain nearly went the way of the other combatants. At the height of the German U-boat campaign in 1917, Britain was reduced to just a few days' supply of sugar and a week of meat.

Food production fell drastically (by approximately 33 per cent across Europe) mainly because of the shortage of farm labour. France was forced to import 639 000 tons of food in 1917. Her grain harvest that year was down by 40 per cent. (Granted, 20 per cent of France's pre-war wheat crop, 26 per cent of her oats and nearly 50 per cent of her sugar beets came from areas occupied by Germany.) Gripped by a short-war mentality, no combatant foresaw a food problem, and therefore nothing was done to stop the exodus of farm labourers into factories and the military. Agricultural production was affected in other ways. Horses were commandeered by armies. Farm machinery could not be replaced when it broke down, since tractor factories were making military vehicles. Chemicals used for fertilizers were suddenly needed for explosives manufacture. (Though German agriculture was nearly self-sufficient before the war, one third of the necessary fertilizers and chemicals was imported.)

The British blockade caused disastrous shortages in Germany and Austria-Hungary. The Central Powers made use of the farm production of allies and of captured areas, but transportation and manpower problems prevented those countries from producing the surplus Germany imagined she would be able to exploit. Nor did German-occupied areas of France and Belgium yield much of value; civilians in these areas were often fed by their compatriots who were allowed to cross battle lines with food convoys. At times, the food situation in Austria-Hungary was so dire that military training regimes had to be relaxed because the soldier's poor diet did not permit rigorous exercise. The army also found that training programmes were constantly disrupted because soldiers were granted leave during the planting and harvesting seasons.

The more serious the food situation, the more inclined governments were to intervene. Government intervention dealt with two concerns: supply and consumption. In the first category, the automatic response was to increase imports. Germany got some food from Scandinavia, Holland and Switzerland, but the Allied blockade prevented her looking further afield. Because the Entente theoretically had access to the rest of the world (as long as U-boat losses could be controlled), its food shortages did not reach crisis proportions.

At home, steps could be taken to secure replacement farm labour. Britain, for instance, encouraged women to work on farms, though with limited success. Germany was forced to use 900 000 prisoners of war, a figure roughly equal (in number, not productivity) to her total agricultural labour force during peacetime. France used women, children, prisoners, and old men, but still had to recall 300 000 soldiers to work the farms.

Wartime shortages encouraged resourcefulness. Pasture was converted to arable land, thus increasing grain production at the expense of meat. Food unfit for human consumption was fed to patriotic pigs. Any citizen with a shotgun found ways to increase his diet. It was a bad time to be a pigeon – many were shot as spies, many others cooked into pies. Nor did the poor turtles of the Mediterranean have a very good war. Ersatz substitutes for coffee, eggs, milk, butter and a host of other commodities were found, much to the disgust of the consumer. In Germany, some 11 000 such substitutes were registered with the government. We can trace the process of adaptation in food production through the wartime history of the humble loaf of bread, the staple of the working-class diet. As the war progressed, the milling process became less wasteful, with the loaf darker and less digestible. Rye, oats, barley, even woodshavings and fine sand were added, while fat, salt and sweetening were removed. By the end of the war the loaf made better artillery ammunition than food.

Consumption could be controlled by making food less appealing: tinned fish instead of fresh, brown bread instead of white, and so on. The British recognized that fresh bread was more appetizing, therefore regulations were passed stipulating that bread could not be sold unless it was at least eight hours old. But governments mainly controlled consumption through price fixing and rationing. Both measures were adopted reluctantly and less than whole-heartedly since they benefited the consumer at the expense of the producer. (Though it has to be said that farmers everywhere had a good war.) Price fixing did cool the temper of the workers, who found that their wages did not keep pace with food price rises. Average real wages declined by 15 per cent in Britain, 23 per cent in

Germany, 33 per cent in Italy and 57 per cent in Russia during the war. Germany started fixing the prices of potatoes, sugar and grain in 1914, France in the following year. Britain did not tamper with prices until 1917, when workers showed signs of serious discontent. Price fixing could, however, result in the opposite effect intended. In Germany, controls on the price of milk and grain simply persuaded farmers to reduce production of both commodities in favour of meat, the price of which was not controlled. Milk became virtually unavailable outside the black market, a phenomenon repeated whenever the price of a commodity was fixed.

Government measures for saving food occasionally backfired. The reduced consumption of luxury goods in Germany seemed a sensible response to shortages and to the import crisis, but it meant that tax revenues so essential to funding the war suffered. In Britain, the middle class took wartime frugality too far, depriving the poor of turnips and potatoes, the only commodities they could afford. The government was forced to persuade the wealthy that it was patriotic to eat asparagus. In Austria-Hungary, a ban imposed in 1914 on the slaughtering of calves for veal led to 10 000 horses being butchered instead, in order to keep a meat-hungry population satisfied. This put added strain on the already over-stretched agriculture and transport sectors. Perhaps half a million horses in Germany died of malnutrition during the war. By late 1916, the shortage of horses in Austria-Hungary was so dire that dogs were increasingly used to pull delivery carts within cities. But dogs who worked also needed to be fed.

Rationing was adopted in France and Britain to reduce worker discontent, since without it food simply went where the money was. In Germany, the problem was much more serious, and rationing had to be adopted (as early as January 1915 for bread) in order to prevent widespread starvation. By 1916, the weekly adult entitlement consisted of 160 to 220 g of flour, 120 g of fish, 100 to 250 g of meat, 60 to 75 g of fats, 200 g of sugar, 270 g of jam or honey substitute, 0.7 litres of milk and one egg. [45, p. 289] Russia, whose export market dwindled because of the war, found herself with a food surplus in rural areas. But because inflation hit manufactured goods harder than agricultural produce, farmers lost much of their purchasing power and thus simply refused to sell their produce. Food shortages in urban areas, already serious because of the collapse of the transport system, therefore worsened.

Government controls sometimes led to an improvement in nutritional standards. Less refined food saved labour and production costs, but also meant a more nutritious (if less desirable) end product. Wholewheat bread was more nutritious than the pre-war white loaf. Shortages of meat sometimes led to a reliance on more nutritional fish, beans and pulses. Consumption of butter and sugar declined drastically, leaving the consumer less happy but more healthy. Shortages of sugar and grain forced reductions in the potency and availability of alcohol, with attendant beneficial effects. Consumption of alcohol in Austria-Hungary was limited to one per cent of pre-war levels, though resourceful citizens did concoct home brews from often rather vile ingredients, to occasionally lethal effect. In Britain, rationing meant that the very poor were provided access to a quantity of food they had not previously enjoyed. The losers in this homogenization of dietary standards were the better off, who were denied access to an amount of food which they could ordinarily afford. But, lest one assume that diets were democratized, it should be emphasized that rationing seldom lived up to lofty ideals. A black market, in which only money talked, did thrive. It is estimated that as much as 50 per cent of all food in Germany was purchased via illegal means.

Dietary improvements occurred only in those countries (particularly Britain) where food shortages did not reach a point of crisis. No amount of tinkering with consumption or production could alter the fact that Germany could not adequately feed her population. It is no wonder, therefore, that food riots were common in the later stages of the war. Generally speaking, in every combatant country, workers found that wages did not keep pace with inflation, therefore dietary standards tumbled. Italian food production declined by only ten per cent during the war, but since workers were already seriously impoverished before 1914, the population could ill-afford even this slight drop in production.

But not all workers suffered equally or indeed absolutely. Many who had struggled to feed families due to unsteady, poorly paid employment suddenly found themselves earning unheard of wages in secure jobs. Often a family enjoyed the benefits of more than one income, as mother or an older child found jobs in war industries. The removal, to the forces, of the male breadwinner meant the loss of his income, but it often also meant that the biggest drain on family income was now fed, clothed and housed by the state. Thus, in some cases, the amount of money (in real terms) spent on food per family member actually increased during the war, with a resultant rise in health standards.

Dietary changes, full employment, disintegration of the housing stock, etc. meant that families were buffeted in different directions. Much depended on the individual family's unique circumstances. German wage rates in war industries rose by 142 per cent during the war, but by just 68 per cent in civil industries. Productivity improvements (in all countries) meant that semi-skilled workers on piece rates often earned more than skilled workers on time rates – up to 33 per cent more in Rhineland munitions factories. If the family had children of working age, if war-related work was available and capricious illness kept at bay, the war might have meant improved health. If, however, father was away at the front and mother had to look after a number of small children in a damp and dingy flat on an income ravaged by wartime inflation, the result might mean serious diet-related illnesses and even death. What is certain is that Europeans were neither universally nor uniformly enfeebled by the war.

Health statistics are, however, notoriously bad at measuring grief and stress, and the physical ailments associated with these mental conditions. A woman whose family income rose because of the war and who was suddenly able to feed her family better would not necessarily have felt that the war had been good to her. She might still have had to deal with constant, corrosive anxiety if a loved one was in danger at the front. Or, worse, she might have to confront the death of a husband, father, lover or son. Given the rigidly patriarchal structure of European societies, this often meant an erosion of the very core of her identity.

War and social change

In the 1960s some historians (chief among them Arthur Marwick) were struck by the apparent connection between war and social change in the twentieth century. Perhaps unconsciously affected by the temper of the sixties, they saw a great ferment of change – much of it positive – brought about by war's disruption. War, they argued, encouraged women toward emancipation, governments toward social responsibility, and workers toward consciousness and assertiveness. Class and gender divisions consequently crumbled.

Thirty years later, these excessively sanguine theories of war and society seem over-cooked. War had some profound (even positive) effects, but it is reckless to postulate an all-embracing theory of war and its effect upon society. In more stable societies, like Britain and France, forces of conservatism and tradition were probably equal to the challenges of war. Germany, Italy and Russia seem to have been more deeply affected by the social consequences of war, but we could argue that the changes apparent in those countries were not borne of war but only stimulated by it. When one studies the First World War one needs to be aware not just of the forces of change, but also of the countervailing forces which constrained or absorbed change. Progress was profound, but so was the power of convention, tradition, authority, repression and nostalgia.

Those who believe that total war fundamentally altered the complexion of society usually focus on two groups: women and the working class. Women, so the argument goes, gained personal esteem and societal recognition by moving into jobs vacated by men. This was supposedly converted, after the war, into political gains, be they concrete reforms like enfranchisement or ideological ones like gender equality. The workers likewise supposedly made gains through their contribution to the war. Wartime shortages of labour increased the power of the working class, at the same time making it more cohesive and assertive. Government was forced to negotiate with trade unions on a more equal basis. A mixing of the classes (especially in the trenches) is supposed to have led to greater harmony between classes and an 'inspection effect' – greater awareness of working class conditions and greater desire to effect improvements.

These positive effects have been grossly exaggerated. Take the case of women. During the war they were but temporary men – cheap labour. The differential between male and female wages in Germany narrowed as a result of the war, but by 1918 women in industry were still earning 50–60 per cent of the average male income. The fact that women could be paid so much less for basically similar work increased antagonism between the sexes and, needless to say, did nothing for gender equality. Women never attained the status of skilled workers, the real source of power in the labour hierarchy. Without that status, they were expendable, in the same way that unskilled or semi-skilled men were before the war. Women who took up male jobs understood that they were to surrender these jobs at the war's end and were often the first to defend this proviso. Very few had their consciousness raised to an extent that they rejected the usual pattern of a working-class woman's life: work, followed by marriage, followed by a family. Most, in fact, appear to have welcomed a return to that status quo. Thus, though their sense of self-worth may have risen during the war, very few found opportunities after it to take advantage of their greater self-esteem by charting a different course for themselves.

A munitions factory was in any case hardly the place to encourage self-belief. The work was unskilled, repetitive and dangerous. Women lost hair, their skin turned yellow and many were killed in catastrophic explosions. They were paid better than they had been before the war, but they were not universally appreciated. Male-dominated unions opposed them at every turn and hardly any effort was made to cater to their special needs with separate washrooms or crèche facilities. Young women also had to put up with the sexual advances of skilled male workers who remained in the factories.

After the war, women workers were told to make way for returning soldiers. As one editorial in a British newspaper remarked, 'The idea that because the State called for women to help the nation the State must continue to employ them is too absurd to entertain. ... women formerly in domestic service should have no difficulty finding vacancies'. [80, p. 266] In Britain, placements in domestic occupations increased by 40 per cent in 1919 over the year before. Nor did the war have any significant long-term effect upon the number of women in work. In 1921, 30.8 per cent of women were employed, down from 32.3 per cent ten years earlier.

There is also a serious flaw in the argument that women can gain status in society by taking up men's jobs. Status in a patriarchal society is calculated according to a male-orientated measure of importance. If a job becomes essentially 'woman's work', its status declines, a decline highlighted by the lower pay attached to it. This is particularly obvious if one looks at clerical work, a predominantly male occupation before the war. Wartime labour shortages resulted in more women becoming clerks and secretaries, with the result that the status of these jobs declined. Few men wanted to return to clerical work after the war, therefore these cast-off jobs were left to women, who were paid less.

War, because it is essentially masculine, can result in a step backward for women. The relaxation of sexual mores during the Great War – often cited as progress – resulted in an increase in illegitimacy. One easily forgets that it was the women who were left to look after the unwanted children. 'Women do not realise', wrote the novelist Storm Jameson in 1917, 'that in any war, their enemy is not on the other side, their enemy is war itself – which robs them of their identity and they cease to be clever, competent, intelligent, beautiful in their own right and become the nurses, the petty joys and at last the mourners of their men'. [54, p. 211] Negative images abound in wartime: gossip-mongers whose loose lips sink ships, prostitutes who spread venereal disease, adulterers who cheat on soldier-husbands.

War reinforces the fundamentally masculine role of warrior and the feminine role of helpless maiden. Women, as sweethearts, lovers or prostitutes, satisfy the sexual and romantic fantasies of men home on leave, roles not conducive to gender equality. War also renders societies more conservative by encouraging nostalgia for a mythical past of prosperity and security. This has a particularly profound effect upon women, who become the icons of tradition – those who keep the home fires burning. During the war, mother-hood took on added importance, as lives became more precious. Women were encouraged to pay closer attention to the needs of their children and were encouraged to have more of them to make up for the loss of life. Deprivation among children was blamed on maternal neglect rather than on poverty. Whilst there was a great deal of male pressure behind this cult of motherhood, one sus-pects that many women welcomed the emphasis upon a nurtur-ing role – one in which they were acknowledged to be proficient. In comparison to the home, the noisy, dirty, tedious factory had few attractions, other than pay. Thus, it is no surprise that immedi-ately after the war, Europeans felt a common desire to rebuild through the family, as evidenced by rising marriage and birth rates. Women were willing partners in this regeneration.

Advances made by workers after the war depended upon retreat by women, therefore it is difficult to imagine how both groups could have benefited from the war. The workers feared that the intro-duction of female industrial labour would permanently erode union power and depress wages. In fact this did not happen. The number of female industrial labourers in Britain after the war was lower than the number before the war, a statistic duplicated in Germany. But, while male workers won this concession, a return to their pre-war status should not be confused with progress.

On the home front, workers derived some benefit from the scarcity of labour. Due to the relaxation of skill differentials, unskilled workers enjoyed the greatest improvement in their standard of living. This meant that the class itself became more homogenous. But that is not the same as political solidarity. In any case, the loyalty of the worker during wartime is usually not to himself, nor to his union, but to the nation. Workers willingly made sacrifices for the good of their country. The idea of the patriotic worker sticks in the gullet of many historians. In most cases, the nation's safety came before the workers' self-interest.

Progress made by workers was also dependent upon the shortage of labour. No matter how much the worker's consciousness may have been raised by the war, his power was, as always, subject to the vagaries of the trade cycle. Thus, while the immediate post-war boom seemed to offer opportunities for the newly assertive working class, when boom turned to bust, the workers were enfeebled. Whatever else might be said about the turbulent interwar years, they were not a time of notable worker solidarity or power.

It is difficult to imagine how a war so lucrative for business and so hard on the workers (who sacrificed lives *and* rights) should be seen as a time of brilliant progress for the latter. In any case, class consciousness is not exclusive to the working class. The middle class also had its consciousness raised by this war. Those on fixed incomes were badly hit by inflation. Others felt that they were unfairly asked, through ever-increasing taxes, to bear the cost of the war. Since this war was particularly deadly for those with the misfortune to be officers, the middle class also suffered disproportionately high death rates. A sense of adversity forced this once amorphous class to become more cohesive and combative. The middle class emerged from the war determined to gain back what had been lost. The most profound example of this assertiveness was their objection to funding (through taxes) the social improvements that the workers felt were their due reward for war service. In Britain, middle class assertiveness took the form of groups like the Middle Class Union and the opposition to the General Strike. In more volatile Germany and Italy, it took the form of support for the fascists.

Change did occur during the Great War. But there were countervailing forces working against change, in particular a prevalent 'for the duration' mood. War is an extraordinary event which engenders a temporary tolerance for disruption. With the armistice comes a widespread desire, among all classes, to return to normal. The extent to which normality is restored is the gauge of how worthwhile the sacrifice was. War is seldom fought to change society, but more often to preserve it.

Postscript

In total war victory goes to the nation or nations which mobilize most effectively. It is not enough simply to place in the field a large professional army, well-trained and led by brilliant generals. The army has to be constantly supplied with reinforcements and munitions. Both have to come from the home front yet each contradicts the other. Every new soldier is a worker removed from the factory or a farmer absent from the field. Balancing the needs of the army, keeping it fed and supplied, while at the same time satisfying the needs of the civilian population, challenges the organizational powers of central government and the tolerance of citizens. All of the belligerents expected a short war, but success went to those that adjusted most rapidly and efficiently to a long one. Gluttony in 1914 often meant starvation in 1917.

There was a fatal contradiction in the German mobilization of the population, which Gerhard Feldman called 'a triumph, not of imagination, but of fantasy'. [50, p. 214] The Hindenburg Programme and Auxiliary Service Law, implemented after it became clear that the war would be long, asked too much of the people, who were expected to tolerate a loss of freedom and an empty stomach. In seeing to the needs of the army Ludendorff paid scant regard for the suffering of civilians. They eventually turned on him. The writer Ernst Glaeser remarked: 'Hunger destroyed our solidarity; the children stole each other's rations. . . . Soon the women who stood in pallid queues before shops spoke more about their children's hunger than about the death of their husbands. . . . Soon a looted ham thrilled us more than the fall of Bucharest.' [45, p. 292] The diet of the average German was 3400 calories per day in 1914. It fell to 1000 calories by 1918. Starvation was tolerable only in the short term, and only if victory seemed certain. Hindenburg and Ludendorff asked the German people to achieve the impossible, motivating them always by a fear of what defeat might mean. Eventually, there came a point when defeat seemed a welcome escape from the tortuous quest for victory.

8
The Soldier's War

The ordinary soldier in the First World War was a beast of burden, a man caged by a life of drudgery, squalor, and limited opportunity. As such, he made the perfect infantryman. Young men died in droves because of a cruel coincidence of technological progress and social evolution. In 1914, the nations of Europe possessed the industrial capacity for mass annihilation *and* millions of deferential donkeys willing to die.

Officers and men

Soldiers in the First World War have often been portrayed as victims, mere cannon fodder sent forward by cold politicians, and mown down by mechanistic weaponry. The image is basically sound, but the conclusions are often over-stated. Sentiment inspires an easy leap from hapless warrior to noble martyr. Since the war in Europe provides few conventional military heroes, the ordinary soldier has been granted heroic status merely for enduring. Thus, the British invented Tommy Atkins, the decent, honest, long-suffering working-class soldier who did his duty and survived by sheer pluck. Parallels can be found in every belligerent culture. Granted, there were men on all sides who conformed to the Tommy Atkins stereotype. But every army had its share of deviants, cowards and criminals. The soldier of the Great War fought with great courage, but he also occasionally cheated, lied, raped and mutinied.

Before the war, prejudice toward soldiers was strong in every society, and often had good cause. Throughout history, soldiers have been models of misbehaviour. Men trained to be violent sometimes used violence indiscriminately. Around any army camp, the incidence of drunkenness, rape and theft was (and remains) much higher than in society as a whole. In 1914, the average soldier came from a life of few opportunities, in which sudden and premature death was relatively common. Often malnourished, he was usually physically smaller than his officers, a fact which reinforced the institutional hierarchy. Men used to a life of poverty and drudgery did not find the spartan conditions and invidious discipline of the military camp all that unfamiliar. Enlisted men, drawn from the lowest classes, were placed within an institution that reinforced traditional social hierarchies and respect for one's 'betters'. Most of these men knew their place and were not inclined to complain. They did not expect much from life. Their social background made them ideal soldiers to fight in this sort of war.

When war broke out, military service was at first very popular. Men rushed forward to join the cause, encouraged by romance, excitement and a feeling that their country needed them. In countries with conscription, very few soldiers went AWOL (absent without official leave) in August 1914. Service was linked with masculinity; women urged their men forward and young girls loitered around camps hoping to pull a soldier. In Britain, where voluntarism remained the rule, there were at first more recruits than the country actually wanted. Granted, some joined up simply because they needed a job, but it is pointless to discount the patriotic nature of the widespread urge to serve. Even in Germany, where most men were already in uniform or in the reserves, an additional 308 000 men volunteered for military service by the end of 1915.

According to myth, the trench experience helped to eradicate class antagonism by forcing officers from the privileged classes to share danger and discomfort with those from the poor, downtrodden masses. This shared suffering supposedly encouraged camaraderie and mutual respect. Yet it is absolute nonsense to suggest that the middle classes were, before the war, completely ignorant of workers or vice versa. The middle class supplied society's managers, owners, landlords, bosses. The workers were their drivers, tenants and labourers – the men who cleaned the chimneys, delivered the coal and tended the fields. The very nature of capitalism meant that these two groups constantly interacted, though within strictly defined patterns. It requires a precarious leap of reason to conclude that those patterns would have been broken down in the army where hierarchy was even more rigid than in civilian life. Class distinctions were essential to a smooth functioning military. Army life was merely another form of the manager–worker relationship. This was particularly true in this war, in which the drudgery of trench life had much in common with the monotonous dehumanization of the factory. Except for the killing, war was not much different from work.

To most middle-class officers, ordinary soldiers were subhuman, virtually a different species. For the élite Prussian officer, the ability to lead was, after all, not something one learned, but a product of birth – in the genes. The British officer A. A. Hanbury-Sparrow thought that ordinary soldiers were 'definitely inferior beings'. [20, p. 165] Army life fostered the officer's élite status. Social barriers were carefully buttressed with separate quarters, canteens, cinemas and even brothels. In the trenches, the junior officer ate separately from his men, usually dining on better food, with freer access to alcohol and cigarettes. A servant often looked after his kit. Perhaps the cruellest differentiation came in the treatment of shell shock. The attitude of Lieutenant-Colonel Frank Maxwell was not unusual:

'Shell shock' is a complaint which, to my mind, is too prevalent everywhere, and I have told my people that my name for it is fright, or something worse, and I am not going to have it. Of course, the average nerve system of this class is much lower than ours, and sights and sounds affect them much more. It means ... that they haven't got our power of self-control, that's all. [14, p. 305]

Officers who suffered 'battle fatigue' enjoyed specialist treatment in comfortable hospitals, an extension of the idea that the mental health of society's élites was better (and therefore more responsive to treatment) than that of workers. In contrast, the ordinary soldier was automatically assumed to be a shirker. He was often tried at court martial for cowardice; if found guilty he was sometimes executed. Others were simply sent back to the front, on the assumption that the ailment could be driven from them by exposure to combat.

Most officers were keen to reinforce the barriers that separated them from their men. Since 'good form' signified authority, officers worked diligently to look like leaders. At the beginning of the war the uniform was carefully tailored, with rank badges large and conspicuous. One French officer, who was not exactly enamoured of the military culture, complained that the uniform made him a walking symbol. Trench life (and the danger of snipers) necessitated greater simplicity and practicality, but, where possible, standards were maintained. Many officers stubbornly resisted the introduction of tin helmets because they made the wearer look too common and heroic, and diluted war's dangerous romance. Subtle distinctions became symbolically important. Officers favoured the élitist revolver over the populist rifle.

Further up the ladder of command, confidence in senior officers was fostered through complicated rituals. Senior commanders cultivated mystery, pageantry and pomp. If the men were sub-human, they were demi-gods. Visual symbols of power reinforced authority: the commander's dress and deportment underlined his superiority and inspired common soldiers to trust in his leadership. A wide brimmed hat shielded his gaze – thus preventing eye contact and accentuating the distance between commander and men. 'I remember being asked on leave what the men thought of Haig', one soldier recalled. 'You might as well have asked the private soldier what he thinks of God'. [20, p. 169] But, though the commanders remained mysterious, in this faceless contest they were often the only warriors recognized by a hero-craving public. The more aloof they were, the more respected they became. Both Haig and Ludendorff exploited their status as populist heroes whenever politicians stood in the way.

Trenches

For a soldier, digging a trench is standard operating procedure – a trained response to enemy fire. But to stay in a trench for years was peculiar to this war and required considerable adaptation, both physical and mental.

At first the trenches were simply muddy slits dug into the ground in haphazard fashion. In areas where the high water table would not permit digging of this type, fortifications were constructed above ground, as raised breastworks of sandbags and wood, with thick protective walls. The trench systems grew more sophisticated as the war progressed and stalemate became the norm. Support and communication trenches were dug in the rear and miles of barbed wire were laid in front to protect the entire system. The system took on a zigzag pattern to deflect blast and to prevent an enemy attacker from firing down the length of the trench. In addition, special dugouts were constructed to give extra protection from artillery bombardment. These also provided sleeping quarters, though usually only for officers. The ordinary soldier had to make do with any available corner to lay out his waterproof sheet and blanket. Often a sleeping platform of sorts would be dug out of the side of the trench, which would at least allow the soldier to avoid the misery of lying on the wet trench floor.

The British soldier Stanley Casson reflected on the sheer size of the trench system on the Western Front:

> Our trenches stood on a faint slope, just overlooking German ground, with a vista of vague plainland below. Away to the right and left stretched the great lines of defence as far as eye and imagination could stretch them. I used to wonder how long it would take for me to walk from the beaches of the North Sea to that curious end of all fighting against the Swiss boundary; to try to guess what each end looked like; to imagine what would happen if I passed a verbal message, in the manner of the parlour game, along to the next man on my right, to be delivered to the end man of all up against the Alps. [33, p. 37]

If the entire system of support, communication, sapper and front-line trenches is considered, the French occupied around 10 000 kilometres of trenches at the height of the war, the British slightly less. On the German side the number easily exceeded 19 000 kilometres. The Germans moved some 46 million cubic metres of soil in constructing their system. Keeping it strong required the shipment of 7112 tonnes of barbed wire from Germany per week. On the British side, it was calculated that one kilometre of line required 900 kilometres of barbed wire, six million sandbags, 28 300 cubic metres of timber and 33 400 square metres of corrugated iron.

Stalemate inspired the trenches and the trenches reinforced stalemate. As construction improved, they became more impregnable. Paul Fussell feels that the character of the trenches reflected crude national stereotypes. 'French trenches were nasty, cynical, efficient and temporary. ... The English were amateur, vague, *ad hoc,* and temporary. The German were efficient, clean, pedantic and permanent. Their occupants proposed to stay where they were'. [33, p. 45]

Since the Germans occupied enemy territory, they did not have to advance to assert supremacy. They learned quickly that an investment in material could overcome a shortage of men. When British troops attacked on the Somme they found some fortifications nine metres deep, with prodigious use of concrete. Floors were occasionally timbered and a host of 'luxuries' were evident, including electric lights, kitchens, water tanks, furniture and wallpaper.

Since the Allies were determined to drive the Germans from France and Belgium, they had no interest in semi-permanent fortresses. The British *Field Service Pocket Book* – the infantry officer's bible – carefully emphasized that trenches were the enemy of mobility. A fortification had to be constructed 'with a view to economizing the power expended on defence in order that the power of offence may be increased'. [33, p. 43] But, on the ground, theory bore little relevance to reality. George Coppard felt that the ordinary soldier paid dearly for principles of war stubbornly upheld by those far from the action:

> The whole conduct of our trench warfare seemed to be based on the concept that we, the British, were not stopping in the trenches for long, but were tarrying awhile on the way to Berlin and that soon we would be chasing Jerry across country. The result, in the long term, meant that we lived a mean and impoverished sort of existence in lousy scratch holes. [17, p. 87]

The Allies were also much more reluctant to surrender ground in order to achieve a more stable, easily defended line. In 1917, the Germans retreated to the carefully prepared Siegfried Line, thus shortening their line by over 48 kilometres and freeing 10 divisions for operations elsewhere. In contrast, the Allies hung on to every bloody salient. Granted, surrendering a piece of France to the Germans was politically sensitive, but the obsession with holding on at all costs did mean that much was sacrificed in defending areas of questionable strategic worth.

The men shared their trenches with rats, lice and the decaying remains of fallen comrades. 'We all had on us the stench of dead bodies', a French soldier at Verdun wrote. 'The bread we ate, the stagnant water we drank, everything we touched had a rotten smell'. [25, p. 152] The rat, symbolic of the miserable depths to which the men had been forced, inspired deep hatred. Soldiers fought over the land and rats fought over the soldiers:

> One evening, whilst on patrol, Jacques saw some rats running from under the dead men's greatcoats, enormous rats, fat with human flesh. His heart pounding, he edged towards one of the bodies. Its helmet had rolled off. The man displayed a grimacing face, stripped of flesh; the skull bare, the eyes devoured. A set of false teeth slid down·on to his rotting jacket, and from the yawning mouth leapt an unspeakably foul beast. [26, p. 55]

Slightly lower down the league table of trench villains was the louse. They were universally loathed, but still managed to inspire ironic comment: 'The lice feared solitude and had a profound sense of family ... Lice have a very warm, very soft bedroom, where the table is always laid. There, in their numerous moments of leisure, they followed the counsels of the creator: they multiplied' [26, p. 56]

Soldiers often felt a martyr's bond with the enemy in the trench opposite. Shared suffering encouraged a common humanity. Amidst the brutality, civility occasionally sprouted like a flower in the desert. Enemies spoke to each other across No Man's Land. The famous Christmas truce of 1914 inspired a football match between Germans and British, much to the dismay of the commanding officers who deemed it bad for morale. In Easter 1916, Austrian and Russian troops left their trenches to gather in No Man's Land. 'We ... shook hands', one Russian soldier wrote, 'and I must confess that they are very kind people'. [14, p. 431] Occasionally, during winter, soldiers threw snowballs instead of grenades. In places, an unofficial understanding allowed soldiers to relieve themselves without fear of being shot. (Neither side wanted the alternative: a trench full of faeces and urine). On almost all fronts, stalemate was occasionally prolonged because of the reluctance of soldiers to disturb it. Charles Sorley recalled

> All patrols – English and German – are much averse to the death and glory principle; so, on running up against one another ... both pretend that they are Levites and the other is a good Samaritan – and pass by on the other side, no word spoken. For either side to bomb the other would be a useless violation of the unwritten laws that govern the relations of combatants

permanently within a hundred yards distance of each other, who have found out that to provide discomfort for the other is but a roundabout way of providing for themselves. [25, p. 105]

Supplies

This war was not only huge in terms of the numbers involved, but also in the complexity of supplying vast armies. The 42nd East Lancashire Brigade, on a front of just 1800 metres, used 5036 bags of cement, 19 384 bags of shingle and 9692 bags of sand in order to construct a single reserve trench. The resulting pile of material weighed over 900 tonnes and had to be transported to the line over very rough ground, the last part of the journey without motorized transport. As defences grew increasingly sophisticated, more and heavier weaponry was needed for the same basic objective of breaking through the enemy line. Thus, in 1914 a British division needed 27 railway wagons of supplies (of all types) to survive for a week. By 1916, the same division needed 20 wagons of food and fodder and another 30 of combat material. But, once supplies were unloaded, they were often heaved into battle on the backs of men. No soldier in this war carried a pack weighing less than sixty pounds.

At the Battle of Verdun, a single German infantry division of 16 000 men and 7000 horses had access to 15 batteries of artillery. Those guns required 36 ammunition trains, or a total length of 56 kilometres. Each train carried 2000 heavy howitzer and 26 880 light field artillery shells. On the other side, the French were forced to rely heavily on trucks, as the rail lines to the Verdun battlefront had been cut. From 24 February to 6 March, 3500 trucks hauled 190 000 troops and 23 000 tonnes of ammunition. At the height of the operation, a vehicle passed every 14 seconds. It is perhaps fortunate that, for all its sound and fury, artillery was not an efficient killer. The German Army Corps VII, which regularly fired one million shells per month during an offensive, found that 100 rounds were required to kill one enemy soldier. This explains why so many shells were needed and why the war was so expensive to fight. The bombardment which preceded the Third Battle of Ypres consisted of over four million rounds, which cost the British taxpayer over £22 million.

The need for vast quantities of weaponry meant that strategic plans were determined to a large extent by the availability of transport. Railway schedules, which influenced the outbreak of war in the first place, also shaped the war's character. Armchair generals often ask why the Great War commanders did not devise more surprise attacks in order to break the deadlock. Not only was such flexibility impossible due to the problems of moving huge munitions shipments from point to point, but the process of movement itself automatically destroyed the element of surprise. Mounting a massive attack meant building roads, railways, camps, hospitals and supply dumps beforehand. Sources of water had to be found, pumped and purified. Food had to be amassed and field kitchens built (think, for a minute, about the complexity of baking bread for two million men). Millions of artillery rounds of various types had to be placed in supply dumps near the battlefield, and then transported to the separate batteries. Granted, this sort of preparation destroyed any possibility of real surprise, but surprise alone, without such preparation, would have achieved nothing.

The tyranny of the machine

Technology shaped this war and the war shaped technology. The unusual stalemate inspired the development of new weapons designed to bring more deadly and accurate firepower on to trenches. By early 1915 the Germans had come up with a range of trench mortars which fired shells varying in size from 9 to 210 pounds and had maximum ranges between 550 and 1100 metres. Though the Allies were much slower in the deployment of weapons of this sort, the British did eventually develop the highly portable and immensely reliable Stokes mortar. The high arc of mortar shells made it easier to land them in the trenches. They were cheap, easily handled, highly accurate and very effective. Mortars seem so basic to this war that it seems curious that their value was not immediately appreciated, especially since they were hardly a new development. But since few expected a static war, the utility of mortars had in effect to be re-learned. The failure to appreciate the implications of technology was universal; examples of it were so frequent that it is pointless to accuse one side of being more Luddite than another.

The French 75 mm gun was the best artillery piece in the war, but the German howitzer was the most fearsome. Because the war was stationary, guns could be placed in essentially permanent positions, which were themselves fortified and protected. This in turn reinforced the static nature of the war, adding another arc to a vicious circle. Though the nature of gunnery at first impeded mobility, improvements in technology and expertise eventually opened the door to greater movement. As fire became more accurate, creeping barrages could be carefully timed with infantry advances, providing protection to the attacking soldier as he moved across No Man's Land. This tactic was not new, having been used to good effect by the British in South Africa. But the skill had to be re-learned by commanders who did not at first think it applicable to a modern continental war. Accurate firing also made accurate location-finding that much easier, since it was a simpler task to plot the position of a gun which fired in a predictable fashion than one whose shells landed erratically. As a result, counter-battery firing improved immensely during the war.

Every soldier feels naked without his rifle. This war was no different, but in few modern wars have rifles been so insignificant. The enemy was seldom seen, therefore shooting at him had little effect. When he was close enough to be seen, he was often too close to be shot at effectively. The grenade proved a far more handy weapon on the Western Front. Lobbing a grenade from a shell-hole into a trench was a very effective way for the individual soldier to bring firepower to bear on the enemy. The weapon did not need to be accurate to be deadly. At first the rate of development was determined by the soldiers themselves, who suffered severely the lack of a simple, mass-produced grenade. Some even devised home-made ones from material available in the trench:

> Take a jam-pot, fill it with shredded gin cotton and ten penny nails, mixed according to taste. Insert a No. 8 detonator and a short length of Bickford's Fuse. Clamp up the lid. Light with a match, pipe, cigar or cigarette and throw for all you are worth. [26, p. 78]

The Germans proved the early leaders in grenade design and production but it was the British who eventually learned how to make them in large quantities. The 'Mills bomb', a highly effective rifle grenade of British design, proved very popular among the troops.

The machine gun was the most effective weapon of defence and, later in the war, also proved invaluable in attack. It was perhaps the most profound application of industrial technology to modern war.

As the name suggests, it was a simple machine applied to the task of killing. As John Keegan writes:

> A succession of 'two inch taps' first on one side of the breach until the stop was reached, then on the other, would keep in the air a stream of bullets so dense that no one could walk upright across the front of the machine-gunner's position without being hit – given, of course that the gunner had set his machine to fire low and that the ground was devoid of cover. The appearance of the machine gun, therefore, had not so much *disciplined* the act of killing ... as mechanized or industrialized it. [55, p. 234]

Machine guns seemed to rule the war. For many men they *were* the war – an enemy more easy to despise than the soldiers in the trench opposite:

> every time a machine gun opened fire in our sector, my men would listen carefully, and when someone said 'It's the coffee mill', his remark would send a tingle down our spines. ... I know nothing more depressing in the midst of battle ... than the steady tac-tac-tac of that deadly weapon. ... There appears to be nothing material to its working. It seems to be dominated and directed by some powerful, scheming spirit of destruction. [26, p. 89]

Machine guns contributed to the stalemate not just because they could mow down attacking troops so effectively, but also because their unwieldy nature at first rendered them inappropriate to the attack. Thus, attacking troops were always outgunned. Since the machine gun consumed ammunition at a prodigious rate, it created its own problems of supply, further exacerbating the static nature of the war. But, eventually, technology solved this dilemma. The lighter and more portable Lewis gun, developed by the British, allowed attackers to move forward supported by machine-gun fire.

The need for a vehicle that could traverse No Man's Land and the enemy trench system was evident from the early stages of the war. In autumn 1914, Churchill provided £70 000 of Admiralty funds for what he termed a 'trench spanning car'. Within months, the idea had developed into one of steam driven machines equipped with caterpillar treads and armoured shelters for the crew. The new machine was given the name 'tank' as a sort of verbal camouflage: covered up, they looked like large water tanks when transported on railway cars to the front. The name simply encouraged that misconception. The guiding light of the British tank programme was Colonel E. B. Swinton, one of the few to appreciate that a weapon so revolutionary necessitated the development of radically new tactics.

Because of their mutual suspicion, Britain and France developed tanks independently of each other, did not share technological breakthroughs, and did not coordinate the manufacture of weaponry once the first prototypes became operational. The British Mark I tank, first used in the Somme Offensive (prematurely, some would argue) weighed 28.5 tonnes, had 0.5-inch armour and a crew of eight. It had a top speed of about six kilometres per hour. But that speed was essentially meaningless since it was measured on smooth ground, which was hard to find on the Western Front. Rough terrain cut the speed in half.

The first successful tank produced in Britain was nicknamed 'Little Willie'. It was quickly replaced by a larger model called, predictably, 'Big Willie'. The latter was then renamed 'Mother', as 'it was the first of all tanks' (even though it was actually the second). 'Mother' came in two forms: male and female. The male 'Mother' was bigger and had better guns, namely two 6-pounder naval guns and four Lewis machine guns, while the female had six Lewis guns. The female, rather inexplicably, had a tiny trap door, rendering it nearly impossible for the crew to escape if the tank caught fire. The crew's worst nightmare was to be trapped inside a burning female tank. For understandable reasons, they preferred male 'Mothers'. (Oh, what a surreal war.)

The French entered the tank race later, but eventually produced more machines than the British. It was not until December 1915 that Colonel Jean Estienne proposed to Joffre that the French should start a construction programme. Joffre agreed and quickly ordered 400 of the new *chars* (for chariots), which were used in the Nivelle Offensive of April 1917. Nearly 5000 were built, around 2000 more than the British. Their tactical deployment was an expression of the prevailing mentalities in the respective countries: the British thought of tanks as steel horses, while the French saw them as 'portable artillery'. [117, p. 111] The latter was perhaps a more enlightened view, but still far short of the outlook which best exploited the weapon's enormous potential. It is nevertheless ironic that the Germans, who would become the leaders in tank warfare two decades later, saw fit to build just 20 during the Great War.

Technological devilry was perhaps most profound when it came to the production of gas. Biologists, physicists and chemists from some of the best universities in Europe eagerly joined the search for chemical weapons to unlock the trench stalemate. The Germans struck first, deploying teargas early in 1915. This had limited results, but did convince them that even more deadly gases might prove effective. Chlorine was used at Ypres on 22 April 1915, with some success, but the problems of delivering the gas remained complex. Gas was at first released from canisters and allowed to drift over enemy lines, making success dependent on a favourable wind.

The British and French denounced the first attacks as a violation of the laws of war, and then promptly stepped up their own gas production programmes. Eventually gas was delivered in mortar canisters and shells, with the French leading the way in the development of the latter. More deadly gases were also developed, particularly phosgene and mustard. The effects of the latter were horrible; those it killed outright were more fortunate than those it assigned an agonisingly slow demise. A nurse wrote:

> I wish those people who write so glibly about this being a holy war and the orators who talk so much about going on no matter how long the war lasts and what it may mean, could see a case – to say nothing of ten cases – of mustard gas in its early stages – could see the poor things burnt and blistered all over with great mustard-coloured suppurating blisters, with blind eyes ... all sticky and stuck together, and always fighting for breath, with voices a mere whisper, saying that their throats are closing and they know they will choke. [26, p. 67]

But while scientists worked hard to develop effective gases and delivery systems, others toiled equally diligently on methods of protection. Eventually, the gas mask virtually cancelled out the gas shell. Chemical warfare was never again as effective as it proved to be early in the war. But it did at least provide temporary relief from rats.

It was a war of machines, assembly lines, accountants, engineers, scientists, managers. Like mere atoms in a chemical process, the soldier was important but not individually significant. Death was measured in hundreds and thousands, not as the destruction of single souls. Louis Mairet wrote:

Now we die. It is the wet death, the muddy death, death dripping with blood, death by drowning, death by sucking under, death in the slaughterhouse. The bodies lie frozen in the earth which gradually sucks them in. [25, p. 153]

In this faceless war, bravery was plentiful but recognizable heroes few. 'Chivalry disappeared for always', wrote Ernst Junger. 'Like all noble and personal feelings it had to give way to the tempo of battle and to the rule of the machine'. [25, p. 144]

Casualties

The soldier faced a range of risks. He could be killed by a sniper's bullet, torn to shreds by a machine gun, choked by gas, strafed by aeroplanes or maimed by mortars or grenades. Stray shells or bullets fired by comrades to the rear killed thousands. The environment also fostered a number of diabolical diseases including trench foot, frostbite, trench fever, and gas gangrene. But artillery was the most deadly and demoralizing feature of this war. Henri Barbusse described the experience of being under fire:

A diabolical uproar surrounds us. We are conscious of a sustained crescendo, an incessant multiplication of the universal frenzy; a hurricane of hoarse and hollow banging of raging clamour, of piercing and beast-like screams, fastens furiously with tatters of smoke upon the earth where we are buried up to our necks, and the wind of shells seems to set it heaving and pitching. [26, p. 63]

Relatively few men were killed by a single merciful bullet through the heart. Most were blown to bits or crushed by the weight of blast. The lucky ones were essentially vaporized – ceasing to exist from one moment to the next. Those less fortunate waited while life oozed from them, with arms or legs torn away like branches of a tree during a hurricane. As the war progressed, bigger guns were brought in to attack ever more impregnable defences. Shrapnel shells, which had little effect against a well-fortified trench, were replaced by shells filled with high explosive. Bombardments became longer and heavier. It was not unusual, after a shelling, for body parts to be found hanging in nearby trees or for a soldier to be killed by the dismembered limb of a comrade. One British chaplain wrote of the aftermath:

> It is a good thing not to be too squeamish ... As usual with a good many deaths, one had the back of his head off, another from the nose downwards completely gone. But it is the multiple wounds that appear worst, men almost in pieces, the number intensifies the horror, we get so few slight cases. [26, p. 114]

Those not killed or wounded still had to suffer the immense mental strain of bombardments that seemed without end. Shells that left no physical scars still tore at the mind.

The weather was the enemy of every soldier. To understand the war, one French soldier wrote, 'you need to have remained for six days and six nights of this winter sitting tight, your belly frozen, your arms hanging loosely, your hands and feet numb, you need to have felt despair, convinced that nothing could ever thaw you out again'. [14, p. 224] On the Western Front, incessant bombardment and heavy rain turned the fields of Flanders into foetid swamps. Soldiers had to watch helplessly as comrades who fell from duck-boards were swallowed slowly by the earth. During one month in 1916 a British Guards battalion on the Somme lost 16 men through drowning. The problem was worst at Ypres in 1917:

> A khaki-clad leg, three heads in a row, the rest of the bodies sub-merged, giving one the idea that they had used their last ounce of strength to keep their heads above the rising water. In another miniature pond, a hand still gripping a rifle is all that is visible, while its next door neighbour is occupied by a steel helmet and half a head, the eyes staring icily at the green slime which floats on the surface. [26, p. 47]

In the East the cold was cruel. Soldiers were buried by avalanches or sank helplessly into snowdrifts. On the Carpathian front in January 1915 the night-time temperature rarely rose above $-15\,°C$. Troops starved because food could not be brought forward. That which did make it to the front lines was too frozen to eat. Soldiers fought sleep, knowing that only by staying awake could they hope to beat the cold. Wolves feasted on those unable to keep sleep or death at bay.

'Humanity is mad! It must be mad to do what it is doing', Alfred Joubaire, a French infantry lieutenant, wrote. 'What a massacre! What scenes of horror and carnage! I cannot find words to translate my impressions. Hell cannot be so terrible! Men are mad!' [26, p. 5] A German soldier fighting near Ypres wrote in a similar vein:

> After crawling through the bleeding remnants of my comrades, and through the smoke and debris, wandering and running in the midst of the raging gunfire in search of refuge, I am now awaiting death at any moment. You do not know what Flanders means. Flanders means endless human endurance. Flanders means blood and scraps of human bodies. Flanders means heroic courage and faithfulness unto death. [26, p. 60]

The war provides sufficient horror to tax any imagination. But it was not unremitting horror. Offensives lasted months but fighting was not constant. On the Western Front, the great offensives took place along relatively short stretches of the line. While some soldiers endured a terrible struggle on the Somme, others experienced a quiet time in Picardy or Flanders. Charles Carrington analyzed how he spent 1916:

> I find that ... I spent 65 days in front line trenches, and 36 more in supporting positions close at hand. ... In addition, 120 days were spent in reserve positions near enough to the line to march up for the day when work or fighting demanded, and 73 days were spent out in rest ... 10 days were spent in Hospital ... 17 days on leave. ... The 101 days under fire contain twelve 'tours' in the trenches varying in length from one to thirteen days. The battalion made sixteen in all during the year. We were in action four times during my ... tours in the trenches. Once I took part in a direct attack, twice in bombing actions, and once we held the front line from which other troops advanced. I also took part in an unsuccessful trench raid. [26, p. 29]

In the East the majority of time was spent manoeuvring for battle (or finding the enemy). Actual battles were quite short. In Salonika over 200 000 men spent nearly the entire war waiting for commanders and politicians to decide how they were to be deployed. On all fronts the boredom was at times so overbearing that many men looked forward to an attack to break the monotony. That said, even quiet could be dangerous. Even on stretches of the front where no battle was in progress, the casualty rate could still be shockingly high. This phenomenon was given a coldly appropriate term: wastage.

War did inspire a minor medical revolution. The development of x-rays was given a boost as were brain surgery techniques. Plastic surgeons were supplied a steady crop of casualties upon whom to practise their art. Psychiatrists gave scientific legitimacy to a heretofore unrecognized category of war neuroses. Though many continued to label the shell shock victim a shirker, there was at least an acceptance that the wounds of war were not always physical. But despite the progress of medical science, many men still died of essentially treatable injuries. The difficulty of getting to the injured and treating them on or near the battlefield meant that even minor trauma sometimes proved fatal. This meant that thousands suffered a slow and agonizing death in No Man's Land. Soldiers from every country recalled one of the war's most agonizing experiences: that of having to listen to the screams of a comrade dying slowly.

For many men, army life represented a more wholesome diet, improved housing, better clothing (especially boots) and more regular medical care than previously experienced. Beer was weaker and access to alcohol considerably restricted. It is therefore no coincidence that many recruits grew a couple of inches and gained considerable weight after enlisting. Health standards often improved during the course of the war, partly in response to the poor health of recruits, but also because of greater public scrutiny. The soldier had become important and his health was essential to the survival of the nation. For this reason, the armies often had first call on the supply of food and medicine. Though, late in the war, Austro-Hungarian soldiers had to survive on just a handful of ersatz bread, 100 grams of horsemeat and some thin broth each day, that, according to Geoffrey Wawro, was a 'feast' by civilian standards. Those considering desertion took note. [14, pp. 408-09]

Morale

In April 1917, when the Nivelle Offensive yielded less than its illustrious commander had promised, French soldiers mutinied. Seventeen men of 108th Infantry Regiment abandoned their posts just prior to the launch of an attack. The demoralization quickly spread, with 46 of 112 divisions eventually affected. The French war effort seemed on the verge of collapse.

The mutinies revealed that the morale of the soldier is a very fragile thing, but also that combat is not its most important determinant. When Pétain, the new French commander-in-chief, investigated the incidents, he found soldiers complaining about mundane matters like food, medical services, frequency of leave, etc., rather than the strains of battle. Being of a pragmatic mind, Pétain recognized that a punitive response would be counter-productive. Thus, of the 35 000 men involved in one way or another, just 2873 were court-martialled and sentenced. Most sentences were suspended and just 43 of the 629 death sentences were carried out.

Though the mutinies were significant, it is important to keep the issue in perspective. If 35 000 men were involved, that is still a very small proportion of the entire French force. In other forces, mutiny was a tiny problem. The Germans had what might be called mutinies late in the war, but they were probably caused by the simple realization that the game was up. In other words, the army was beaten before it mutinied. The same can be said of the Russian army, where collapse had more to do with the political turmoil in the country and defeat on the battlefield than with an identifiable disenchantment with the war. Much has been made of the British revolt at Etaples in 1917, when soldiers briefly rioted over conditions at a training camp. But that incident is significant only because, in the wider picture, it is insignificant. It takes a historian obsessively interested in the unusual to devote much attention to that teacup-sized storm.

There was no more stable fighting force than the British army. Granted, the British conducted 169 040 courts martial during the war, but if one takes into account the extraordinary circumstances of war and an army obsessed with discipline, the figure does not suggest a crime rate significantly higher than existed in peacetime civilian society. Courts martial could pertain to relatively minor offences like drunkenness. Those pertaining to mutiny, cowardice and self-inflicted wounds together account for less than one per cent of the total number of fighting men. Bearing in mind what Pétain discovered about the factors affecting morale, it is perhaps no wonder that issues as small as the availability of jam might serve as the proverbial straw that broke the soldier's spirit. This perhaps explains why the British, whose logistical apparatus was second to none, suffered the least severe problems of morale. British soldiers were, on the whole, better fed and clothed, and enjoyed better medical care than any of the other combatants.

The availability of small comforts might also in part explain the Russian collapse, given that the Russian army stood on the other end of the scale of logistical efficiency. 'It is very bad now', one soldier wrote to his mother. 'We haven't received bread for two weeks, only rusks; that's what we are expected to fight on. There is a shortage of rusks too and no snuff [tobacco] at all'. [14, p. 428] Similar shortages crippled the Austro-Hungarian army. 'I think we will die of hunger before a bullet gets us', an Austrian soldier wrote in despair to his mother. [50, p. 182] Turkish soldiers fought with incredible tenacity but deserted in droves when boots were not replaced, food was poor and pay stopped. But while all armies seem to have understood the intricacies of the morale problem to one degree or another, few could address it completely. When German soldiers ran out of socks or fell short of wholesome food, it was not because of a cruel government or inefficient command, but because the German war machine was stretched to the limit. The Ottoman Empire had more than enough food to feed its soldiers, but lacked the ability to get it to them.

Each army developed its own method of maintaining morale that was itself a reflection of distinct cultural values. The spit and polish, rigid discipline of the British army worked in part because of the cohesive class structure of Britain and the ingrained respect for authority among the working classes. It would not have worked in the French army where a high proportion of soldiers were of peasant stock and therefore a great deal more self-reliant. In contrast to British infantrymen, fewer French soldiers had suffered the dehumanizing experience of the factory. British officers often remarked scathingly on the indiscipline of French troops and the slovenly nature of their officers, drawing a connection between the two. But, in truth, a peculiarly French equilibrium had been established which suited the army's socio-cultural background.

Every army had an outlaw element who resented authority and looked for ways to escape duty. Given the rigidly controlled military environment, it was difficult for these men to express their discontent without incurring severe retribution. Thus, mere hooligans were often turned into criminals by a system intolerant of even the most minor offence. Nevertheless, some very serious crimes were committed on all sides. Atrocity stories were grossly exaggerated (often intentionally so for propaganda purposes), but many had a grain of truth. Soldiers did steal, rape and pillage. Civilians who found themselves in the path of an advancing army (or, worse, a retreating one) did suffer terribly. There is also no doubt that unpopular officers in the Great War were occasionally murdered by their men or left to die in a shellhole when rescue might have been possible.

Military training aims to destroy a man's individuality, so that he becomes a mere cog in a fighting machine. 'War in England only means putting all men of military age in England into a state of routinal coma, preparatory to getting them killed', Sorley commented. 'You are ... given six months to become conventional; your peace made with God, you will be sent out and killed'. [103, p. 27] Though soldiers entered the army for a variety of reasons (from compulsion to service to a misguided sense of adventure), they continued to fight for different ones. Habit, duty, discipline and fear of punishment all played a part. One German soldier forced to endure the horror at Verdun later confessed:

We never understood the sense of the entire operation ... The soldier does his duty and does not question why. It was duty alone that kept us together and held our courage up. At such a place, one cannot speak of enthusiasm; everyone wishes they were a thousand miles away. [45, p. 193]

Fatalism set in, allowing the men to cope with the horrors around them and to avoid being smothered by the proximity of death. Men who seemed glass-eyed and vacant had actually turned themselves into very effective fighters. Gone was the reckless quest for heroism, in its place a sturdy pragmatism:

The skin seemed shinier and tighter on men's faces, and eyes burned with a hard brightness under the brims of their helmets. One felt every question as an interruption of some absorbing business of the mind. ... One by one, they realised that each must go alone, and that each of them already was alone with himself, helping the others perhaps, but looking at them with strange eyes, while the world became unreal and empty, and they moved in a mystery, where no help was. [26, p. 97]

'In truth, courage has nothing to do with it', an Alsatian soldier reflected. 'The fear of death surpasses all other feelings and terrible compulsion alone drives the soldier forward'. [45, p. 193] They fought not for their country but for their own survival and out of loyalty to their comrades. This loyalty was itself a manifestation of self-protection since all soldiers realised that survival was impossible without the help of friends.

But while the war anaesthetised many men, in others it inspired a deep camaraderie. Men who were culturally conditioned to repress feelings found emotional release in a horrible war. A British private wrote:

> To live amongst men who would give their last fag, their last bite, aye, even their last breath if need be for a pal – that is comradeship, the comradeship of the trenches. The only clean thing borne of this life of cruelty and filth. It grows in purity from the very obscenity of its surroundings. [26, p. 202]

The mixture of terrible danger and deep emotional intensity gave the war a perverse attraction for some. Men hated it, but couldn't bear to be away from it. A German soldier on leave confessed:

> I am restless. I hate the kitchen table at which I am writing. I lost patience over a book. I should like to push the landscape aside as if it irritated me. I must get to the Front. I must again hear the shells roaring up into the sky and the desolate valley echoing the sound. I must get back to my company ... live once more in the realm of death. [26, p. 202]

The worst war in history was for many the best years of their life.

9
Peace of Sorts

The Germans settled for an armistice because they wanted to avoid the stigma of defeat, and hoped to hold on to some of their conquered territory. They were, by the end of 1918, in desperate straits, and desperation encouraged ridiculous fantasies about the sort of deal they might arrange. An armistice was technically a peace between equals, leading to a negotiated treaty. But this technicality did not remotely interest nor trouble the victorious powers. They had no doubt that Germany had been defeated. If the Germans chose to debate that point, they could do so on the battlefield. In truth, the harsh terms of the armistice ensured that a resumption of hostilities was out of the question. The idea of a peace between equals was, therefore, equally fantastic.

Woodrow Wilson might once have made vague assertions about the need for a 'peace of understanding and conciliation', [100, p. 192] but the Germans had, as far as he was concerned, squandered that opportunity with the astonishingly harsh Treaty of Brest-Litovsk. That treaty had led Wilson to conclude that Germany was only interested in justice if she was the chief beneficiary. His European partners needed no convincing; they had always been determined to make Germany atone for her transgressions. It is nevertheless entirely understandable that Germany should have been confused by mixed signals emanating from Washington. Wilson tended to become intoxicated by the sound of his own moral pronouncements. As for the American people, they delighted in the way he had made the war and the peace into a noble cause. Thus, even though Wilson was a great deal more hardbitten by the end of the war than he had been when he entered it, he still could not resist playing to the crowd with his moralistic nonsense. If the Germans were confused it was in large measure his fault.

One of Wilson's gravest errors was to state openly that he refused to negotiate with the 'military masters and monarchical autocrats' who ruled Germany. [100, p. 194] This sent a signal to the Germans that if they got rid of the Kaiser and his entourage and replaced them with an ersatz democracy, they could expect a softer peace. No such peace was ever remotely possible. By the time Wilson made his pronouncement, the three protagonists – France, Britain and the United States – had all decided that Germany should be punished severely. That Wilson should have suggested otherwise raised German expectations and eventually left the Allies open to charges of deceit.

It was appropriate that the peace conference should take place in Paris – appropriate, but also wildly inappropriate. The war had been won in the West and victory had meant a liberation of France. But the choice of Paris was, for that reason, symbolic of Allied victory and, as such, a calculated snub to the Germans. It underlined the notion that vengeance for the crimes of 1870 would be sought. Though it is unlikely that the Germans would have received a sympathetic hearing in another Entente capital (a neutral one was out of the question), it has to be said that malice ran deep in Paris, since France had suffered from the war so directly.

The twenty-seven national delegations present in Paris included many of the bit players in this war. The desire by every delegate to have his say quickly put paid to optimistic notions of open negotiation, originally favoured by Wilson. Instead, the main proceedings were soon dominated by the Council of Ten, which included two representatives each from Britain, France, the United States, Italy and Japan. It was in fact a council of eight, since Japan had no real interest in European affairs but was keen to use her influence on such an esteemed body to gain important concessions in Asia, at the expense of the old German Empire and of China. Thus, the body was essentially the Supreme War Council by another name. The representatives were used to talking to each other, even though they were not very good at agreeing. Whenever a representative from a smaller power tried to get a word (or demand) in edgewise, he was reminded that the four powers had together lost 12 million men in the war. That sacrifice apparently allowed them to shape the peace.

Mutual suspicions among the Big Four ran deep. Relations between the French and the British had always been difficult and did not improve under the pressure of trying to agree upon terms. Clemenceau was widely suspected by the other powers of wanting to dominate the proceedings in order to create a new Europe suited to French interests and which addressed French fears. Lloyd

George seemed interested only in a Europe ideally suited to British commerce and in harmony with the British Empire. His overriding mendacity provoked distrust among his colleagues. For instance, there seemed no way to square the Lloyd George who argued that 'We cannot both cripple [Germany] and expect her to pay' with the one who whipped his people into righteous fury at the 1918 election. [101, p. 32] Orlando rightly called him a 'slippery prestidigitator [illusionist]'. [66, p. 107] As for the Italians, due to their rather cynical decision to enter the war, they had never been accepted as a bona fide member of the alliance. Orlando was not a sufficiently dominating individual to make amends for the low esteem in which his country was held. His disillusionment with the peace process as it affected Italy led to his marginalization and the Big Four became, in effect, the Big Three.

The European leaders reserved their greatest suspicion for Wilson who, they thought, seemed determined to hijack proceedings in order to pursue his moralist impulses. His *naïveté* was deeply worrying, but the fact that it was combined with a messianic zeal seemed dangerous. 'You wish to do justice to the Germans', Clemenceau warned Wilson. 'Do not believe they will ever forgive us; they will merely seek the opportunity for revenge'. [101, p. 192] Lloyd George, Orlando and Clemenceau felt that Wilson's criticism of their demands for reparations seemed utterly hypocritical in the light of his simultaneous insistence that all debts owed to the United States by the Allied powers had to be paid. As for Wilson, he publicly stated his feelings that the Americans were 'the only disinterested people at the Conference' and that 'the men with whom we are about to deal do not represent their own people'. [136, p. 574] The comments did nothing to endear him to his colleagues. In any case, the defeat of Wilson's Democratic Party in the 1918 congressional elections meant that the president could hardly claim to represent a popular will.

Germany's absence seems a bit strange and, in retrospect, rather unfortunate. Granted, since this was not going to be a negotiated peace, there was no reason for the enemy to be present. But had German (and Austro-Hungarian) representatives taken part they would at least have been forced to answer the charges against them, for instance on the issue of war guilt. The result would not have been in doubt, but, as every good propagandist will admit, show trials do serve a purpose. At the very least, Germany's subsequent claim that the treaty was merely a *diktat* would have lost a great deal of force. Denying the Germans a presence gave credibility to the martyred image Hitler and his cronies so assiduously constructed after the war.

For understandable reasons, Russia was also not present. One-time allies had been transformed into bitter enemies, to the extent that the Entente Powers had even agreed to send troops to assist the anti-Bolshevik forces fighting in the Russian hinterlands. The new rulers in Moscow were confident enough in the advent of the communist revolution to believe that the forces gathered in Paris would soon crumble under the weight of capitalist contradiction. But that feeling went both ways, since the British, French and Americans had little confidence in Lenin's ability to hold his country together. Russia's absence nevertheless meant that a diplomatic vacuum existed as far as the fate of Eastern Europe was concerned.

Though the Russians were not physically present, the Russian problem hung like a black cloud over the conference. Countering the Bolshevik threat worried the Big Four as much as did the problem of punishing Germany. 'Our real danger now is not the Boches but Bolshevism', argued Henry Wilson shortly after the war. [39, p. 321] In fact, the two problems were intrinsically related, as the delegates were painfully aware that harsh punishment of Germany might increase her susceptibility to Bolshevism. In his Fontainebleau Memorandum of March 1919, Lloyd George warned that

> The greatest danger that I see in the present situation is that Germany may throw in her lot with Bolshevism . . . Once that happens all Eastern Europe will be swept into the orbit of the Bolshevik revolution and within a year we may witness the spectacle of nearly three hundred million people organised into a vast red army under German instructors and German generals equipped with German cannon and German machine guns and prepared for a renewal of the attack on Eastern Europe. [75, p. 582]

Nor was the Russian danger restricted to Europe. The imperial powers – Britain, France, and Belgium – were alarmed by the way Russia had projected herself as a supporter of anti-colonial revolutionary movements.

The Big Four were not free agents. Wilson, as has been suggested, was essentially a lame duck president. He also felt, as he confessed, 'the dumb eyes of the people' upon him. 'What is expected of me only God could perform', he once complained. [101, p. 187] That was perhaps true, but if the people wanted miracles it was because he encouraged them to do so. Lloyd George was a leader without a real party; his every move was closely monitored by the Conservatives who dominated his coalition government. And, like Orlando and Clemenceau, he was buffeted by a raging current of populist xenophobia – emotions he had encouraged by his promises during the election campaign to hang the Kaiser. The war itself had been a great democratic act; the participation of the masses in the victory implied that those same masses would influence the shape of the peace, if only indirectly. The people were both assertive and impatient for a return to 'normality' but also determined that Germany should pay. Delays in the settlement would not be tolerated. This impatience in part explains the absence of the Germans. What we know as the peace conference was not originally meant to be that at all. The delegates had gathered at Versailles to agree on the terms of the settlement, before dealing with German representatives at the formal conference. But that preliminary process proved so difficult and time-consuming that it became, in essence, the conference itself.

The German settlement

The settlement with Germany, known afterwards as the Treaty of Versailles, had five principal parts. The first pertained to the establishment of the League of Nations, an aspect duplicated in each of the separate treaties with Austria, Hungary, Bulgaria and Turkey. The League was the great noble ambition of Wilson, who insisted that discussion of it should have priority over all other matters. Here he clashed with Clemenceau, who was more interested in hard regulations that would limit the future power of Germany and would punish her for the suffering she had caused. But, eventually, the French gave way when they became convinced that the League might be useful in enforcing the punitive resolutions they wanted.

The French disagreed with Wilson on the form the League would take. Again reflecting their prevailing security concerns, they sought a body in which membership would be mandatory and which would have its own independent military force. Wilson considered this impracticable and ideologically absurd. It would, he felt, be counterproductive for an international organization formed to promote peace immediately to make enemies of those states that refused to join. Eventually, the representatives agreed to implement the general plan put forth by the American David Hunter Miller and the Englishman C. J. Hurst, which conformed quite closely to what Wilson had envisaged. The plan called for a Secretariat with executive functions, a Council (consisting of France, Britain, Italy, Japan and the United States as permanent members, and four other members selected by the Assembly), and an Assembly consisting of all member nations.

The second part of the Versailles Treaty pertained to the requirement that Germany surrender territory annexed in previous wars. German expansion had been one of the most contentious issues before the war, and indeed was one of the reasons why France approached what should have been a defensive war in an offensive fashion. Here, the delegates appear to have had a long memory. Territories stripped from Denmark and France were relatively easy to restore to their former owners. But in the case of Polish territory, some of which had been acquired during the partition struggles of the eighteenth century, dispersal was not quite so easy. There was enormous resentment within Germany toward the establishment of an independent Polish state, but the Wilsonian principle of self-determination implied that such an outcome was justified.

A viable Polish state, it was felt, needed access to the sea, through the port of Danzig. But that city had a predominantly German population. It was eventually decided that the port itself should become a free city administered by the League of Nations, a solution which simply replaced one problem with another. The 'Polish Corridor' to Danzig cut off approximately 1.5 million Germans in East Prussia from the rest of Germany. They were guaranteed free transit across the corridor, but that concession did little to cool tempers. It would henceforth be easy to whip up German nationalism in East Prussia, as Hitler later discovered.

The Eastern border of Poland was also a vexing problem, made more so by the fact that Russia was not present at the conference. In December 1919 a commission headed by Lord Curzon devised a boundary which managed to annoy both the Russians and the Poles. The issue was eventually settled on the battlefield, with the Poles victorious. The Treaty of Riga of March 1921 subsequently set a border acceptable to the Poles and grudgingly accepted by the Russians.

In Silesia, the Germans had carried out a systematic policy of colonization in the decades before the war. As in all colonies, the master race took over the positions of power, while the native peoples provided the labourers. Around two million Germans were firmly ensconced in the region, living a life that they did not wish to surrender. Their absorption into the new Poland not only flew in the face of self-determination, but created a ready source of tinder for future conflagrations. Lloyd George recognized as much when he warned in March 1919 of the dangers of placing so many Germans under foreign control:

> I cannot imagine any greater cause for future war than that the German people, who have proved themselves one of the most powerful and vigorous races of the world, should be surrounded by a number of small States, many of them consisting of peoples who have never previously set up a stable government for themselves, but each containing large masses of Germans clamouring for reunion with their native land. [85, pp. 113–14]

Lloyd George's concerns exposed the conflict between *realpolitik* and self-determination. Under the Wilsonian formula, small states like Poland had justification for existence. Their instability was in large measure due to the German contempt for self-determination over the previous century. Dispossessed Germans in the new states were only there in the first place because of the imperial ambitions of their forebears. But, however much Wilson might have wished, the past could not be erased. There was a certain rough justice in the new configuration, but not a great deal of stability.

The third part of the Treaty dealt with measures designed to limit the ability of Germany to wage war in the future. The British and the Americans were satisfied to restrict Germany to a small professional army of a size not dissimilar to their own. But the French feared that this would be made into a force designed for rapid expansion. In response to this problem, the representatives decided to limit the German army to 100 000 men who would serve 12-year enlistments. This ruled out the creation of a reservoir of trained men through a short enlistment period. It was furthermore decided that Germany should be prohibited an air force, tanks, or heavy artillery. The navy was to be limited to six pre-Dreadnought battleships, six light cruisers and twelve destroyers. Still feeling the bruises of the undersea war, the delegates further stipulated that Germany would be allowed no submarines.

The question of preventing future German aggression brought to mind another issue, that of protecting France, the likely victim of such aggression. The French wanted a series of buffer states in the territory west of the Rhine. Wilson and Lloyd George vetoed this idea, partly because of the military commitment it implied, but also because they feared that it would simply create a powerful stimulus for German retribution – a sort of Alsace-Lorraine in reverse. Clemenceau remained steadfast, though he insisted that he had no desire to annex the area for France. It was eventually decided that the region would be permanently demilitarized and the eastern side of the river would be kept free of military activity to a depth of 50 kilometres. Clemenceau accepted this concession only after the British and Americans promised to come to the aid of France if Germany ever attacked. In the meantime, the area would be divided into three sectors. The British would police the northern sector around the Rhine bridgehead at Cologne for five years, the Americans the middle sector around Koblenz for ten years, and the French the southern sector around Mainz for fifteen years.

The fourth part of the Treaty dealt with reparations. Behind the subject of reparations lay the question of guilt. Recompense could not be sought unless it was established that the war itself and the damage it caused were the fault of the Germans. The representatives plainly felt that Germany was to blame, but they were hardly unbiased. German culpability was formally established through the notorious Article 231, the 'war-guilt clause'. Seldom has an issue of such profound long-term implications been decided with so little deliberation. Related to this issue was the stipulation that around 100 'war criminals' should stand trial for 'acts against the laws and customs of war'. At the top of the list was the Kaiser, but it also included almost all U-boat commanders.

Guilt thus established, the representatives moved on to the question of damages. Here, two forces crashed head-on. The first was the powerful desire for retribution by those countries that had suffered terribly in the war, namely Britain, France and Italy. In January 1918, Lloyd George had asserted the right of the Entente Powers to 'political and economic restoration of the invaded countries, and for reparations for injuries done in violation of international law'. [136, p. 548] That desire had been transformed into a formidable populist political force, as the case of Britain illustrates. At the 1918 election, the British were whipped into righteous fury by promises of squeezing the German lemon until the pips squeaked.

The second force was that of reason and morality, of which the United States was the self-appointed arbiter. Wilson felt that the negotiations presented an opportunity to move away from old style diplomacy and the idea of a vengeful peace, which reparations implied. He had stated quite clearly that there should be 'no annexations, no contributions, no punitive indemnities'. [100, p. 193] It was also argued that a harsh peace would merely sow the seeds of the next war; reparations would be a constant reminder of a humiliation that needed to be righted. Others, including the British economist John Maynard Keynes, chief treasury representative at Versailles, argued that reparations would destabilize economies, not just within Germany, but within the whole international system of trade.

Reparations were designed both to provide recompense and to keep Germany weak. But the latter goal was riddled with pitfalls and contradictions. A weak Germany could not very well pay the reparations, while a strong Germany might feel sufficiently confident to refuse payment. Keeping Germany poor might also increase the appeal of Bolshevism within the country and strengthen the desire for revenge. Pragmatists, though few in number, also realized that the recovery of European trade required a healthy German economy. Impoverished Germans were not likely to buy foreign goods.

It was inevitable that the forces of retribution would prove more powerful than those of reason. But, though the support for reparations was overwhelming, there was little agreement on their appropriate level. Since the war had been fought in areas outside Germany, the victors had suffered a great deal more than the vanquished. Whole areas of France and Belgium lay desolate. The damage to British shipping was likewise immense. There was also considerable argument about whether the damages suffered by the soldiers should be included in the calculation. Should, for instance, Germany be required to contribute to British and French war pensions? To include these damages would go against the traditional definition of the soldier, for whom suffering and loss are an implied part of the job. But others argued that the soldiers in question were not professionals but mere civilians whose lives had been disrupted against their will.

Reparations came in two kinds: land and money. In the former category, the Saar industrial region was separated from Germany and was to be administered by the League for the benefit of France and Belgium, in compensation for the damage caused by Germany to the industrial regions of those two countries. After fifteen years, a plebiscite would be held to determine whether the area would be returned to Germany. If the people voted to do so (as they almost certainly would) Germany would still be required to buy back the mines in the region.

As for the issue of monetary recompense, there was at least some recognition that it was illogical (other than in a purely symbolic sense) to set a figure wildly in excess of what Germany could pay over a reasonable period of time. But even with this limitation, estimates still ranged from £2000 million to £24 000 million, figures which were, it must be said, well below the total value of the damage caused. Eventually Article 232 defined the limits of Allied claims:

> The Allied and Associated Governments recognise that the resources of Germany are not adequate, after taking into account permanent diminutions of such resources which will result from other provisions of the present Treaty, to make complete reparation for all such loss and damage. The Allied and Associated Governments, however, require, and Germany undertakes, that she will make compensation for all damage done to the civilian population of the Allied and Associated Powers and to their property during the period of the belligerency of each as an Allied or Associated Power against Germany by such aggression by land, by sea and from the air. [136, p. 555]

The delegates also disagreed about how to distribute the money collected. Each country inflated its claims not out of greed toward Germany, but in order to gain a higher proportion of whatever final amount was imposed. In the end, deciding on a figure proved far too divisive and problematic for the delegates, who eventually commissioned a body of experts to report on the matter within two years. In the meantime, the Treaty stipulated that Germany should pay an immediate £1000 million, in addition to interest bearing bonds of another £4000 million. In April 1921, the final figure was set at £6600 million. The decision to confine the calculations to civilian damage took some of the sting out of the tail of Article 231. But for Germany, post-war resentment was founded not on the amount of the reparations but on their existence at all, and what that implied – namely war guilt.

The fifth part of the Treaty dealt with the dispersal of former German colonies to the Allied powers. The importance of this matter was more symbolic than real. The colonies had been accumulated by a jealous Germany to try to gain late admission to the imperial club. The question of who controlled them had always been more important than their inherent value. Germany's exports to her African colonies, for instance, constituted just one third of one per cent of her total foreign trade. The British, in particular, wanted to ensure that the colonies ended up in the right hands, since they might otherwise be used as naval bases to threaten British control of the seas.

During the war the forces of the British Empire, South Africa, and Japan had conquered German colonies. No power wanted to give up what it had conquered, even if the prize was hardly worthy of possession. But the ideal of self-determination militated against a cynical carving up of colonial spoils. A legal fudge was invented to deal with this embarrassing contradiction: the territories were not annexed outright, but instead were mandated under the authority of the League of Nations, which held ultimate power over their administration. But, beyond the legal definition, there was little difference between a colony and a mandated territory – at least according to enthusiastic imperialists in Britain. Nor could anyone pretend that mandated status meant an automatic improvement in the fortunes of the former colony. A transfer from German rule to Belgian or South African did not necessarily benefit native peoples.

On 7 May 1919 the terms of the peace were presented to the Germans. They were given fifteen days to respond. On receiving the terms, Count Brockdorff-Rantzau, the German foreign minister, showed no sign of contrition. He proceeded to condemn the Allies for killing hundreds of civilians through the continued imposition of the blockade and also demanded a neutral commission to investigate the question of responsibility for the war. Needless to say, this response only served to confirm the feeling within the Allied countries that retribution was justified. It also raised fears that Germany would refuse to sign the Treaty, to the extent that Lloyd George concluded that an occupation of Berlin might be necessary as 'an outward and visible sign of smashing the Junkers'. [136, p. 562]

In a series of responses, the Germans objected to the harshness of the Treaty and to the fact they had been swindled – made to believe that 'Germany's lot would be fundamentally altered if it were

severed from the fate of its rulers'. [136, p. 564–6] In intentionally apocalyptic tones it was argued that 'those who will sign this
Treaty will sign the death sentence of many millions of German
men, women and children'. Brockdorff-Rantzau warned that it
would condemn the German people to 'perpetual slave labour' and
accused the Reparations Commission of seeking 'dictatorial powers
over the whole life of our people in economic and cultural matters'.
[112, p. 87]

In reply, the Allies argued that the change of government had
been all too cynical. It was, in other words, difficult to accept that
the German people who, throughout the war, had 'obeyed every
order, however savage, of their government', had now undergone
such a rapid and profound transformation. As to the German claim
that the terms were an affront to justice, the Allies replied:

> Justice is what the German delegation asks for, and says that
> Germany had been promised. But it must be justice for all. ...
> Somebody must suffer for the consequences of the war. Is it to be
> Germany, or only the peoples she has wronged? ... Not to do
> justice to all concerned would only leave the world open to fresh
> calamities. ... if there is to be early reconciliation and appease-
> ment, it will be because those responsible for concluding the war
> have had the courage to see that justice is not deflected for the
> sake of a convenient peace. [136, pp. 564–6]

There followed a period of bickering over the specific terms of the
Treaty - the surrender of German colonies, the formation of the
new Polish state, the question of reparations, and so on. Finally, on
16 June the Germans were presented with a slightly modified set of
terms and told that their reply had to be forthcoming within a week.
The government subsequently fell, with the irascible Brockdorff-
Rantzau replaced by Hermann Müller. He tried to secure further
concessions, but without success. On 28 June the Treaty was signed
in the Galerie des Glaces at Versailles. It was, in truth, neither
a treaty nor an agreement, but a set of terms imposed upon a
defeated power.

Division of the Hapsburg spoils

The war had destroyed the Hapsburg and Ottoman Empires,
neither of which could be reassembled, even if a desire to do so

existed. The British briefly toyed with the idea of maintaining the Hapsburg Empire after the war, as long as it could be detached from Germany. This certainly seemed attractive in comparison to the instability that would inevitably result from the formation of a number of independent states in south-eastern Europe, all with a grudge to bear. But by the time the war was over, the glue that had held disparate peoples together had disintegrated. The peace-makers could either create new nations, or split the Hapsburg spoils among existing ones. Thus, delegates approved the establishment of Czechoslovakia and Poland, while enlarging Romania and Italy. The remaining Balkan regions were amalgamated into the King-dom of the Serbs, Croats and Slovenes, which formally became Yugoslavia in 1929. The ethnic quarrels that had weakened the old Empire now troubled a new set of states.

In addressing the ethnic question, the delegates found themselves on a hiding to nothing. Wilson's adherence to the principles of self-determination did not take into account the fact that ethnic groups lived amongst each other in central and south-eastern Europe. To separate them and give each a distinct nation with which to identify was impossible. The new states had to be viable, and economic viability often conflicted with self-determination. Thus, in the case of Czechoslovakia, the new nation consisted of the Czech provinces of Bohemia and Moravia (formerly administered by Austria), in addition to Slovakia (formerly part of Hungary), and Ruthenia. Viability dictated the inclusion of the Sudetenland, despite the fact that the inhabitants were mainly Austrians (Sudeten Germans). No one ethnic group was dominant, and the German population in the west was ominously large. Yet there was at least a will among the people to make the new state succeed, and a healthy industrial base.

The Yugoslav problem was even more complex. In 1917 the Corfu Manifesto established the intention of the ethnic groups in the region to unite under one national banner. The new state was inevitably dominated by Serbia, whose rulers were not particularly interested in ethnic diversity. They hoped instead to create a mini-Empire in the Balkans, not unlike what they had been trying to achieve before the war. The linguistic, cultural and religious differ-ences that divided the various ethnic groups did not bode well for the future. One needs only to bear in mind the troubled state of the region in the 1990s to understand how difficult it was to establish a peaceful and harmonious nation.

Romania did well out of the peace, mainly because the Allied powers were keen to punish Russia and build a state strong enough to resist any moves toward a Hapsburg restoration. Romania was given the Dobrudja, the eastern Banat and Transylvania, and, somewhat surprisingly, was gifted Bessarabia, in order to keep the latter out of Russian hands. Bulgaria, punished for its role in the war, was forced to give western Thrace to Greece and western Macedonia to the new state of Yugoslavia. This meant that she was now cut off from direct access to the Mediterranean, which adversely affected her economic viability.

The secret Treaty of London promised Italy the opportunity of eastward expansion in exchange for her agreement to fight on the side of the Entente. Aside from the obvious greed that lay behind this agreement, there was a legitimate feeling on the part of the Italians that they needed the territory in order to protect themselves from Austro-Hungarian aggression. But therein lay the fallacy in the treaty: if the Allies won the war the buffer zone would not be needed because Austria-Hungary would be defeated, leading to her disintegration. A dead dog does not bite. Yet if the Allies lost the war, the agreement would be moot, since Italy could hardly press her claim against a victorious Hapsburg Empire.

When it came time to discuss this aspect of the settlement, the Hapsburg Empire had ceased to exist. Italy could hardly make a case for needing protection in a region where she was now the dominant power. Wilson, in any case, had no intention of honouring secret treaties of this nature since they went against his sacred principles. Italy nevertheless managed to secure the Trentino (or Austrian Tyrol) up to the Brenner Pass, the coastal province of Gorizia-Gradisca, and the ports of Trieste and Istria. Orlando also wanted the city of Fiume in Dalmatia, but Wilson refused on the grounds that, though the city itself was largely Italian, the surrounding countryside was Slavic. He felt, therefore, that the area should rightly go to the newly formed Yugoslavia. Orlando then threatened to refuse to join the League of Nations, and received some support from Clemenceau and Lloyd George, both of whom were keen to score points with the Italians in order to gain concessions in other areas. Wilson, supremely sure of himself, was determined to win this point. Confident that Orlando did not enjoy the support of the Italian people, he astonishingly made a direct appeal to them to reject the their leader's demands. Orlando left the conference in disgust and Wilson had his way – for the moment.

But, he had misread the feelings of the Italian people, who cheered when Gabriele d'Annunzio marched into Fiume at the head of a band of Italian volunteers in September 1919. Shortly over a year later, Yugoslav and Italian delegates agreed at Rapallo that Fiume should go to Italy.

The areas that were left became independent Austria and Hungary. In trying to punish those two peoples for their part in the war, the Allied representatives created states that had little ethnic logic and were not economically strong. Austria consisted of just 6.5 million people, a third of whom lived in Vienna. There was little in this new creation upon which to base a viable national identity and groups within the country argued vehemently among themselves over whether the state should exist at all. A powerful lobby pressed incessantly for *Anschluss* (union with Germany), which was formally prohibited under the terms of the treaties. The determination of Britain and France to block such a union made the idea all the more attractive to Germans and Austrians. But the fact that self-determination was quite clearly not being applied to the German people left the victorious powers open to charges of hypocrisy.

The new Austrian nation had few friends in Eastern Europe. The successor states, especially Yugoslavia and Romania, delighted in seeing Austria reduced to an ineffectual rump. They still harboured great bitterness toward the Austrians and were therefore determined to make life difficult for them, mainly through trade barriers restricting access to traditional markets. In contrast, Hungary was a great deal more economically viable than Austria, but was still troubled by a lack of self-confidence as a nation. Sixty-five per cent of its former territory had been distributed among the successor states, including Transylvania with its large Magyar population.

Thus, the new states in Eastern Europe may have had more logic ethnically than the old Hapsburg Empire ever had, but ethnic ties were not enough on their own to make strong nations. The Allied representatives were adept at drawing boundaries on maps, but seemed to give little consideration to the problems of nation-building. They had created new states in a once-turbulent region, but had not removed the source of the turbulence. The compromise between economic viability and self-determination resulted in a number of ominous contradictions, as in the case of the Sudetenland. That problem troubled the representatives, but not as much as it might have done had they possessed either a good crystal ball or a keen sense of history. The possibility that they were bequeathing terrible problems to the next generation did not divert them from their course. In truth, their main aim was to sort out matters on their doorstep, namely the problem of Germany. The rest of Europe had been a sideshow during the war and continued to be so after it.

The Eastern question

The same ethnic difficulties that plagued the settlement of the old Hapsburg Empire repeated themselves when it came to the dispersal of Ottoman territories. The British had an extra agenda, namely that, in order to ensure their hegemony in the area, they had to keep the Turks as weak as possible. Lloyd George even wanted to deny the Turks Constantinople, but was persuaded otherwise by his Cabinet. The Treaty of Sèvres was largely an expression of British interests in the old Ottoman region. Turkey was forced to give up her non-Turkish populations, with Palestine, Transjordan, and Iraq being mandated to Britain, and Syria and Lebanon to the French. The straits – the object of such bitter fighting during the war – were internationalized.

British imperialists felt reasonably satisfied with the spoils of victory in the Middle East. As the arch-imperialist Leopold Amery saw it, in order to defeat Germany, Britain had been

> compelled to complete the liberation of the Arabs, to make secure the independence of Persia ... to protect tropical Africa from German economic and military exploitation. All these objects are justifiable in themselves and don't become less so because they increase the general sphere of British influence. ... And if, when it is all over, ... the British Commonwealth emerges greater in area and resources who has the right to complain? [2, vol. 2, p. 161]

Wilson certainly felt that he had right to complain. His policy of self-determination inspired Arab separatists and angered British imperialists. British indebtedness to America meant that Wilson's scruples could not be ignored. Technically, the new possessions were not colonies, but territories mandated under League authority. Britain was supposed to help them along the road to self-determination. But, as Amery confessed, 'I do not think that the Mandate is likely to impose upon us any conditions which we would not impose upon ourselves or which we have not been in the habit of imposing upon ourselves whenever we deal with subject peoples.' [138, c 2175]

The striking feature of the Ottoman settlement and indeed of the way the former German colonies were redistributed, was the continued assumption of the European right to govern. The Middle East was not yet considered a problem between Arab and Jew, but instead remained one between France and Britain. The same could be said of Africa. The settlements reached were therefore designed to insure European harmony rather than the stability of the native peoples who lived in the region. The war had not shaken European confidence in the right to rule.

In retrospect

Despite the popularity of the Wilsonian formula at the start of the conference, what emerged was not an American treaty. The settlement reflected the characters of all the participants, but, in general, Clemenceau's political savvy and Lloyd George's cynicism got the better of Wilson's moralistic egotism. Clemenceau did not get the buffer states he hoped for, but the map of Europe was redrawn with French security in mind. Self-determination was implemented not because of its moral value, but because it proved a useful tool for containing German ambitions. Germany was held in check by giving encouragement to Slavic nationalism. Austria was emasculated. Thus, the old German partnership was now surrounded by an angry pack of dogs. Granted, this meant the Balkanization of the Balkans, but the merits of that solution have to be judged by its alternatives. At the time, it seemed better, and certainly more just, to have south-eastern Europe broken into pieces than dominated by Germany or Russia. It is all very well to claim that the area was unstable and torn by tribal jealousies, but, as the last years of the Hapsburg Empire had demonstrated, there was no real stability in denying self-determination. The aspirations of the Poles, Serbs and Czechs would not simply disappear if they were once again herded into a sup-ranational state.

But the system required a strong France to work, and in 1918 France was not strong and had little prospect of becoming so. Though Britain agreed to the shape of the settlement, she was not warmly inclined toward its implications. She had always feared French hegemony as much as German. Four years of war had not altered those fears all that much. 'I am seriously afraid', wrote Lord Curzon (a member of the War Cabinet) in December 1918, 'that the great power from whom we have most to fear in future is France'. [101, p. 191] Britain was therefore keen to welcome Germany back into the fold as quickly as possible (the better to improve the British balance of trade), yet the Versailles formula depended on Germany being kept weak.

The Versailles settlement has been blamed for causing the Second World War. Because we know that a Second World War occurred, it is easy to judge in retrospect that the treaty was too harsh. All told, Germany was required to surrender 13 per cent of her area, 12 per cent of her population, 16 per cent of her coal production, 48 per cent of her iron production, 10 per cent of her manufacturing capacity and 15 per cent of her agricultural land. This harshness had a dual effect: it encouraged a desire for revenge within Germany and an embarrassed feeling of contrition among some groups in Britain. Thus, when the time came that Germany felt able to exact her revenge, the British were less inclined to react because many believed that her anger was warranted.

Another school holds that Germany was not punished enough. There are those, for instance, who argue that the war ended too soon, that Germany's offer of an armistice should have been refused and that her army should have been pushed back across the Rhine so that its defeat would subsequently have been undeniable. (Pershing, at one point during the final months, put forth such an argument, but quickly realized that it was not likely to gain approval.) Those who adhere to this school often also feel that the Treaty established the principle of war guilt, which encouraged German resentment, but did not sufficiently destroy the German ability to act upon that resentment. Bearing in mind the way Hitler manipulated the propaganda value of the 'unjust' peace, it seems the argument has some merit. But punishment, be it of nations or children, often has the opposite effect intended. Could Germany's aggressive power be destroyed by any means? And, if those means were available, would the Allies have been prepared to make the sacrifices necessary to implement them? As with the idea of a push across the Rhine, so too with an extremely harsh peace: which country would have been prepared to forfeit the lives of its citizens in order to make the victory more emphatic and the peace more severe?

It is difficult to imagine a treaty that would have satisfied the Entente Powers and left the Germans feeling that they had been treated fairly. France and Belgium required some compensation given the physical destruction wrought in those two countries. Germany – in contrast – was hardly touched. A more liberal treaty might have brought into being a more peaceful, secure Europe, but the populist mood was not liberal. Colonel House, Wilson's aide, confessed that he would have 'preferred a different peace'. But, he admitted, it was 'too much too expect of men come together at such a time and for such a purpose'. [66, p. 105] The Treaty was flawed, but it was not unworkable, as long as it was seen as the beginning rather than the end of the peace process. In July 1919, Lloyd George told the House of Commons that he hoped that the League of Nations would remedy the 'crudities' of the settlement. Wilson had similar hopes. Unfortunately, the League never had the power to fulfil their wishes.

The flaws in the Treaty did not alone cause the Second World War. Germany was able to act upon her resentment because the country that emerged most powerful from the First World War decided subsequently to absent herself from European affairs. Republicans led by Senator Henry Cabot Lodge, refused to ratify the Treaty and, in the process, vetoed American membership of the League of Nations. Guarantees made to France were also left unratified. Power implies responsibility, yet the US, in the interwar period, sought an isolationist haven, where it would not have to apply its power at all. It is by no means clear that American membership in the League would have prevented the Second World War. But it is certain that America's decision to turn her back on Europe created a power vacuum that Hitler was able to exploit.

10
'The Rank Stench of those Bodies Haunts Me Still'

The psychological effects of the war are often commented upon, but seldom seriously studied, perhaps because of the difficulty of measuring grief. Across Europe, the losses caused by the war were prodigious. France lost 1.3 million men killed, Russia and Germany nearly 2 million, Italy 500 000 and the British Empire almost a million. Demographers argue that post-war baby booms and changes in patterns of emigration quickly rectified these losses. But not in the hearts of those who suffered a loved one's departure or those who had to witness the carnage. 'The best of me died at Bapaume', wrote the poet Olive Lindsay; 'When the world went up in fire'. [92, p. 64]

For the ex-soldier, the war experience was a fully laden pack which he could not easily discard. Some wrote memoirs or poetry in an ambitious, but usually futile, effort at purgation. Many simply reminisced with other old soldiers, in pubs or ex-servicemen's clubs. Others were driven mad remembering. The horror of war slowly consumed them like a relentless cancer. They existed in limbo between madness and sanity, suffering from what might today be called post-traumatic stress. Some eventually exorcised the past; others were plagued by ghosts for the rest of their lives. Smells, sounds, faces would suddenly bring to the surface long forgotten horrors. 'The rank stench of those bodies haunts me still,/And I remember things I'd best forget', wrote Siegfried Sassoon. [102, p. 124]

The dead had to be remembered, but remembrance was often too painful. The ubiquity of death challenged traditional processes of mourning. Guillaume Apollinaire wrote:

> Here you are beside me again
> Memories of my companions killed in the war
> The olive branch of time
> Memories that make only a single memory

200

As a hundred skins make only a single coat
As these thousands of wounds make only a single
    newspaper article [102, p. 243]

Charles Hamilton Sorley wrote:

When you see the millions of mouthless dead
Across your dreams in pale battalions go,
... should you
Perceive one face that you loved heretofore,
It is a spook. None wears the face you knew.
Great death has made all his for evermore. [102, p. 89–90]

Whereas the literature of those who fought evokes memories of the 'pale battalions', when civilians grieved, they grieved alone over a very personal loss. Those at home might not have been able to grasp the millions of mouthless dead, but they had no difficulty comprehending an empty chair at dinner. Sorley's sense of futility is understandable, but so is the desperation of those civilians intent upon remembering that 'one face'. It is no wonder that, across Europe, the popularity of spiritualism increased massively in the immediate post war years.

Coming to terms with the war often meant honouring the lost loved one as a hero whose cause was worthy. Death had to have justification, for futility combined with loss was too much to bear. In Britain, immediate postwar evocations of the conflict bear a striking resemblance to perceptions of it in August 1914. The war was a 'great triumph and a great deliverance', the *Daily Mail* commented on Armistice Day 1919. [20, p. 281] John Stanhope Arkwright, perhaps the most widely read poet during the war, managed to maintain visions of heroic sacrifice throughout the conflict – explanation, perhaps, of his extraordinary popularity. His poem 'Armistice' seems a far cry from the sense of futility evident in the work of Owen or Sassoon:

Bow down, Old Land, at the altar-steps of God;
Thank Him for Peace – thank Him for Victory;
But chiefly thank him that thy feet have trod
The path of honour in the Agony. [13, p. 340]

It may have been a modern war, but the British mourned their dead according to very traditional patterns.

In France, there was a sense of deliverance but not really of victory. Measured in terms of the percentage of the population killed, the French sacrifice was greater than any of the other major belligerents. The loss was too great to permit any real sense of celebration, which might explain why Armistice Day was observed in a much more muted fashion than in Britain. Henri Barbusse, whose writings reflected the French sense of duty and determination at the beginning of the war and the sense of unretrievable loss at the end of it, counselled his countrymen on the best way to mourn the dead:

> The only acceptable attitude ... is to bring to their tombs ... impeccable silence. At least, if we do not speak in their name, no one else should dare to do so. A father has no moral right to use the heroic death of his son to add bluster to his personal prestige, to draw admiration to himself. ... [or] to support a politico-commercial doctrine which, consciously or not, would provoke new massacres and lead humanity into the abyss. [130, p. 182]

In *Les Croix de Bois,* by Roland Dorgelès, the protagonist, Sulphart, takes issue with an acquaintance who argues that the end of war came too late for anyone to claim victory. When challenged to explain how it might be seen as a victory,

> Suphart, disconcerted, hesitated for a moment, groping for the words which eluded him, to explain his wild happiness. Then, without even understanding the terrible significance of his statement, he answered simply: 'I think it's a victory because I've got out of it alive ...' [13, p. 344]

It was difficult for the French to make sense of a war in which victory was defined as mere survival.

In Germany, where a sense of triumph was obviously inappropriate, those who had served and those who had died were still considered heroes, even if their efforts had fallen short of victory. There was great confusion and argument over how to remember the war. When a national war memorial was unveiled in 1924, the occasion prompted rioting between rival political groups, each with a different spin on the past. In *Otto Babendiek,* Gustav Frensen urged his countrymen to see the war as a triumph of the German spirit:

> We have no need to feel ashamed, for we have suffered a thousand
> times more, both officers and men, and have been a thousand
> times braver, than our enemies. So let us march back covered with
> laurels ... back to our homes under old Hindenburg! [13, p. 342]

The soldiers' heroism gave added weight to the sense that they had
been betrayed. They were transformed into martyrs stabbed in the
back by a cowardly government. The myth of swindle had power
because there were so many victims to give it force and because
of the indisputable fact that German soldiers were still an army of
occupation at the time of the Armistice. Soldiers who felt betrayal
most acutely found in right-wing movements a way to recover pride
and to plot revenge. In *The Road Back* by Erich Maria Remarque,
Heel, a quintessentially German officer, vents his frustration by
joining the *Freikorps* so that he can continue to wage war against
those whom he blames for Germany's emasculated state. 'It cannot be that two million Germans should have fallen in vain' Adolf
Hitler proclaimed in 1922. 'No, we do not pardon, we demand –
vengeance!' [56, p. 3]

The Americans celebrated victory most enthusiastically, for the
simple reason that it had come at manageable cost. William J.
Newlin, Professor of Philosophy at Amherst College, expressed a
popular sentiment when he praised the way men of widely diverse
ethnic origins had joined together to save the world:

> from English to Greek, from French to Slav – Americans all.
> What force welded such widely diverse elements into unity?
> Something that makes them give up life itself if thereby they
> can help to win for their fellows that which they all value in
> common – freedom and liberty and justice for all men, every-
> where, the right of self-determination; and the opportunity for
> unhindered self-development. [76, p. 195]

It was the opportunity for unhindered self-development which
seemed the juiciest fruit of victory. Lieutenant John Seerly wrote in
the magazine *The New Success*:

> every man in the American army ... 'got together' in a comradely
> fashion that would have stopped class struggles over here long
> ago if each of us had not been too stubborn in the past to give

way an inch on account of misunderstanding. A better world and a better spirit of business is bound to come with the returning soldier. [76, p. 199]

This glorious war apparently produced neither cripples nor emotional wrecks. The same magazine celebrated the story of a bakery wagon driver who before the war earned $11 per week. After service in France, he returned suffering from heart disease and neurasthenia. Unable to resume his previous employment, he was sent on a stenography course and landed a job earning $100 per month. Disillusion was a decidedly un-American emotion.

The rank stench of those bodies haunted nations as well as individuals. The various belligerents tried, each in their own way, to construct a world that would honour the dead but, more importantly, would also prevent such a catastrophe happening again. The imperfect peace is a manifestation of these competing visions of the post-war world. France, haunted by Verdun, assumed a defensive mentality in the mistaken belief that fortifications could keep war itself at bay. Britain felt guilty about the peace, and eventually guilty about the war. The belief that the sacrifice had been worthwhile lasted perhaps ten years. But by 1928, Haig was dead and it was open season on those commanders deemed to have squandered the lives of the innocent. The war poets like Sassoon, Owen, Rosenberg and Sorley grew immensely popular because the sense of futility they evoked harmonized with a common disillusionment. The popular temper was translated into public policy, manifested in a desire to appease Germany and to reject rearmament. Those who embraced pacifism were oftentimes simply frightened of war.

The French and British abhorrence of war provided the perfect hothouse in which the German desire for revenge could grow. In Britain, hatred of war and scorn for the peace were two sides of the same coin. Those not tortured by memories were driven by pragmatism: there was a widespread recognition within the British business community that economic growth depended upon German revival. French bitterness was less easily erased. France remained deeply suspicious of Germany and fearful of a German resurgence but lacked the energy to turn her fears into spirited resistance. In any case, the agreements made at Versailles, which were designed to guarantee France's safety, turned out to be hollow promises. Hitler's cleverness lay in exploiting the pusillanimity of Germany's former enemies.

As for the Austrians, they still craved the limelight even if they no longer lived under it. Those who found enforced insignificance intolerable now saw redemption in pan-German terms. *Anschluss* (union with Germany) was increasingly given a patriotic presentation, despite the fact that its proponents were fully aware that any sort of amalgamation meant in truth a subservience to Berlin reminiscent of the war years. It is ironic that those who argued for a separate Austrian identity were often branded traitors to the Austrian cause.

The Russians were keen for the moment to turn their back upon Europe. But fear of Germany was still deeply felt. That fear led to clumsy contradictions in the application of Marxist ideology. The new Russian government liked to project itself as the friend of anti-colonial movements, but could not resist the temptation to pursue its own imperialist inclinations, supposedly out of self-protection. European socialists often turned a blind eye toward Russian excesses in the belief that Marxism remained the last best hope for mankind. But for most of Europe, the presence of the Russian bogey inspired greater tolerance toward Germany. For the British in particular, friendliness toward the Germans seemed a sensible way to build a bulwark against the communist tide.

The rank stench did not apparently haunt Americans. They went to war believing in their righteous cause and afterwards maintained a sense of noble accomplishment even if the world was not remotely safe for democracy. A history devoid of bitter memories is easily forgotten. The Americans are, in any case, expert at turning their backs on the past. One American soldier, fed up with having to guard the Rhine bridgehead at Koblenz, looked forward to his return Stateside:

> Yes, Coblenz town's a fine town, as towns in Europe go,
> But give me towns to westward, where life moves
>   not so slow,
> With fewer castles, maybe, – more future and less past,
> And then I'll give up roaming, and settle down
>   at last. [76, p. 207]

Any residual feeling of disappointment with the peace was quickly subsumed by the euphoria which the new economic order inspired. America, alone among the combatants, emerged from the war richer and more economically powerful than when she had entered it.

In these circumstances, it was no struggle to turn away from sordid Europe. Isolation seemed morally right and economically feasible. 'We have had a panoramic view of Europe from Russia to Italy and the more we see of the world the better we love America', one soldier wrote. 'Regardless of what our politics have been in the past our votes in the future will be controlled by one policy – America first.' [76, p. 211]

Americans saw their country as 'a lovely flower having its roots in mire ... [which has] sprung up out of the chaos of the muddy bloody ruin into which the War has plunged the world'. [76, p. 209] Though nauseatingly egocentric, that view was not altogether inaccurate. For the nations of Europe, the war had been fought either for protection or aggrandizement. Yet all had lost. Even the victorious were plunged into steep decline. The United States, on the other hand, did not seek the war, but was massively enriched by it. One soldier was certain that the war experience would strengthen America because it had hardened her sons:

> The tooth-brush, the daily drill, the regular meals, the smooth shave, the clean shirt, the daily bath, the easy footwear, have all played their part. We are heavier, we are taller, we are stronger and returning, we will infuse the iron of our blood into the nation and give her vigour. [76, p. 212]

For most of Europe the war had meant carnage, futility, mud and blood. For Americans, it meant clean socks and healthy teeth.

Before the war, restless modernists bemoaned the stability, predictability and complacence of pre-war Europe. In the chaos of war, they argued, lay the discovery of a deeply buried soul. The war certainly brought chaos. Those who craved instability enjoyed brief satisfaction. But there was little redemption in carnage. After the war, the Versailles settlement and economic dislocation ensured that chaos became the natural order. The map of Europe might perhaps have been a more accurate representation of national identities than that which had existed before 1914, but the price of respecting those identities was greater instability. Before 1914, a stable world was cause for restlessness; after 1918, the chaos and uncertainty of the world made stability and order seem very attractive.

Appendix: Guide to Further Reading

Full details of the books listed below are provided in the bibliography which follows.

General histories

For understandable reasons, most of the general histories of the war which have been published in English betray a British perspective. By the far the best is Keegan's *The First World War*. It covers a huge amount of ground in a relatively short book, yet still manages to include the essential detail which gives the account its dramatic impact. Among the other surveys, Cruttwell's *A History of the Great War* and *The First World War*, by Falls, remain very useful. Both are written in a lively style which students will find sustaining. For a general history which pays attention to the cultural dimensions of the war, see Ferro's *The Great War, 1914–1918*. A very useful collection of essays on a wide variety of topics can be found in *Facing Armageddon*, by Cecil and Liddle.

Origins and war plans

The most complete study of the origins of the war remains Albertini's mammoth three-volume work, *The Origins of the War of 1914*. Students might, however, find it a difficult read. One of the more coherent accounts of the events leading up to the war is Lafore's *The Long Fuse*. Students should also play close attention to four books which look at the origins from the standpoint of a single country, namely Steiner's *Britain and the Origins of the First World War*, Keiger's *France and the Origins of the First World War*, Williamson's *Austria-Hungary and the Origins of the First World War* and Berghahn's *Germany and the Approach of War in 1914*.

They provide detail and perspective not available in the more general texts. On the question of war plans, Ritter's *The Schlieffen Plan* is invaluable, and Kennedy's series of essays in *The War Plans of the Great Powers* provides a stimulating introduction to the problems of preparing for continental war. On the question of the pre-war mood, Eksteins provides a fascinating (though at times somewhat rarefied) discussion in *Rites of Spring*. Wohl's *The Generation of 1914* is also very useful.

The Conduct of the war

Recent scholarship on how the war was fought has been outstandingly well researched. Of particular note are the volumes by Travers, namely *The Killing Ground* and *How the War Was Won*. For a detailed analysis of the command of Hindenburg and Ludendorff, see Kitchen's *The Silent Dictatorship*. Herwig's *The First World War: Germany and Austria-Hungary 1914–1918* covers a wider canvas, and does so with great panache. It is outstanding book which provides considerable depth, yet still manages to be lively and very readable. Stone's *The Eastern Front* remains the standard bearer on that campaign, and is likely to do so for some time. The best source on the naval war remains Marder's *From Dreadnought to Scapa Flow*, though it has an unashamedly British perspective. Students will probably find Halpern's *A Naval History of World War I* and Hough's *The Great War At Sea, 1914–1918* much more useful for the purpose of writing essays or for getting a sense of the entire naval war.

Individual battle histories vary immensely. Many are long on drama but short on accuracy. It is advisable, therefore, that they be read in conjunction with more scholarly military histories like those by Travers and Stone mentioned above. Students will, however, derive great enjoyment out of Middlebrook's *The First Day of the Somme,* Wolff's *In Flanders Fields* and Horne's *The Price of Victory*, the latter a harrowing account of the Verdun battle. *Gallipoli,* by Rhodes James, offers fascinating insights into the controversial campaign to seize the Dardanelles, and Farwell (*The Great War in Africa*) is excellent on the African campaigns.

The generals have received a great deal of attention, especially those whose performance is open to question. Terraine has conducted a one-man campaign to vindicate Haig, and the sheer energy of his effort is impressive. His *Haig: The Educated Soldier* is well researched and written with considerable style, but students should not use it without also consulting De Groot's *Douglas Haig, 1861–1928*. Winter's *Haig's Command* is an example of what happens when the obsession to vilify rages out of control. Liddell Hart's *Foch: Man of Orleans* and Goodspeed's *Ludendorff* are both dated but remain worthy of attention, as does Magnus on Kitchener. Holmes has written a fascinating and sensitive biography of Sir John French (*The Little Field Marshal*) which provides a valuable insight into the character of the British army before 1914.

The most welcome development in military studies in recent years has been the way social history has merged so well with the study of war. This has been most noticeable in scholarship on the British army, with Beckett and Simpson's *A Nation in Arms* particularly noteworthy. The collections by Cecil and Liddle (*Facing Armageddon* and *At the Eleventh Hour*) demonstrate that the First World War continues to inspire the interest of highly skilled specialist historians. Porch (*The March to the Marne*) is excellent on the French army, as is Smith (*Between Mutiny and Obedience*). On the Russian army, see Menning's *Bayonets Before Bullets*. Useful studies of the German army are difficult to find unless one reads German, but Herwig (mentioned above) provides a wealth of valuable material. For the war through the eyes of the soldiers, *Eye-Deep in Hell* by Ellis remains a wonderfully rich source.

Home fronts

In recent years, social historians have also been active in examining the effect of the First World War upon domestic society. Winter's *The Upheaval of War* provides useful comparisons of the various belligerent countries, while Hardach's *The First World War 1914–1918* is particularly good on the war economies. Horne's *State, Society and Mobilization in Europe during the First World War* is a collection of very important essays on the way the various belligerents reacted to mass mobilization. The most up-to-date study of the British home front is De Groot's *Blighty*, which questions the standard wisdom regarding war and social change. For France, see Becker, *The Great War and the French People*. The cultural and intellectual history of the war is covered in Fussell's *The Great War and Modern Memory*, a book which, despite its numerous flaws, remains enormously important. In the same vein, though concerned exclusively with Britain, is *A War Imagined*, by Hynes. The best book on dealing with the war's destruction is Winter's *Sites of Memory, Sites of Mourning*.

The Peace Process

The collection of articles in Cecil and Liddle (*At the Eleventh Hour*) is very useful for understanding the mood and intentions of the various belligerents in November 1918 and the deliberations over the armistice terms. Meigs (*Optimism at Armageddon*) provides a fascinating look at the end-of-war mood in the United States, the country which would emerge strongest from the conflict.

On the peace process. Mayer's *Politics and Diplomacy of Peacemaking Containment and Counterrevolution at Versailles, 1918–1919* is dated but still very useful. Sharp's *The Versailles Settlement: Peacemaking in Paris, 1919* is a solid text which students will find informative and accessible. Trachtenburg's *Reparation in World Politics-: France and European Economic Diplomacy, 1916–1923* remains a very useful source on the mood within France, and Lentin (*Lloyd George, Woodrow Wilson and the Guilt Of Germany: An Essay in the Pre-History of Appeasement*) does likewise for Britain. Also worthy of note is Dockrill and Goold's *Peace Without Promise*.

Bibliography

Please note that items are numbered in accordance with the numbers appearing in square brackets in the body of the text.

1. ALBERTINI, L., *The Origins of the War of 1914*, 3 vols (London, 1952–7)
2. AMERY, L. S., *My Political Life*, 3 vols (London, 1953)
3. ASPREY, R., *The German High Command at War* (New York, 1991)
4. BARKER, A., *The Neglected War: Mesopotamia 1914–1918* (London, 1964)
5. BARNETT, C., *The Swordbearers* (London, 1963)
6. BECKER, J-J., *The Great War and the French People* (Leamington Spa, 1985)
7. BECKETT, I., and SIMPSON, K., *A Nation in Arms* (Manchester, 1985)
8. BERGHAHN, V., *Germany and the Approach of War in 1914* (New York, 1973)
9. BOND, B., and CAVE, N. (eds), *Haig: A Reappraisal 70 Years On* (Barnsley, 1999)
10. BURK, K. (ed.), *War and the State* (London, 1982)
11. CAMPBELL, N., *Jutland: An Analysis of the Fighting* (London, 1986)
12. CASSAR, G., *The French and the Dardanelles* (London, 1971)
13. CECIL, H., and LIDDLE, P. H., *At the Eleventh Hour* (London, 1998)
14. CECIL, H., and LIDDLE, P. H., *Facing Armageddon* (London, 1996)
15. CHAMBERLAIN, M., *Pax Britannica?* (London, 1988)
16. CLARK, C. M. H., *A History of Australia*, 6 vols (Melbourne, 1962–81)

17. COPPARD, G., *With a Machine Gun to Cambrai* (London, 1969)
18. CROSS, T., *The Lost Voices of World War I* (London, 1988)
19. CRUTTWELL, C. R. M. F., *A History of the Great War* (London, 1982)
20. DE GROOT, G., *Blighty: British Society in the Era of the Great War* (London, 1996)
21. DE GROOT, G., *Douglas Haig, 1861–1928* (London, 1988)
22. DE GROOT, G., et al., *Military Miscellany I* (Stroud, 1997)
23. DEMM, E. 'Propaganda and caricature in the First World War', *Journal of Contemporary History*, vol. 28 (1993), pp. 163–92
24. DOCKRILL, M., and GOOLD, J., *Peace Without Promise* (London, 1981)
25. EKSTEINS, M., *Rites of Spring* (Boston, 1989)
26. ELLIS, J., *Eye-Deep in Hell* (London, 1976)
27. FALLS, C., *Caporetto* (London, 1966)
28. FALLS, C., *The First World War* (New York, 1959)
29. FARWELL, B., *The Great War in Africa* (London, 1987)
30. FELDMAN, G., *Arms, Industry and Labor in Germany, 1914–18* (Princeton, 1966)
31. FERRO, M., *The Great War 1914–1918* (London, 1973)
32. FRENCH, D., *British Strategy and War Aims* (London, 1986)
33. FUSSELL, P., *The Great War and Modern Memory* (Oxford, 1975)
34. GOOCH, J., *Army, State and Society, 1870–1915* (New York, 1989)
35. GORDON, A., *The Rules of the Game* (London, 1996)
36. GORDON, M., 'Domestic conflict and the origins of the First World War: the British and German cases', *Journal of Modern History*, vol. 46 (1974), pp. 191–226
37. GREGORY, A., *The Silence of Memory* (Oxford, 1994)
38. GRIFFITH, P., *Battle Tactics of the Western Front* (London, 1992)
39. GUINN, P., *British Strategy and Politics* (Oxford, 1965)
40. HALPERN, P., *A Naval History of World War I* (London, 1994)
41. HALPERN, P., *The Naval War in the Mediterranean, 1914–18* (London, 1987)
42. HANKEY, M., *The Supreme Control at the Paris Peace Conference* (London, 1963)

43. HARDACH, G., *The First World War 1914–1918* (Harmonds-worth, 1987)
44. HARRIS, B., 'The demographic impact of the First World War: an anthropometric perspective', *Journal of the Society for the Social History of Medicine*, vol. 6 (1993), pp. 343–66
45. HERWIG, H., *The First World War: Germany and Austria 1914–1918* (London, 1997)
46. HERWIG, H., *Luxury Fleet* (London, 1980)
47. HOLMES, R., *The Little Field Marshal* (London, 1981)
48. HORNE, A., *The Price of Victory* (London, 1962)
49. HORNE, J., and KRAMER, A., 'German "atrocities" and Franco-German Opinion, 1914', *Journal of Modern History*, vol. 66 (1994), pp. 1–33
50. HORNE, J. (ed.), *State, Society and Mobilization in Europe during the First World War* (Cambridge, 1997)
51. HOUGH, R., *The Great War At Sea, 1914–1918* (Oxford, 1983)
52. HYNES, S., *A War Imagined* (New York, 1990)
53. JAMES, L., *The Rise and Fall of the British Empire* (London, 1994)
54. JAMESON, M. S., *No Time Like the Present* (London, 1933)
55. KEEGAN, J., *The Face of Battle* (Harmondsworth, 1976)
56. KEEGAN, J., *The First World War* (London, 1999)
57. KEIGER, J., *France and the Origins of the First World War* (New York, 1983)
58. KENNEDY, P., *The Realities Behind Diplomacy* (London, 1981)
59. KENNEDY, P., *The War Plans of the Great Powers* (London, 1979)
60. KITCHEN, M., *The Silent Dictatorship: The Politics of the German High Command under Hindenburg and Ludendorff* (London, 1976)
61. KNOX, A., *With the Russian Army, 1914–17*, 2 vols (London, 1921)
62. LAFORE, L., *The Long Fuse* (Philadelphia, 1965)
63. LAPPING, B., *End of Empire* (London, 1989)
64. LAWRENCE, T. E., *Seven Pillars of Wisdom* (London, 1940)
65. LEED, E., *No Man's Land: Combat and Identity in World War I* (Cambridge, 1979)
66. LENTIN, A. A., *Lloyd George, Woodrow Wilson and the Guilt Of Germany: An Essay in the Pre-History of Appeasement* (Leicester, 1984)

67. LIDDELL HART, B. H., *History of the First World War* (London, 1970)
68. MACFIE, A. L., *The End of the Ottoman Empire* (London, 1998)
69. MACKAY, R., *Fisher of Kilverstone* (Oxford, 1973)
70. MAGNUS, P., *Kitchener* (New York, 1959)
71. MANSFIELD, P., *A History of the Middle East* (London, 1992)
72. MARDER, A., *From the Dreadnought to Scapa Flow*, 5 vols (London, 1961–70)
73. MARQUIS, A. G., 'Words as weapons: propaganda in Britain and Germany during the First World War', *Journal of Contemporary History*, vol. 13 (1978), pp. 467–98
74. MASEFIELD, J., *Gallipoli* (London, 1916)
75. MAYER, A. J., *Politics and Diplomacy of Peacemaking Containment and Counterrevolution at Versailles, 1918–1919* (London, 1968)
76. MEIGS, M., *Optimism at Armageddon* (London, 1997)
77. MENNING, B., *Bayonets Before Bullets: The Imperial Russian Army, 1861–1914* (Bloomington, 1994)
78. MIDDLEBROOK, M., *The First Day on the Somme* (London, 1971)
79. MIDDLEBROOK, M., *The Kaiser's Battle* (London, 1978)
80. MITCHELL, D., *Women on the Warpath* (London, 1966)
81. MONTAGU, E., *An Indian Diary* (London, 1930)
82. MOOREHEAD, A., *Gallipoli* (London, 1956)
83. MORRIS, J., *Farewell the Trumpets* (London, 1978)
84. MOYER, L., *Victory Must be Ours* (London, 1995)
85. NORTHEDGE, F. S., *The Troubled Giant : Britain Among the Great Powers, 1916–1939* (London, 1966)
86. OSUNTOKUN, A., *Nigeria in the First World War* (London, 1979)
87. PADFIELD, P., *The Great Naval Race: the Anglo-German Naval Rivalry, 1900–1914* (London, 1974)
88. PLAYNE, C., *The Pre-War Mind in Britain* (London, 1928)
89. POLLEN, A. H., *The Navy in Battle* (London, 1918)
90. PORCH, D., *The March to the Marne* (Cambridge, 1981)
91. PORTER, B., *The Lion's Share* (London, 1975)
92. REILLY, C., *Scars Upon My Heart: Women's Poetry and Verse of the First World War* (London, 1981)
93. RHODES JAMES, R., *Gallipoli* (London, 1965)

94. RITTER, G., *The Schlieffen Plan* (New York, 1959)
95. ROBBINS, K., *The First World War* (Oxford, 1984)
96. ROSHWALD, A., and STITES, R., *European Culture in the Great War* (Cambridge, 1999)
97. ROSSKILL, S., *Earl Beatty* (London, 1980)
98. ROTHENBURG, G., *The Army of Franz Joseph,* (West Lafayette, 1976)
99. SCHMITT, B. E., and VEDELER, H. C., *The World in Crucible, 1914–1919* (New York, 1988)
100. SEAMAN, L. C. B., *From Vienna to Versailles* (London, 1964)
101. SHARP, A., *The Versailles Settlement: Peacemaking in Paris, 1919* (London, 1991)
102. SILKIN, J. (ed.), *The Penguin Book of First World War Poetry* (Harmondsworth, 1979)
103. SILKIN, J. (ed.), *The Penguin Book of First World War Prose* (Harmondsworth, 1990)
104. SIMKINS, P., *Kitchener's Army* (Manchester, 1986)
105. SMYTHE, D., *Pershing* (Bloomington, 1986)
106. STEINBERG, J., *Yesterday's Deterrent* (London, 1965)
107. STEINER, Z., *Britain and the Origins of the First World War* (Houndmills, 1977)
108. STONE, N., *The Eastern Front, 1914-1917* (New York, 1975)
109. TEMPLE PATTERSON, A., *Jellicoe* (London, 1969)
110. TERRAINE, J., *Business in Great Waters* (London, 1989)
111. TERRAINE, J., *Haig: The Educated Soldier* (London, 1963)
112. TRACHTENBURG, M., *Reparation in World Politics: France and European Economic Diplomacy, 1916–1923* (New York, 1980)
113. TRAVERS, T., *How the War Was Won* (London, 1992)
114. TRAVERS, T., *The Killing Ground* (London, 1987)
115. TUCHMAN, B., *The Guns of August* (New York, 1962)
116. TUCHMAN, B., *The Proud Tower* (New York, 1978)
117. TUCKER, S., *The Great War 1914–1918* (London, 1998)
118. VACHELL, H. A., *The Hill* (London, 1905)
119. WAITE, F., *The New Zealanders at Gallipoli* (Auckland, 1921)
120. WELLS, H. G., *Mr Britling Sees it Through* (London, 1917)
121. WHALEN, R., *Bitter Wounds; German Victims of the Great War* (Ithaca, 1984)
122. WHEELER-BENNETT, J., *Brest-Litovsk: The Forgotten Peace* (London, 1966)

123. WHEELER-BENNETT, J., *Hindenburg: The Wooden Titan* (London, 1966)
124. WILDMAN, B., *The End of the Russian Imperial Army* (Princeton, 1980)
125. WILLIAMSON, S., *Austria-Hungary and the Origins of the First World War* (New York, 1991)
126. WILSON, T., 'Britain's "moral commitment" to France in August 1914', *History*, vol. 64 (1979), pp. 380–90.
127. WILSON, T., 'Lord Bryce's investigation into alleged German atrocities in Belgium, 1914–15', *Journal of Contemporary History*, vol. 14 (1979), pp. 369–83
128. WILSON, T., *The Myriad Faces of War* (Cambridge, 1986)
129. WINTER, D., *Haig's Command* (London, 1991)
130. WINTER, J., *Sites of Memory, Sites of Mourning: The Great War in European Cultural History* (Cambridge, 1995)
131. WINTER, J., and WALL, W. (eds), *The Upheaval of War: Family, Work and Welfare in Europe, 1914–18* (Cambridge, 1988)
132. WOHL, R., *The Generation of 1914* (Cambridge, Mass., 1979)
133. WOLFF, L., *In Flanders Fields* (London, 1958)
134. WOODWARD, D. R., *Lloyd George and the Generals* (London, 1983)
135. WOODWARD, D. R., *Trial by Friendship* (Lexington, Kentucky, 1993)
136. WOODWARD, L., *Great Britain and the War of 1914-1918* (London, 1967)
137. ZEMAN, Z., *The Break-up of the Habsburg Empire* (London, 1961)

Other sources

138. *Daily Mail*
139. *Daily Telegraph*
140. *The Times*
141. *Parliamentary Debates*

Index

217

Nicholas II, Tsar, 18, 52, 69
Niemen, River, 55
Nietzsche, Frederich, 4
Nigeria, 101
Nineveh, 107
Nivelle, Robert, 42–3, 47, 115
North Sea, 77
Noyon, 121
Nyasaland, 105

Ocean, 94
oil, 107
Olympic Games, 2, 21
Operation Michael, 116–23, 147
Orange River colony, 101
Order No. 1, 70
Orlando, Vittorio, 69, 183, 185, 194
Ostend, 19
Otto Babendiek, 202
Ottoman Empire, 6–7, 14, 92, 106,
    133, 178, 192, 196–7
    see also Turkey
Owen, Wilfred, 147, 201, 204

Pacific Ocean, 76, 79, 102–3
Painlevé, Paul, 69
Palestine, 108–9, 196
Paris, 12, 30, 32, 63, 87, 116, 122–6
Paris Peace Conference, 103,
    181–92
Passchendaele, 45
patriotism, 8, 74
Pax Britannica, 9–10, 110–11
Payer, Friedrich von, 131
periscopes, 84
Pershing, John, 114, 123, 126, 198
Pétain, Henri, 39, 43, 114–15, 119,
    122–3
Petrograd, 69
Petrograd Soviet, 69
Piave, River, 68, 132–3
Picardy, 175
Pig War, 13
Piraeus, 99
Plan 1919, 128
Plan XVII, 27, 137
Playne, Caroline, 20–1
Plumer, Herbert, 44
Poincaré, Raymond, 17

Poland, 52, 55–6, 61, 144, 186–7,
    192–3, 197
Polish Corridor, 186
Pollen, Arthur, 74
Port Arthur, Battle of, 73
Port Stanley, 80, 91
Portugal, 102, 124
Posen, 60
Princip, Gavrilo, 16
Prittwitz, Max von, 53
profiteering, 139
progressivism, 4
propaganda, 145–9
Provisional Government, 70
Prussia, 12, 30, 52–3, 59–60, 63, 186
Prut, River, 64
Przemyśl, 56, 59–60
Putnik, Radomir, 55

railways, 19, 24, 52–3, 61, 65–6, 89,
    117, 123, 130–31, 167–8
Rapallo, 69, 195
Rawlinson, Henry, 40, 128
Reims, 43, 125
Reinsurance Treaty, 9
Remarque, Erich Maria, 203
Rennenkampf, Pavel, 49, 53–5
reparations, 130, 188–90, 192
Rhine, River, 45, 188, 198, 205
Rhodesia, 102, 134
Ribot, Alexander, 99
Riezler, Kurt, 20
rifles, 29, 58, 169
Riga, 61, 71, 117
Riga, Treaty of, 186
Romania, 6, 14, 51, 65–6, 71, 91,
    193–5
Rome, 62
Rosenberg, Isaac, 204
Rovno, 61
Royal Navy, 3, 9, 21, 28, 72–90,
    94–5, 107, 136
Rupprecht, Crown Prince, 45
Russia, 26–7, 44, 53, 58–61, 64,
    70–3, 75, 79, 91–2, 94–6,
    112–13, 116, 131–2, 137, 184,
    186, 194, 197, 200, 205–6
    army, 30, 49, 52–9, 62–5, 70–1,
    121, 166, 177–8